THE SOCIOLOGY OF INDUSTRIAL RELATIONS

STUDIES IN METHOD

Power in Trade Unions
Trade Union Leadership
Trade Unions and the Government
Militant Trade Unionism
International Bibliography of Trade Unionism

V. L. Allen

The sociology of industrial relations

Studies in method

Longman

LONGMAN GROUP LIMITED
London

Associated companies, branches and representatives
throughout the world

© Longman Group Limited 1971

First published 1971

ISBN 0 582 44482 9 cased
ISBN 0 582 44483 7 paper

Printed in Great Britain by
The Camelot Press Ltd, London and Southampton

Contents

Preface

This book consists of essays written on aspects of industrial relations at various times since 1958. The main purpose in bringing the essays together is to illustrate the use of one particular conceptual approach to the study of industrial relations. For this reason the arrangement of the essays is not historical nor in the order in which they were written. The arrangement has been made as far as possible to facilitate the illustration of the conceptual approach. This approach is described broadly in Chapter 1, supplemented by the first chapter in each Part. Each chapter in some way provides evidence of its use though in some cases this comprises little more than the way in which data is selected and categorized. This unevenness in the chapters reflects the unevenness in my thinking about the matter. I have become increasingly concerned about the need for a logically consistent set of analytical tools for studying industrial relations and more inclined to expose methodology as a necessary condition for understanding what is written about the subject.

The book has four sections. Part I describes the methodology and shows its relevance for the study of industrial relations in general. Part II shows the manner in which contemporary and historical issues are analysed through this method. Part III, in the main, illustrates how secondary sources depend upon methodology for their meaning. In other words how the data drawn from existing histories can take on a different meaning when used within a different conceptual framework. Lastly, Part IV shows how the study of industrial relations in under-developed countries is dependent upon the conceptual framework of the social analyst.

The book consists of an interpretation of both historical and contemporary issues in industrial relations which is contrary to the one which is generally dominant in Western capitalist countries. Although the methodology involved is described briefly in the first chapter of each Part, at no point is it given a name, nor is any source quoted. It is difficult to describe the methodology in the way that conventional sociological theory is described as functionalism or structural-functionalism. The term structuralism could possibly have been used as an indication of the approach, but it has been used so indiscriminately by American sociologists who feel the need to give themselves a progressive label so as to distinguish themselves from other sociologists using much the same approach as themselves. In any event structuralism indicates only one prong in an essentially two-pronged approach. As I state in Chapter 1 of Part I the methodology comprises a combination of historical materialism and the dialectical process. The unique combination of these prongs originates in the work of Karl Marx and Frederick Engels. The approach, therefore, is a Marxist one. There are, of course, different facets to Marx's contribution and there are many interpretations of it and for this reason it may be misleading to call my approach a Marxist one without some qualification. Nonetheless Marxism is an explanatory generic term which covers what is attempted here.

My debts to people over the period during which these chapters have been written are legion. I have been involved in many discussions, formal and informal, concerning the construction of a dynamic conceptual approach. They have taken place in Britain, France, Yugoslavia and Italy. It would take a long time to list the names of all those involved and it would be invidious to make a selection. I thank them all. I owe a special debt, however, to Sheila Allen, for she, arguing from the same assumptions, has been my most pointed and persistent critic during the whole of this period. In my experience, argument between people who broadly agree is the most fruitful.

V.L.A.

Acknowledgements

Ten of the 18 chapters have been published before and I wish to thank the editors and publishers of the following for permission to reproduce my articles here:
Chapter 2, *The British Journal of Sociology*, Vol. X, No. 3, 1959; Chapter 3, *The British Journal of Sociology*, Vol. XIV, No. 1, 1963; Chapter 13, *The British Journal of Sociology*, Vol. XI, No. 1, 1960. This Journal is published jointly by Routledge & Kegan Paul Ltd., and the London School of Economics. Chapters 5 and 14, *The Socialist Register*, 1964 and 1968 respectively, published by Merlin. Chapter 6, *International Review of Social History*, Vol. IX (1964), Part 2. Chapter 8, *The Listener*, 30 November 1961. Chapter 17, *The Listener*, 22 March 1962. Chapter 9, *The Manchester School*, Vol. XXVIII, No. 3, 1960. Chapter 16, *The Journal of Modern African Studies*, Vol. 7, No. 2, 1969, published by the Cambridge University Press. Chapter 18 was written whilst I was working on a study of trade unionism in Africa and Asia at the International Labour Office, Geneva, in 1958–59.

PART I

PART 1

The sociological method

My main concern during the period covered by the writing of this book was to locate the causes of industrial behaviour and not simply to describe what I saw. Description has a static form: it portrays what is seen to exist at a particular point of time and gives no assistance in understanding the movement from the past, through the present, into the future, which is necessary if we are to be able to anticipate developments in industrial relations. In order to avoid the defects of descriptive studies I had to reject not only such studies, but all types of static or equilibrium analytical models, and adopt an approach which was based on a dynamic conception of industrial reality. The implications of making such a choice are profound in a variety of respects.

Theorizing in the social sciences is necessarily tautological. The investigator invariably and inevitably commences his work with some view of the situation he intends to investigate. His view may not be precisely formulated and it may not be explicit. It may not even be recognized as a view. But it will be present because the investigator will have been subjected through family, school, work and general environmental influences to socializing pressures which will have created for him a particular generalized picture or interpretation of social reality with some detailed aspects. The generalized picture will depict reality either as a mainly static or as a dynamic phenomenon. Whichever it is, it will carry its influence through the process of perception into the collection, selection, interpretation and collation of data, and through this process will intrude into the conclusions. Thus research based on an initial view that reality is static will inevitably conclude that reality is static.

The tautological nature of social science research is more apparent in industrial relations than in most other aspects of social behaviour because it involves a conflict situation which is obviously dominated by movement. It is difficult to disguise a static interpretation of conflict or to confuse it with a dynamic interpretation. The implications of the conclusions drawn from research based on the two assumptions stand in marked contrast to each other. Research based on a static view of reality assumes that the structure of industrial relations, that is, the nature of the society which gives rise to them, is fixed. All movement, therefore, is of a limited kind with no structural implications. Any changes which might result from such movement can, likewise, have no impact on the structure of industrial relations. They are temporary, remedial and constitute no threat to the established order of things. A dynamic analysis, on the other hand, assumes that the structure of industrial relations is changing and is capable of qualitative changes. No relationships or interests are impervious to change in a dynamic situation. Such an analysis can produce disturbing conclusions for those who wish to keep things as they are.

The dominant paradigm in the social sciences which provides models for the analysis of industrial relations is based on a relative static view of reality. It assumes a basic consensus in societies which can only be temporarily broken. It has provided the conceptual approach for the great majority of books, articles, speeches and general comments on industrial relations. It is taken to be the common-sense attitude to industrial relations, but it is also highly theoretically refined. The models have resulted in a multiplicity of studies which by and large fall into two main categories.[1]

There is first the descriptive category. This is largely concerned with general descriptions of institutions, such as trade unions or collective bargaining. The aim of such works has been to present facts on the assumption that facts speak for themselves. Facts, however, do not speak for themselves. They represent the view of the authors within the framework of the dominant paradigm. *An Introduction to the Study of Industrial Relations* by J. H. Richardson (Allen & Unwin, 1954) is a classic example of the descriptive type. There are many others of this type such as *The System of Industrial Relations in Great Britain: its history, law and institutions*, edited by A. Flanders and H. A. Clegg (Blackwell, 1954), *British Trade Unions* by N. I. Barou (Gollancz, 1947), *Industrial Conciliation and Arbitration in Great Britain* by I. G. Sharp (Allen & Unwin, 1950), *Trade Union Government and Administration in Great Britain* by B. C. Roberts (London School of Economics, 1956) and my own book, *Power in Trade Unions* (Longmans, 1954). It represents the commonest approach to the study of industrial relations.

[1] See 'An essay on analytical methods in studies of trade unionism' in *International Bibliography of Trade Unionism*, London, Merlin, 1968, V. L. Allen, for an examination of these categories.

The second category concerns empirical, problem centred studies. These are of two sorts: the fact collection sort which rejects explicit theorizing and the small group research sort which uses theory openly. These two differ in reality only to the extent to which they acknowledge the use and significance of theory. Both have a theoretical framework and it is the same one. Empirical studies have been less frequently undertaken in Britain than in the USA, largely because the supply of research funds has been more limited. They are of much less significance than general descriptive studies and, in the main, have concerned either segments of the work situation or issues arising out of the methods employed in industrial relations. The problems examined have been those of employers, and have related to such matters as labour instability, incentives, productivity, strikes and other forms of industrial action. The problems have been written up in articles rather than books, but in incomplete, unpublished reports more than anything else. A study of democracy in a branch of the Transport and General Workers' Union by J. Goldstein resulted in *The Government of British Trade Unions: A Study of Apathy and the Democratic Process in the Transport and General Workers' Union* (Allen & Unwin, 1952). An empirical investigation of the role of trade union officials was made by H. A. Clegg, A. J. Killick and R. Adams in *Trade Union Officers, branch secretaries, and shop stewards in British trade unions* (Blackwell, 1961). A number of problem centred studies have been published by the Department of Social Science at Liverpool University, most notably *The Dock Worker* (1954) and *Technical Change and Industrial Relations* (1956). Both these books have a strong theoretical setting as has a much more recently published collection of essays and case studies about industrial conflict by J. E. T. Eldridge, *Industrial Disputes* (Routledge & Kegan Paul, 1968). There are works which have been written within the dominant paradigm which do not fit neatly into these categories. Many histories of trade unions are written in a static form. *The History of Trade Unionism* by Sidney and Beatrice Webb (1894; second edn, 1920) and *The Trades Union Congress, 1868–1921* by B. C. Roberts (Allen & Unwin, 1958) are good illustrations of this type. In *The Growth of British Industrial Relations: A Study from the Standpoint of 1906–1914* (Macmillan 1959), E. H. Phelps Brown uses an historical analysis to explain industrial relations but he assumes that British capitalist society in all of its historical phases has basic consensus qualities. A short analysis by Allan Flanders, *Industrial Relations: an essay on its theory and future* (Faber, 1965), is concerned with manipulations within a given structure and is, in consequence, a form of systems analysis.

It is not necessary to give detailed expositions of the above works or the many others which are methodologically similar to them in order to show that they originate from a static paradigm and in consequence constitute a rationalization of the existing structure of industrial relations. It simply has to be shown that they possess the characteristics of systems analysis, or alternatively make the assumption of organic unity or consensus. Whenever an assumption of consensus or organic unity is made anything which penetrates the consensus or breaks the unity is seen as a disruptive factor. As any kind of movement may have penetration qualities, then movement itself is seen as a disturbing element. In order to cope with the possibility of undermining the primary assumption the analyst has to define change so that it cannot disrupt or cause permanent disunity, or he has to assume that the system has self-correcting qualities. The outcome is that change is regarded as undesirable. It is in this sense that static analysis is a rationalization of what exists, of the present, and can be called *status quo* analysis.

The abundance of published works written within the dominant paradigm makes it unnecessary to reproduce any part of them in this book, even as illustrations. This is not a sign of a lack of objectivity, impartiality or balance. Most people who come to the study of industrial relations know only the conventional static approach. And most of these people continue using that approach throughout their studies and afterwards. They consider it to be adequate because it is the only approach they know. Because the static paradigm is generally used and provides the framework for common-sense interpretations there is little reason why people should question its use. If there is a lack of objectivity or balance at all it is in the attitude of conformist theorists to nonconformist approaches to the subject. It is for this reason that a book devoted to a single nonconformist methodology requires an explanation. Conventional sociologists are so accustomed to being in an unchallenged position that they are intolerant of minority views which might threaten the validity of that position. Their concept of fairness requires that the conventional view should always be put by its opponents. It does not require that nonconformist studies should be published alongside the conformist ones.

Criticisms of what is theoretically conventional are usually received with silence, outrage or derision. They are rarely seen as positive contributions to an understanding of social behaviour. The critics are either studiously ignored, or accused of 'tilting at windmills', of 'putting up straw men', of being polemical for its own sake, of introducing ideology or politics into scientific discussions. There are few things so sacrosanct as a conventionally accepted social theory. There is a good reason for this fact. A social theory achieves acceptability and hence dominance not through its capacity to explain reality alone but through its capacity to explain reality in the context of a given power structure. Any theory which leads to the questioning of basic power relationships is unacceptable to those who dominate the power structure. This is the case at all levels; in all types of power situations. In order to be accepted a social theory has to assume that the structure of the system with which it is concerned is unchanging. It then provides both a rationale of the system and a framework for action which will protect it because it never questions its legitimacy.

The extent to which a nonconformist approach evokes hostility depends on the intensity and immediacy of its impact. A completed logically consistent causal analysis which can at all points be seen as an alternative to the dominant one is more threatening than one which is vaguely formulated or poorly constructed. An analysis which refers to the past is more readily tolerated than one which relates to contemporary events.

Two points can be made about the approach used in this book. Firstly, it is presented as an alternative to the dominant conformist one not because it is valid or true but because it is the better of the two. It would be both unscientific and arrogant to claim more than this. The approach used here is simply the most useful that social scientists have at their disposal at the moment because, so far as we know, it approximates more closely to reality than its alternative. Secondly, the approach used here is not presented as a complete model. In the main it merely represents a form of perception, showing how the selection, interpretation and general use of data are influenced by the initial assumptions made about the nature of social behaviour. The first assumption which is made is that social behaviour is a dynamic phenomenon. This means that it is subject to pressures both from within and without which can lead to social change, sometimes of a qualitative kind. This assumption, which has substantial empirical backing from both contemporary and historical sources, stands in complete contrast to the one implicit in most contemporary sociological analyses, and it has contrasting consequences. Once social behaviour is assumed to be dynamic it is assumed that it can change its form. Nothing, in the long run, can be said to be fixed or immutable. Even in the short run whether or not the structure of social behaviour, its forms or boundaries, remain unchanged is a matter for empirical investigation and not something which can be dealt with by an assumption. In a dynamic situation the relationships between social phenomena are fluid and may be causal in character. Behaviour is environmentally determined.

The next step is to decide which elements in environments have greatest causal significance and in what way they create movement. It cannot be assumed that the elements have no given priority rating because this would mean first that nothing could be said about any issue until it had been investigated, and secondly that there need be no causal relationship between two or more issues. Both of these consequences are inconsistent with the initial assumption that social behaviour is dynamic. In order to be consistent with the notion that social behaviour is environmentally determined, and, therefore, that all forms of social behaviour have causal connections, there has to be one consistently present interconnecting element. This element is the economic one. It is always present and always has causal priority over other elements. The economic pressures in environments mould and shape the sociological and psychological factors. There is not a mechanistic relationship between economic and other factors. In some situations, particularly over short periods of time, and at some levels of analysis, sociological factors may have priority over economic ones. For example, in the short run, institutional phenomena such as rules and procedures, the distribution of authority and job categories obviously exercise preponderant influences over organizational behaviour. All that environmental determinism involves is that there is a causal connection between all elements in an environment and that the economic one is the most important. Thus in every analysis one has to identify the economic factors first and, if they are present, give them priority. In an analysis of strike action in a particular firm one would first ask questions about the economic circumstances of the employees and the firm and proceed from there. It does not follow that that particular strike has to have an economic cause. It may have been prompted by a question of discipline or victimization but unless it is to be merely descriptive then the analysis has to have an economic context.

Movement in a dynamic situation must occur in a manner which ensures that it does not lapse, that it is not sporadic. Unless there is a mechanism whereby a continuous impulse for movement is created then the initial assumption is violated and we return to an empiricist position which is that there may or may not be movement. Just as conventional sociologists assume that systems have homeostatic qualities to ensure the maintenance of organic unity, so those who assume that social behaviour has dynamic qualities must adopt a working hypothesis which maintains their prime assumption. This working hypothesis is that movement is generated and perpetuated by the existence of contradictions at every level of social behaviour and in all of its aspects. A contradiction, in its process towards resolution, creates further contradictions so that the stage of resolution is never reached. It is on the notion of contradiction that the possibility of model building for a dynamic analysis really rests. Relatively little work has so far been done in this direction and there is little evidence of the use of such a model in the following chapters. But implicit in the book is the assumption that movement occurs through contradictions.

The existence of contradictions and the relationship between them both in relation to contemporary action and over time constitute the dialectical process. This process spells out the necessity for an historical approach to all social issues. There is no break in the continuity of the dialectical process. Every contradiction is derived from earlier ones and cannot be understood without reference to them. The significance of an historical approach is emphasized through use in the rest of this book. The dialectic transforms environmental determinism, which by itself is a static approach, into historical materialism, which is dynamic in conception.

Historical materialism provides the conceptual framework for all that follows. It determines the selection and interpretation of data and the manner in which it is arranged. It stipulates that a part cannot be understood without reference to the whole, that segments of systems cannot be analysed in isolation from each other or their environments. It also stipulates that the present cannot be understood without reference to the past; that no point in history should be examined without consideration of its past. As contemporary situations should be analysed by taking all elements into account, so should historical situations. If historical analysis is to provide meaningful explanations it must constitute sociological studies of the past. By the same argument, the present must be viewed as history.

A further and final consequence follows from the use of historical materialism which is directly relevant to the subject matter of this book. The title of the book is *The Sociology of Industrial Relations*, yet it is largely about trade unionism. Surely, it might be argued, industrial relations covers more than simply trade unionism. The answer is that it does, but that the core of the subject is trade unionism. Industrial relations arise out of the prime economic relationship in society which is the buying and selling of labour power. There is perpetual interaction between the buyers and the sellers for three main reasons. Firstly because there is an enormous imbalance of economic power between the two classes. There are many sellers and relatively few buyers. The buyers who own the means of production are dominant over individual sellers in every sphere of activity. Second, it takes place because members of the labour market possess various degrees of freedom to exploit the power position for their own advantages. And lastly it exists because there are constant unremitting pressures on buyers and sellers to use this freedom. The sellers, or employees, depend on the price of labour power for their subsistence and, therefore, are forced to maximize it, while the buyers, or employers, treat that price as a cost and are perpetually trying to minimize it. The result of these factors is a dynamic conflict situation. Trade unionism is an attempt by otherwise relatively powerless individual employees to rectify the power imbalance. It is a substitute for individual action and is an integral part of the relationship between the buyers and sellers of labour power.

All other relationships in industry have developed out of that between employees and employers. They are of a derived or secondary character. Economic market pressures on employers to reduce costs led them to use their power to discriminate between employees, to combine them with machines, to displace them by machines. Friction between crafts and between various types of work categories resulted from these pressures. But no matter how many machines were used, or how complicated the technological processes were, the central relationship continued to be that between employees and employers and the constant protective reaction of employees throughout all the changes was to organize collectively. The complex authority structures which exist in contemporary industry, giving rise to a number of relationships such as those between managers and employers, managers and managers, and managers and managed, are a consequence of the inability of employers to cope singlehandedly with the management of expanding and increasingly complex industrial enterprises. The first decision of an employer to delegate authority led immediately to new relationships. Every subsequent decision to create categories of authority led to further relationships. The whole paraphernalia of personnel management is of a secondary character.

Industry consists of a hierarchy of social relationships which together constitute industrial relations. The hierarchy rests on the prime relationship between employees and employers, and is made up of a succession of relationships which are derived from each other and which differ, therefore, in degrees of importance in relation to the whole. A comprehensive book about industrial relations would range over the complete hierarchy but one lacking in completeness must, in order to warrant the description 'industrial relations', give preference to trade unionism.

2

The need for a sociology of industrial relations

The task which I have set myself in this chapter is neither popular nor easy. It is not popular to claim recognition for a new discipline in a field of study which is already occupied by many vested interests. It is not easy because those already working in the field have rationalized their presence and justified their approaches and methods. Those who are now examining labour problems are not likely to be readily convinced that by going their separate ways they are preventing a correct understanding of the behaviour of labour being reached. But the task must be tackled, for its rewards are so obvious not only in the sphere of labour activity but in understanding human behaviour generally.

I propose to do it by describing first how the present haphazard study of labour problems has developed, by showing its limitations; then by explaining how these limitations can be removed.

Diffusion and Confusion

A representative collection of people who profess to study labour problems today would consist of members of almost every social science faculty. There would be economists, historians, philosophers, anthropologists, sociologists, lawyers, political theorists, psychiatrists, psychologists and others. Each would be looking at labour behaviour from his specialist point of view; convinced, justifiably, that his view was important, but rarely if ever taking account of the views of others. This state of affairs has evolved because the factors which aroused the interest of academics in labour problems have been many and varied.

Early political economists were interested in the wages of labour and in the quantity of labour used in production. Adam Smith examined wages as a price but his approach had width as well as depth, as befitted a moral philosopher. Political economists who followed paid less attention to wages and more to the quantity of labour in production. They developed a theory which eliminated the need for them to consider labour problems. Provided the right institutional framework in the economy existed these problems, they considered, would be non-existent.

David Ricardo first propounded the theory. It was based on economic and political individualism and its principal task was to establish a theory of value.[1] The determinant of the relative value of commodities was the relative quantity of labour used in their production. Differences in the skill and intensity of work had no effect on values in Ricardo's theory and were therefore ignored.[2] Movements in wages were considered to be equally unimportant,[3] but a wage was a price and therefore required an explanation. Here his assumption of individualism became evident. 'Like all other contracts,' he stated, 'wages should be left to the fair and free competition of the market, and should never be controlled by the interference of the legislature.'[4] Trade union interference, if it had been important, would have been considered equally undesirable.

Ricardo's theory was modified but his basic assumption was left unquestioned. Consequently collective action by workers had no theoretical basis and was therefore ignored by political economists, just as imperfect competition and unemployment were ignored. An interest in wage determination was aroused by Marx's labour theory of value but it was shortlived. Economics, by the end of the nineteenth century, was firmly in the grip of marginal analysis. Wage determination, by now a part of the economists' exclusive field, got lost in the models which marginal analysis inspired. Understandably, it has never been satisfactorily explained.

Interest in other aspects of labour behaviour had then to be inspired by others. It came about through the work of nineteenth-century social reformers. It was they who first investigated the uses of labour, to expose the maltreatment of children and females, and who revealed the conditions of factories. Investigations once started widened and drew the investigators to examine related problems. Political economists remained consciously unconcerned. Having written their value judgements into their theories they had recoiled from observing facts which might disprove them. They falsely repudiated the task of

---

[1] David Ricardo, *Principles of Political Economy and Taxation* (1817), in *The Works of David Ricardo*, ed. J. R. McCulloch, 1846, p. 5.

[2] *Ibid.*, pp. 14–15.

[3] *Ibid.*, pp. 19–20. Ricardo later admitted that wage movements could affect value; see *Letters of Ricardo to Malthus*, ed. James Bonar, Oxford University Press, 1887, p. xvii.

[4] *Principles of Political Economy and Taxation*, p. 57.

making moral judgements. As early as 1850 a distinguished commentator said: 'It quite disgusts me to hear the cold, calculating economists throwing aside all moral considerations, and with entire ignorance of the state of the people who work in factories, talk of its being an infringement of principle to interfere with labour.'[5] This commentator has been followed by others equally disgusted, for many economists have maintained this façade of scientific detachment.

Until the fragmentation of political economy occurred and the social sciences emerged, labour problems, wage determination apart, received academic treatment from very few people. The National Association for the Promotion of Social Science—an association of liberally minded intellectuals formed in 1857—produced a well-documented report on *Trade Societies and Strikes* in 1860. In 1870 L. Brentano published an erudite description of the history and development of guilds and the origin of trade unions. Thorold Rogers's mammoth work on *The History of Agriculture and Prices*, which contained material relating to labour, came out in 1893. An occasional article appeared in the *Economic Journal* or the *Economic Review* which bore some connection with labour problems.

It was already common, towards the end of the century, for novelists and journalists to indulge in social reporting in the tradition of Dickens and Mayhew, but organized empirical investigations were new until Charles Booth started his inquiry into the life and labour of London people in 1886. The situation was ripe for investigation. Trade unions had emerged as militant industrial and political bodies. They drew attention to themselves and to the working and living conditions of workers whom they represented.

Those who were drawn into the field of social investigation belonged to the world of philanthrophy—a world consisting of public-spirited, benevolent rich. Some of them were there as a result of their own observations, but conversion was not uncommon. The world of philanthropy, like all other worlds, had its divisions. Out of one of these emerged a group which based its philanthrophy on a study of facts.[6] The emphasis of the new empirical investigators was on the condition of labour: its theme was exploitation but it led some into other channels.

Beatrice Potter was the first of these investigators to move away from the philanthrophic approach—though never to desert it wholly —and to examine the working class to reveal an explanation for its

[5] Quoted in O. R. McGregor, 'Social research and social policy', *British Journal of Sociology*, June 1957, p. 149.
[6] Beatrice Webb, *My Apprenticeship*, Longmans, 1926, p. 195.

actions. This led her as a first step to look at working-class institutions. Description had to precede explanation. Beatrice Potter was one of a closely related group of people who inspired or simply led each other to investigate. She owed much of her interest to Frederic Harrison, who was an intellectual friend of labour and had sat on the Royal Commission on Trade Unions in 1867–69. Her first connection with the working class was made through her sister Kate, who became a rent collector in Whitechapel after working with Octavia Hill; it was extended by a visit to Lancashire arranged by a servant of her family in 1883. Beatrice Potter also became a rent collector. She wrote: 'It was in the autumn of 1883 that I took the first step as a social investigator, though I am afraid the adventure was more a sentimental journey than a scientific exploration.'[7] She worked with Charles Booth, whose wife Mary was her cousin. From there she went on to examine the 'virtues and vices of trade unionism'. At the time of her marriage she was already working on a description of trade unionism. Her husband, Sidney Webb, came to write it with her through their efforts at undertaking joint projects. His was a fortuitous entry.

The Webbs attempted to write a 'scientific analysis of the structure and functions of British Trade Unions, in order to discover the tacit assumption and social implications underlying their activities; and . . . the relation of manual-working trade unionism to other forms of social organization: notably, to profit-making enterprise, to political democracy, and to the consumers' co-operation'. This was an auspicious beginning. Their *History of Trade Unionism* was regarded as an historical introduction. It was published in 1894. The main work came out in 1899 under the title of *Industrial Democracy*. These works were a sound basis for further research. They had shown that the behaviour of labour was capable of academic treatment. Very little further research was undertaken. It is pertinent to ask why.

The advent of the fact-finding philanthropists coincided with the impact of Marxism on the British trade union movement, which helped in the creation of a class-conscious labour movement and equipped it with the terminology befitting a conflict. The new general unions formed after 1889 were militant and politically conscious. Their leaders were responsible for persuading the trade union movement to accept a socialist programme and to establish its own political party. From the end of the nineteenth century to 1914 there was a situation of developing class conflict in industry and politics. Thus industry was no longer a field where philanthropists could safely and anonymously work. Those who remained did so mainly in support of

[7] *Ibid.* p. 151

labour in the struggle, and became in effect propagandists for the cause of labour. The long-term aims of socialism encouraged conjecture and theorizing about the role of labour in achieving it. Thus theories about organized labour were developed before sufficient facts about it had been collected and collated. The work of the Webbs was considered factual enough for the purpose.

The examination of the structure and activities of organized labour was eschewed in academic circles because of its political implications. Economists would not undertake it, for not only did it raise moral issues but it conflicted with the basic assumptions in their theory. Sociologists, who were then emerging, were still too busy trying to find universal laws of human behaviour to be concerned with detail, least of all that which it was politically unsavoury to touch. When they eventually looked at detail they did so as pathologists. They were concerned with the marginal man, woman and child—the broken homes, the deliquents, the maladjusted. The economic historians who were new to the academic scene worked on the sound principle of first things first and started at the beginning of economic institutions. They had long to go before they reached trade unions.

No attention was given to man as a worker either by those sympathetic towards the aims of organized labour or by others. In terms of the class war he was a victim whose only means of retribution was to be uncooperative in industry—to do nothing to increase profits or to bolster up capitalism—and to join his trade union. Employers were not interested either, for with the threat of unemployment they had the means to compel a worker to be cooperative.

And so, until the third Labour Government came into office faced with an economic problem which demanded high productivity for its solution and without the pressure of unemployment to extract it, only the organizations of labour were examined. This emphasis, of course, was not to be disparaged, for description was necessary. But unfortunately the description was mundane and based largely on the Webbs' research. Sometimes it was even preceded by analysis.

There was very little work done in universities on labour organizations in the interwar years. The only serious contributor was G. D. H. Cole. His work for the Carnegie Endowment for International Peace and his books, which were inspired by his intense identity with the aims of labour, all written shortly after the First World War, were both sympathetic and erudite. But Cole too soon took on the part of a propagandist and his serious contributions in this field fell away. The study of industrial relations made a formal entry into three universities, Cambridge, Leeds and Cardiff, in the early 1930s through the beneficence of Montague Burton, but the situation remained unchanged. The subject continued to be neglected.

In 1945 the economists, constructing even more complicated models, were preoccupied with repairing the breach caused by Keynes; sociologists were still social pathologists; and economic historians were continuing to read the Webbs for their lectures. The collective or individual activities of labour played virtually no part in their university curricula, and no part at all in their researches.

Then quite suddenly the situation changed. Labour in all its aspects became nationally important. The level of wages influenced the level of prices which influenced the demand for exports. What determined the level of wages? Strikes reduced the national product. What caused strikes? Workers' attitudes were influenced by long-established traditions. What was their history? Full employment had removed the 'economic whip'. What was the substitute? These and other questions became of vital national importance. Various members of the social science faculties rushed to the colours and gave the answers, without, it should be noted, doing much appreciable further research.

The emphasis shifted from regarding trade unions purely as vehicles for social change to looking at them as production agents. Individual workers were brought prominently into the picture. What could make them work harder? Here was an opening for the psychiatrist. Coloured machines? Worktime music? How did they work best? In groups or as individuals? What was the principal incentive? Money? Here was an opening for everybody.

We are approaching now the heterogeneous group I mentioned at the beginning. As the postwar years moved to the present others joined in. Some sociologists widening their horizons, took to examining industrial communities such as firms, but this interest was confined to a small group. And social anthropologists, running out of primitive societies, turned slightly to segments of modern industrial society to apply their methods.

A branch of sociology?

Universities no longer consider it politically disreputable to examine labour problems; but it is not yet academically reputable to do so. Labour problems are matters which individual members of social science faculties can examine if they wish but they must do so within the confines of their special disciplines, and normally in addition to other work. Consequently there are many approaches to labour problems and equally varied conclusions. There has been a substantial increase in the volume and quality of the work done. The Webbs are no longer the prime source for information about trade unions, though they have been by no means displaced. And we know more about the motives and behaviour of individual workers as well as organizations. There have been micro as well as macro studies. Yet we are still not in a position to give answers to important questions concerning, for instance, wage determination, strike behaviour, productivity. Why is this so?

The reason lies in the inadequacy of the methods which have been used. Workers are men and women who sell labour power in a competitive market; who work under conditions which lend themselves to exploitation; and who, in various ways, collectively and individually, have sought to protect themselves from that exploitation. The reason for their behaviour lies in the organization of industrial society, but the determinants of it consist of the whole environment in which they find themselves. One cannot abstract a worker from his environment and expect to understand him properly. We are concerned then with the study of people who spend part of their lives under certain recognizable industrial conditions. These people are ordinary because they are so numerous; they live in homes, urban conglomerations, villages, new housing estates; they are literate or illiterate; they get married, have children and educate them; they grow old. All these factors have interrelated consequences. It should be clear that the study of workers is a branch of sociology.

One can point to many an aspect of human behaviour which is worthy of examination, but that does not constitute it a branch of sociology; and one can indicate recognizable branches of sociology which do not justify the treatment of a discipline. I maintain that the sociology of work, or more aptly of industrial relations, is a discipline within the compass of sociology.[8]

Why, it may be asked, advocate fission? Is this not a tendency which is opposite to the best interests of sociology? On the contrary, the development of sociology, and certainly the development of sociological theory, depends on fission. It is necessary for detailed observations to be made in various aspects of social behaviour, for expert analyses to follow, for partial conclusions to emerge, so that we get an intensive picture of social activity and so that those sociologists with panoramic minds, the Comtes and the Spencers of this generation,

---

[8] I am not going to delay here over the definition of a discipline. It is clear in the following paragraphs what I mean by it. For an apt description of the use of the term discipline see Donald G. MacRae, 'Some sociological prospects', *Transactions of the Third Congress of Sociology*, viii, 1956, 297.

can have substance on which to build their theories of social action.

Another question may be 'Why not leave the developing subject of industrial sociology to develop and do the job I want done?' In the first place industrial sociology is not a subject. It is a name for the work which those sociologists who are interested in industrial problems do. It is not a distinctive aspect of human behaviour, for what men and women do in industry cannot be separated from their collective behaviour outside industry, in trade unions, in politics, in social institutions such as Co-operative Societies. A glance at any of the American textbooks on industrial sociology (fortunately there are no British ones yet) shows that there is confusion about what it entails. As if someone has selected chapter headings out of a hat. Moreover, one gathers that industrial sociology is management oriented. The sociology of industrial relations is not concerned with the practice of management *per se*. But I will return to this later.

At this point I want to mention why I think the sociology of industrial relations should be treated as a discipline. Then I shall describe its scope and method.

Qualifying as a discipline

The sociology of industrial relations covers a large segment of human behaviour in which actions are coherently related, spring from common causes and are directed towards similar ends. It is a segment in which there are principles governing action which, when related to the facts of situations in which workers live and work, lend themselves to prediction. The behaviour in it has an identity of his own. Just look at some of the factors involved in it: wages, productivity, incentive schemes, strikes, ca'canny, security, employment, political action, workers' control, victimization, discipline in trade unions. These are all variables in a single situation, which if analysed in relation to each other would reveal significant principles of social action.

The fact-collecting and the analysis cannot be undertaken by anyone; they demand persons, academic ability apart, with special qualifications. It is known among sociologists that in many fields of their study sympathy is necessary for understanding. This is especially true with the sociology of industrial relations. People who are antipathetic towards the aims of organized labour, who do not sympathize with the conditions in which so many working people find themselves, are not likely to get very far with their investigations. They will not get adequate responses and they will be incapable of understanding the responses they do get. I am not suggesting that those who engage in the sociology of industrial relations should adopt a partisan approach, I am suggesting that they should be motivated by an element of social purpose. There is no room here for the economist without value judgements, for the political theorist who deals only with systems and neglects their *raison-d'être*, for economic historians who simply narrate chronological events, except as technical subscribers.

Some consider it repugnant to associate academic research with social policy; hence the yearning to make the social sciences into exact sciences. What such people really want is to deal with inanimate objects which can be analysed and tested and because they do not have them they create them. So we get the 'economic man'. In fact there are strong elements of purpose in many forms of social research. Many people who investigate crime, the family, conditions of old people, do not do so with an attitude of complete neutrality.[9] Their views about these subjects have often led them to investigate. This does not lead to distortion but to a better understanding.

The central institutions in the sociology of industrial relations are trade unions, and if they are not understood then the validity of many conclusions is lost. One cannot get to know about them through examining their constitutions alone or by submitting their actions to rational tests. Trade unions, whilst they have a strong rational basis for their present existence, derive much of their motivating power from the historical tradition of struggle. The tradition is reflected in the values of trade unions, which in turn are shown in their actual behaviour. Trade union actions are inexplicable except in the context of the tradition of struggle. It has to be understood and understanding is a specialist function.

One can study ancient Greek literature without having to make out a case for its value to present day society, because the classics are a social institution. One cannot launch upon a study of sociology in the same carefree manner. In what way will the study be useful? How will that affect *us*? Is this capable of *objective* research? Who else is interested in your work? These are the questions one has to answer. Yet sociological studies can be so obviously useful to contemporary society. Research into the sociology of industrial relations is especially useful.

It is so in three main ways. First it has a technological value. Labour problems result from the application of technology in a society which is ill-fitted to receive it. An examination of these problems may help

---

[9] See G. D. H. Cole, 'Sociology and social policy', *British Journal of Sociology*, June 1957.

to ease the friction which will result from an extension of technology. In consequence it would increase production. In this sense it can be compared with fundamental research in the physical sciences in that its results, if applied, would act on industry like technical innovations. But what a difference it would make if one could *see* its results like an enormous telescope or a nuclear weapon. Secondly, it has a political significance. It can show the trend in the distribution of power in society. It can reveal how political power is exercised and by whom. It can give an insight into the sources of the impetus for social change. Lastly it can show in detail the institutional behaviour of man; how he acts under duress, under compulsion, what his collective values are, what is meant by loyalty.

The scope of the sociology of industrial relations

I have already made references to the scope of the subject. Here I must define it more precisely. The subject deals with the individual and collective activities of labour. We are concerned with the individual at work, not in his home or during his leisure unless it becomes clear that influences from those environments are determining his worktime behaviour. At work a man or woman will have relationships with fellow workers, with supervisors and managers, with union representatives, with machines. From these relationships and the effects of cross-relationships, arise many problems which are individual ones. Absenteeism, attitudes to work, labour turnover, are examples.

The collective behaviour of workers takes different forms and extends well beyond the confines of work places. It is concerned with workshop organizations of shop stewards as well as trade unions, unofficial as well as official bodies. And it includes the obtrusion of these bodies into all manner of activities in the community. So one would deal with the hierarchy of the Labour Movement and the role and rights of individuals in it; its political activities at local and national levels; its industrial relations and the manner in which they have been institutionalized; its relations with the Government; its aspirations and ideologies and its history. This is not an exhaustive list.

So far I have described the subject as if it were confined to phenomena in a single state. Given industrial conditions, a permanent working class, and a freedom to combine, it is a worldwide subject. Except in a limited examination of wage policies there have been no effective comparative studies. The scope of our subject would include the individual and collective behaviour of workers in all communities, industrially developed and developing. There is vast scope here. In Africa, Asia and Latin America there are labour problems which are new and revealing.

The scope of this subject can never be fixed. All the time one has to look over one's shoulder to see what influences are acting on labour— to see what policies the Government is pursuing; what changes are taking place in the geographical and occupational distribution of labour and in the location of industry; what is happening to the educational system and how ethical values are altering. The scope is set by the nature of the problem. The most complex problems are found in developing economies. There the scope is very wide.

Take, for instance, the attitude to strikes in India. There is general hostility and suspicion against strikes over wages and working conditions in India, while strikes for political ends are condoned by the employers, public and even the Government. This situation, which is the exact reverse of that in Britain, only makes sense in the context of the deeply embedded customs of social immobility which are applied through the caste system, and the long lived civil disobedience campaign for independence, during which the right to engage in mass political protests became ingrained. An analysis of strikes in India would take the research worker well beyond the limits of his specific field of learning.

One could give many other examples. The emergence of trade union leaders in developing economies can only be meaningfully explained through an examination of local or national social customs, the extent of illiteracy and the growth of political opportunities. An analysis of attitudes to work should take one further afield. Workers may dislike work because they are easily exhausted, due to malnutrition and chronic debilitating disease. They may belong to social systems where manual work is only undertaken by certain groups. Most of them will have moved relatively recently from societies where relationships were based on kinship and status to environments dominated by contractual obligations. They will be subjected to seemingly harsh individual disciplines and fresh leaders, and judged according to new moral values. Regular working hours, disciplined supervision, foremen and managers with authority only at work, industrial groups which disregard tribal, racial or caste distinctions, are all strange phenomena in the lives of most industrial workers in Asia or Africa. In developing economies, then, the sociology of industrial relations would necessarily be as complex as anywhere else.

Its method

My last points concerns method. We have no technical vocabulary to assist us in description and designation. Nor do we need one. Labour sociologists must deal, like other sociologists, with ordinary people and if we are to make our points intelligible to them then we must use their language. This means, of course, that common imprecise terms must be used—like politics, class, compulsion, discipline, sanctions. The lack of precision, however, is a lesser disadvantage than the confusion which arises from the introduction of new terms. The terms are never uniformly accepted. Devised to aid understanding, in fact they hamper it. It is possible for sociologists to be unintelligible to each other. But put the heterogeneous group of specialists in labour problems mentioned earlier together to discuss a common problem in their specialist vocabularies, and the result would be like a comedy.

The methods we use must necessarily be related to the stage we have reached in the development of the subject. We are still in the fact-collecting, classifying, defining process. In such a situation it is fatuous to talk of 'institutional' and 'scientific' schools in the subject; more so to make comparisons between them.[10] The stage of development is so elementary that we need to learn all we can about the framework of formal institutions and about the situations in which these institutions operate. No one approach can be wholly satisfactory, but each has its value. Much of the research done so far has been based on documentary evidence; but there have been 'situational' studies[11] and in-plant studies in which workers have been observed, and questioned by interviews and questionnaires.[12]

The emphasis needs to be changed from documentary studies to empirical investigations only because information is lacking about situations. But in order to understand current situations they must be related to their historical developments. It has been rightly pointed out that much published work about situations in factories 'shows a deplorable lack of historical understanding and sometimes a failure to appreciate the nature of the "situation" studied due to ignorance of the framework of formal institutions which surround it'.[13] There must not be the dichotomy between history and empirical research

[10] See M. P. Fogarty, 'Industrial relations: studies in the universities', *The Times Review of Industry*, January 1955; and A. Flanders and H. A. Clegg, eds, *The System of Industrial Relations in Great Britain*, Blackwell, 1954.

[11] F. Zweig, *Productivity and Trade Unions*, Blackwell, 1951, is a good illustration.

[12] For example, W. H. Scott, A. H. Halsey, J. A. Banks and T. Lupton, eds, *Technical Change and Industrial Relations*, Social Research Services, Liverpool University Press, 1956.

[13] Flanders and Clegg.

which exists between social anthropology and ethnology. History, as I explained earlier, provides a motive force in the collective behaviour of labour; to leave it out is like neglecting the need to eat when examining attitudes to work.

The need in method is for a modified anthropological approach merged with an historical analysis. How to synthesize the two is a problem which has not yet been tackled effectively in sociology generally. But it must be done in this aspect of sociology. The breadth of the approach depends on the nature of the issue. Obviously more external data would be required in an investigation of a labour problem in Malaya than in London. In the first place a lot of information about workers in London can be assumed to be known, whereas the same is not true for Malaya; and secondly labour problems in Malaya are superimposed on a society which has deeply entrenched non-industrial traditions and customs. The method of anthropological abstraction should be used wherever possible. That is, a labour problem should be treated for a particular and limited investigation.

In the choice of a problem for study some thought should be given to the use to which the results should be put. The sociology of industrial relations will not develop usefully unless comparative studies can be made. An investigation of a minute factory situation, such as is frequently carried out in the USA, may be a useful exercise for a postgraduate student but it is not likely to be of further value except to provide conclusions about that precise type of situation. The issues should be broad enough to have some general significance and to make it a feasible task to relate the conclusions which have been reached about them.

If the sociology of industrial relations is approached in the manner I have described we may equip ourselves to talk sensibly about commonplace behaviour, and, who knows, we may even be able to predict with some degree of accuracy.

3

Valuations and historical interpretation[1]

The social scientist derives values from his environment which inevitably intrude in some degree into his work, for a person cannot abstract himself from the attitudes and pressures of the society in which he lives. Nor can he prevent them from influencing his choice of a subject to study, the selection and collation of data and the assessment of it. A social scientist cannot be impartial about his subject. He can strive for objectivity through his use of scientific method and by taking into account his own bias, but he can never produce a truly impartial study, whether it be of social, economic, political or historical phenomena.

It follows that each sociological work is to some extent a reflection of its author and his environment and that, therefore, in order to understand it one must pay some attention to the author, his values and attitudes. In this paper *The History of Trade Unionism*[2] by Sidney and Beatrice Webb is examined in this way. First, the manner in which the Webbs approached their subject is considered; then an attempt is made to show how this distorted the narration of events the Webbs were endeavouring to record.

The Webbs brought different but complementary qualities to bear on their work. Sidney Webb, by and large, was the assimilator of facts, the note-taker and the draughtsman, while Beatrice was the social investigator, the one who dealt in ideas and worried about method. For this reason, when considering the methodology of the Webbs, more importance should be attached to the background and values of Beatrice Webb and to her conception of the purpose of history than to those of Sidney Webb.

There is no mechanical relationship between social position and ideas but they are closely associated. Beatrice Webb came from a rich

[1] A version of this paper was read to the Society for the Study of Labour History on 27 January 1962.

[2] First published 1894; second 1920 edition, printed by the authors for the trade unionists of the United Kingdom, 1920. Page references are to the 1920 edition.

upper-middle-class family. She had had no contact with working-class people until she began her work as a social investigator. So she brought to bear on her social work and research activities the values of this insular, socially superior environment. It is not surprising to note that she came to social investigation through a belief in philanthropy. She typed men according to the values of her social group, preferring men who were steady, reliable, diligent and hard-working.[3] This preference was reflected in the Webbs' treatment and assessment of union leaders.

Beatrice Webb always regarded herself, before writing *The History of Trade Unionism*, as an apprentice to the craft of social investigation, and she looked on history as an aid to improvement in the craft. She wrote in 1885 that 'having sampled the method of observation and experiment and discovered my field of inquiry, what I needed most was historical background'. Six months later, after much reading, including *Das Kapital* in French, she had decided that historical studies had two uses, namely to provide an 'indispensable knowledge of fact as it enlightens social structure, and the equally indispensable cultivation of imagination to enable you to realize the multiform conditions and temperaments which make up human society'.[4] In short, the purpose of history was to provide a detailed background for the understanding of contemporary problems.

In her pursuit of craft skill, Beatrice Webb was interested in methodology, but not until she worked for Charles Booth did she formulate clear ideas about it. Then she became a firm supporter of what she called Booth's scientific method. This involved collecting as extensive a range of facts and figures as possible about the matter under investigation, and in taking pains to eliminate the subjective elements, particularly those which may have entered into the observations. Beatrice Webb was aware of the difficulty of avoiding bias. She recognized that some was inevitable; some, indeed, was desirable as a quality in a social investigator. But it had to be prevented from distorting the narrative or analysis and in order to achieve this it was desirable for the investigator to hold a number of hypotheses. For her, objectivity entailed being uncommitted to a single or prime explanation of events. Dogmatism was unscientific.

Sidney Webb, before meeting Beatrice, had shown no interest in the phenomenon of trade unionism. His contribution to the *Fabian Essays*

[3] She wrote about 'English working-men of the better type' (*Our Partnership*, Longmans, 1948, p. 22), and the 'sterling integrity and capacity' of Will Thorne, leader of the Gas Workers and General Labourers' Union (*History of Trade Unionism*, p. 402).

[4] *My Apprenticeship*, Longmans, Second Edition, pp. 244, 245.

in 1889, the 'Historic groundwork of socialism', contained no reference to it. But in that essay he did formulate his view of the nature of historical change. He regarded society as being in a constant process of change, evolving gradually from the old to the new 'without any breach of continuity or abrupt change of the entire social tissue at any point during the process. The new becomes itself old often before it is consciously recognized as new. . . .' Change was inevitable but it would occur only gradually. 'History shews us', he added, 'no example of sudden substitutions of Utopian and revolutionary romance.' He thought also that change involved improvement—there occurred 'a constant growth and development of the social organism'. Sidney Webb had formulated his ideal type of society, namely one which was both democratic and socialist, and thought that the economic history of the nineteenth century showed a continuous record of progress towards it. A knowledge of this continuous process, and therefore the purpose of history, Sidney Webb believed, gave 'the clue to the significance of contemporary events'.[5] To this extent his conception of history was similar to that held by Beatrice Webb.

The expectations which historians have had of their subject have varied as related subjects have developed. The tools of analysis at their disposal have become more numerous and complex and have altered the nature of the questions which they have expected to answer. Just as biographers of today have been influenced by Freudian analysis and therefore see a significance in relationships which previously they would have passed by, so have economic historians been influenced by developments in economic and sociological theory, such as Keynesian analysis. The economic historians of today make correlations which nineteenth-century historians never made because they had no analytical significance then.

In the nineteenth century, largely because of the absence of analytical sophistication, historians concentrated on the collection of facts. They regarded themselves by and large as fact-finders in the belief that facts told their own story. The Webbs moved in this tradition. They were interested in telling a story, not in explaining why during the history of trade unionism certain things happened. Because they never intended their history to provide explanations it may be unfair to criticize them for not doing so. 'To us', Beatrice Webb wrote, '*The History of Trade Unionism* seemed little more than an historical introduction to the task we had set before us: the scientific analysis of the structure and function of British Trade Unions.'[6] In the preface

---

[5] *Fabian Essays in Socialism*, ed. G. B. Shaw, 1889, pp. 31, 32.
[6] *Our Partnership*, p. 43.

to their scientific analysis, *Industrial Democracy*, the Webbs called their *History of Trade Unionism* a description of the external characteristics of trade unionism.

But what they set out to do and what they achieved turned out to be different things. 'The reader', they stated in the preface to the 1920 edition of the *History*, 'must not expect to find in this historical volume either an analysis of Trade Union organization, policy and methods, or any judgment upon the validity of its assumptions, its economic achievements, or its limitations.' They referred those who wanted to know 'Whether the trade unionism of which we now write merely the story is a good or bad element in industry and in the State' to a bibliography at the end of the book. They believed that they had laid fact upon fact in such a manner as to exclude judgements altogether.[7] But they had done no such thing.

The history of trade unionism which has been repeated in a succession of books and reiterated in endless lectures was made by the Webbs. There was, in a sense, no trade union history until they wrote it. The information for it was collected by them or under their guidance; they arranged it, sifted what they deemed to be relevant from the irrelevant. Their decisions turned mere information into historical facts. The consequences can be seen in the emphases, the phases, the developments which are now accorded historical importance. The Webbs did in fact tell us about causes.

The history of social phenomena, the Webbs believed, could only be written through a description of continuous organizations.[8] This explains why their book, though called *The History of Trade Unionism*, is about formal, continuously operating trade union organizations. An organization, however, can operate continuously for a week or a hundred years, and how long it has to operate continuously for it to be historically significant is a question for historians to answer. The question cannot be left unanswered. The Webbs did not answer it. It seems that they were thinking about continuity when they were

[7] It is surprising that Beatrice Webb thought that she could write history in this manner. After the *History* had been published she wrote: 'No doubt the sequence involved in history is as artificial as are the groups involved in classification. How silly it is to suppose that facts ever tell their own story—it is all a matter of arranging them so that they may tell something—and the arrangement is a purely subjective matter' (*Our Partnership*, p. 44). Later, when almost overcome by the structural problems of analysis, she wrote: 'With history the threads are supplied by the chronological order—you can weave these threads into any pattern; bring one of them to the surface and then another . . .' (*ibid.*, p. 47). One can only conclude that she and her husband regarded themselves as being sound accurate weavers of historical threads.

[8] *The History of Trade Unionism*, p. viii.

referring to ⌈continuously operating organizations,⌉ for when deciding whether to examine an organization they looked backwards for evidence of continuity of existence and if they found none then they lost interest.

Their preoccupation with unions which showed evidence of continuity led the Webbs to neglect ephemeral bodies or to dismiss their existence as being of no historical significance. But, more important, it led them to neglect the eighteenth century. Yet it is from the conditions of that century that trade unionism emerged and spread, until in the last quarter it was widespread. But even if the Webbs had been interested in the eighteenth century it is unlikely that they would have been able to give adequate answers about the emergence of trade unionism because of the narrowness of their conceptual framework. They made formal union organizations central and dominant in their work and mentioned other factors only in so far as they impinged directly on trade union affairs. For instance, they described changes in the law relating to trade unions and the activities of some politicians and intellectuals. Occasionally the state of trade or the structure of industry was mentioned but rarely were any correlations established between them and trade union action. The Webbs, therefore, discarded factors that are now regarded as causative ones and emphasized factors which are now treated as being of limited explanatory influence.

If history is to provide explanations it must be equivalent to sociological studies of the past. This means, in the case of trade unions, that they must be examined in the context of their whole environments with the primary economic and secondary social and political forces isolated and assessed. The justification for this approach lies in the recognition that industrial and social and political behaviour is a created thing; arising as a consequence of the interaction of many forces, conditioned by them and perpetuated or ended by them. This behaviour may develop self-operating mechanisms which may tend to insulate it from the effects of these forces to some extent but never wholly or for very long. The behaviour, too, may be influenced by personalities, but these must always be seen in their contexts. Persons respond to situations rather than create them; they may influence timing and intensity but rarely direction.

It is in this way that the historical process should be viewed. A history of no matter what institution or event should reproduce this moulding, shaping activity between its pages. If the work covers only a brief period then the activity can be described in some detail, but if it covers a long period, as does the work of the Webbs, then it should describe the movement of general forces and their interaction with each other. Whether or not an historian has attempted to satisfy this standard can be seen first from an examination of the framework of his book and secondly from an examination of the treatment of events within each section of the framework.

The framework used by the Webbs is revealed by their table of contents. The chapters are arranged in a time sequence and each chapter indicates what the Webbs thought was a main phase of activity. It is often difficult to distinguish meaningful phases, particularly to date them. But the Webbs had little difficulty because they regarded obvious formal events as marking the transition from one phase to another. In the remainder of this paper some aspects of the phasing of trade union history by the Webbs will be examined and then their treatment of activities within them will be assessed.

The first formal event of any importance in the history of trade unionism, according to the Webbs, was the passing of the Combination Acts in 1799 and 1800. Before 1799 lay the largely uncharted gestation period which they called The Origins of Trade Unionism, and after it came what they termed The Struggle for Existence which lasted until the Combination Laws Repeal Act Amendment Act replaced the Combination Acts in 1825. The implication of the emphasis on the years 1799 and 1825 as the years marking the limits of a phase is that the Combination Acts had a decisive impact on trade union action. This was not the case. The Combination Acts were not the first acts of repression against trade unionism. Trade unionists firstly, could be prosecuted under common law for acting in restraint of trade. Secondly, by 1799 there were already about forty special Acts of Parliament directed against them.[9] Perhaps then the Combination Acts were more repressive or were more effectively applied than the other measures. This was not so either. The penalties under the Acts were milder than could be enforced through alternative means and, in any case, when employers wanted to take action against trade unions they often sought special means to do so rather than invoke the Combination Acts. The Acts had a greater significance in the North than elsewhere and their application varied over time, but they did not cause trade unions in general to have to struggle for their existence.

The significance of the Combination Acts is that they indicated the state of mind of a ruling class which had witnessed from fairly close quarters a revolution in France by the under-privileged. For the first

[9] A. Aspinall, ed. *The Early English Trade Unions: documents from the Home Office papers in the Public Record Office*, Batchworth 1949, p. x.

time combinations seemed to have political implications. In so far then as there was a change in the environment of trade unions it was brought about by the French Revolution in 1789 and it did not last until 1825. Political repression continued well into the nineteenth century but it was not engendered by the fear of revolution in the same intensity after 1820. By then the French Revolution was long past; the French had been defeated at Waterloo; different politicians were making the decisions and the unions themselves had consolidated their positions. In 1818 the Combination Acts were regarded by the Under Secretary of State for the Home Office as being 'almost a dead letter'.[10] Their removal from the Statute Book in 1824, like the removal of so much legislation, came long after they had lost their utility. It may be argued, of course, that the wave of strikes in 1825 and the reintroduction of restrictions on combinations through the Combination Laws Repeal Act Amendment Act the same year reveal that the Acts had some significance. The news of the repeal may have been taken as an impulse to organize by some workers, but it should be noted that 1825 was a year of good trade and that during previous years of good trade, 1818–19 for instance, there had also been much strike action. The reimposition of restrictions through the 1825 Act only indicates that the legislators saw a correlation between the repeal of the Acts and the strike action of 1825; it does not follow that such a correlation did in fact exist. The words and actions of legislators can rarely be explained in simple meaningful terms.

The next phase in the framework of the Webbs is called a revolutionary one and covers the years from 1829 to 1842. It starts with the attempt by John Doherty to form a general trades union and ends with the Plug Riots in the Midlands and Lancashire. In this period the Webbs saw insurrection, expressed mainly through an endeavour to apply the ideals of Robert Owen through the medium of trade unions, as the dominant feature. Owen, however, flirted very briefly with the trade union movement and had little effect on the aspirations and methods of the thousands of trade unionists who belonged to the lodges of the Grand National Consolidated Trades Union which Owen was instrumental in forming. The interests of the ordinary trade unionists, as a perusal of the papers at the Public Records Office shows, were confined to wages and conditions of work. What is significant about the activities of the trade unionists is that they were related through membership of a single large organization which catered for workers irrespective of their trade. It was experiments in the formation of large general or trades unions which characterized

[10] *Ibid.*, p. xix.

the period. But not the period the Webbs had selected. The attempts at general union, as G. D. H. Cole pointed out, started in 1818 and ended in 1834.[11] After 1934 purely sectional developments, which in some trades had always been pursued, were carried on in all trades. They were pursued irrespective of the prevailing political movements.

The political activities which workers engaged in until 1842 were never alternatives to trade union action but were complementary. There were many parallel streams of activity in the 1830s and 1840s— trade unionism, factory reform agitation, the Corn Law repeal movement and Chartism. Because these streams were products of different forces they did not often coincide in intensity. For instance, unemployment weakened trade union action but provided the material for mass political support. This has often been taken to mean, though falsely, that workers turned in frustration from one course of action to another.

The historical distortion created by the Webbs' preoccupation with formal institutional matters was most probably greatest in their treatment of the mid-century years. They saw a phase stretching from 1843 to 1860 which they called the New Spirit and the New Model and which was pivoted on the formation of the Amalgamated Society of Engineers in 1851. They had what can only be described as an obsession for the administratively tidy, centralized constitution of the ASE and they proclaimed it as the New Model. This ranks as a piece of historical fiction. The main characteristics of the constitution of the Amalgamated Society of Engineers had appeared in a number of unions since the early 1830s. They had been forced on them by economic and industrial pressures. The movement of skilled workers such as bookbinders, printers, brushmakers and engineers of various kinds, in search of work during the depression years of the 1830s and 1840s, brought about attempts to link up local societies catering for the same trade; the high incidence of unemployment revealed the defects of the tramping system and impelled trade unionists to consider uniformly applied benefit systems; improvements in transport and postal communications helped to break down local insularity; the introduction of machines affected craft skills by diluting them; and employers, controlling larger, expanding industrial and financial units, revealed the weaknesses of small insular trade societies. In the face of these factors piecemeal adjustments were being continually made in union organizations. The impact of the factors varied between industries; in some instances, as in the mining and cotton textile industries, there were strong countervailing forces which preserved and consoli-

[11] G. D. H. Cole, *Attempts at General Union*, Macmillan, 1953.

dated local societies or led to a federal system of government. G. D. H. Cole, in a neglected article in the *International Review for Social History* for 1937,[12] described the constituent parts of the factors leading to centralized and decentralized organizational forms. Certainly the Amalgamated Society of Engineers warrants recording as an historical event but not because of its constitutional uniqueness. It provided one of the first illustrations of a union which could wage a major strike without subsequently suffering from insolvency. The formation of the ASE was not the most significant event for trade unionism of 1851. That event was the Great Exhibition in the Palace of Industry: 1851 marked not the middle of a phase but the beginning of one.

The Great Exhibition epitomized the cult of progress in Victorian England, a cult which gave Sidney Webb a particular conception of history. It signified a change in the environment of trade unions. In the years that followed it until about 1874 the history of trade unionism is about the manner in which the belief in progress affected the composition, methods and leadership of trade unions. From 1874 until after the year which closed the Webbs' *History*, trade unionism is about the irrelevance of this belief to the experiences of working men and women and the consequent changes in their collective behaviour. The Webbs did not see things in this way. They explained events largely in terms of leadership policies. They regarded the small group of London-centred union leaders in the 1860s and 1870s as the men who 'steered the Trade Union Movement through its great crisis . . .'[13] and considered that the failure of these men to remain in control was due to the combined effects of changing personalities and the retention by those who remained of laissez-faire views. The Webbs believed in the primary importance of crusades, propaganda and lectures to working men and women. In other words, they believed in conversion irrespective to a large extent of the nature of the economic and social conditions which existed. It is not surprising, then, that the Webbs gave the Junta a phase all to themselves instead of looking at the operation of the group as a part of a complex process. The last phase designated by the Webbs, called the Old Unionism and the New and spreading over the years 1875 to 1890, is explained mainly in similar terms.

There is a strong case for rephasing trade union history so that it provides the kind of explanations which satisfy the standards of

[12] G. D. H. Cole, 'Some notes on British trade unionism in the third quarter of the nineteenth century', *International Review for Social History*, ii, 1937, 1–23.
[13] *The History of Trade Unionism*, p. 297.

contemporary historians. But there is more to it than this for the Webbs, through their neglect of primary economic forces and a lack of sociological understanding which was implicit in Sidney Webb's conception of history, have either provided partial explanations or have introduced distortions in the treatment of events within each section of their historical framework. It is only possible to give a few such illustrations in the remainder of this paper.

In their description of the origin of trade unionism the Webbs attributed a causative influence to the meeting of journeymen together to get work, to provide themselves with security through benefit clubs and to protest against the excessive use of apprentices. These factors indeed brought journeymen together, but what forces created them with such intensity and why in the second half of the eighteenth century and not before? In many trades the necessary conditions for trade unionism had existed since the seventeenth century.

The timing of collective action can be explained in terms of the economic pressures on employers which arose from the combined effects of an intensification of production, wars and inflation in the second half of the eighteenth century. These pressures resulted on the one hand in employment fluctuations of a greater intensity than hitherto and on the other hand in attempts to cut labour costs through using cheap apprenticeship labour. They did what previous pressures had not succeeded in doing; that is, they made journeymen realize the primary importance of production relationships and revealed their positions of inferiority in those relationships. This explanation was not given by the Webbs.

A quick move to the other end of the time span of the Webbs' *History* reveals a superficial explanation of the extension of trade unionism to unskilled workers. The Webbs could not account for the extension then contraction of collective action among the unskilled workers in the 1870s and they did not think that there was any comparison between that period and the late 1880s and early 1890s when similar movements took place. They did, however, think there was an analogy between 1833-34 and 1889-91. They were impressed with the gains made in 1889, made comparisons between the policies which were pursued and concluded that the 'empirical Socialism of the Trade Unionist of 1889, with its eclectic opportunism, its preference for municipal collectivism, its cautious adaptation of existing social structure' would be proved superior to the 'revolutionary and universal Communism of Robert Owen'.[14] They also believed that the

[14] *The History of Trade Unionism*, p. 417.

methods of 1889 were more effective because 'they aimed, not at superseding existing social structures, but at capturing them all in the interests of the wage-earners'. The Webbs acknowledged that the circumstances had changed but listed only the formal political structure as a relevant factor in the circumstances. At no point did they regard as important the factors, such as the widening of the permanent industrial labour force, the extension of educational facilities and the increasing intensity of trade depressions, which had brought about a consciousness of class among the skilled as well as unskilled workers which had been absent in 1834 and weak in the 1870s.

Sometimes the Webbs were inconsistent in their explanations. Occasionally they related trade union action to the state of the labour market. For instance, they wrote that the years between 1825 and 1830 were years of trade contraction and distress during which strikes invariably ended in disaster.[15] But they did not often take the correlation further and were not able to account for the wage and strike movements which occurred so regularly. One particular movement was that of 1834. Sidney and Beatrice Webb attributed the collapse of the Grand National Consolidated Trades Union to its own internal defects and its pursuit of Owenite ideals. They wrote:

> The records of the rise and fall of the 'New Unionism' of 1830–4 leave us conscious of a vast enlargement in the ideas of the workers, without any corresponding alteration in their tactics in the field. In council they are idealists, dreaming of a new heaven and a new earth; humanitarians, educationalists, socialists, moralists: in battle they are still the struggling, half-emancipated serfs of 1825, armed only with the rude weapons of the strike and boycott.[16]

This is an exaggerated description, reflecting their preference for the bureaucratic and their dislike of the idealistic. There is no doubt that the membership of the Grand National Consolidated Trades Union did outrun the capacity of the Union's administration to deal with it, but this does not account for the rapid and complete decline of the Union. The Webbs mentioned the two key features in the situation but did not relate them. They described how the employers used the 'document' on a large scale and mentioned that the year it happened was one of rising trade. The unions 'get beaten', they noted, 'in a rising market instead of, as hitherto, only in a falling one'.[17] They did not ask why the employers were willing to forgo the benefits of an expanding market for as long as six months in some cases, for that is as long as some of the strikes and lockouts persisted. They did not

[15] *Ibid.*, p. 111.   [16] *Ibid.*, p. 153.   [17] *Ibid.*, p. 154.

note that the factor which distinguished this year from earlier ones was the uniform determination of the employers to stamp out the form of trade unionism which the Grand National Consolidated Trades Union represented, regardless of the short-run economic costs to them. Nor did they consider whether a union without the defects they deplored could have withstood the employers' attack.

The emphasis which the Webbs placed on the causative roles of individuals resulted in undue attention being given to certain people. The most glaring case is that of Francis Place, the Charing Cross tailor. Place warrants a mention in trade union history as the man who agitated in the years leading up to 1825 for the repeal of the Combination Acts. But his activities in obtaining the repeal have no historical trade union significance. What is significant are the conditions which led to such an uneventful repeal. Maybe the Prime Minister was not aware that the Acts had been repealed but what is more important is that apparently he was not interested either. This is a case where the Webbs' admiration for the qualities of a man distorted an historical emphasis.

Throughout *The History of Trade Unionism* one can detect the influence of Sidney Webb's view that the economic history of the nineteenth century is a record of continuous improvement. Instead of examining all the time the manner in which unions were coping with their changing environments, the authors inspected the unions for improvement and rated them accordingly. In the beginning democracy was primitive, but not at the end. They were eulogistic about the representative government of the cotton spinners and the miners. In the beginning the local trade societies were administratively crude but not so the New Model unions. Likewise the policies of Robert Owen were impracticable but not those of the Municipal Collectivists. Collective bargaining, Government recognition, public acceptance, industrial moderation, were each viewed as an improvement on what went on before rather than as a response to situations in which unions were functioning.

PART II

PART II

4

Contemporary and historical issues in industrial relations

The manner in which trade union development, the role of unions and their response to situations are interpreted depends upon which of the two conceptual approaches mentioned in Chapter 1 are used.

One approach sees industrial relations occurring within a dynamic conflict situation which is permanent and unalterable so long as the structure of the society remains unaltered. This situation was mentioned briefly towards the end of Chapter 1. It occurs because on the one hand the sellers of labour power enter the labour market in order to subsist so that the price of labour power is a vital subsistence matter for them, while on the other hand the buyers enter the market because they own the means of production and have insufficient labour power to make production possible so that the price is an important cost factor which has to be minimized in order to make production profitable. These two interests are irreconcilable. They are engaged in a perpetual conflict over the distribution of revenue. It might be stated that the interests have a common purpose in increasing total revenue and so they may have. But the conflict over distribution is in no sense lessened by this for the actual distribution of additional increments of revenue is determined by the power situation. Employees with no power may get nothing. There is no automatic distribution based on a sense of fairness or equity. Shares have to be fought for, sometimes bitterly.

The conflict which arises out of the primary market relationship is not like an argument over the price of a commodity. The buyers of labour power assume that they can control the commodity they buy. As labour power cannot be separated from the persons who provide it the control is exercised over people. Employers have constructed complex authority structures to ensure that the requisite amount of effort is provided at the rates and the times they require. The power they have, to choose and discard labour, is supplemented by the control they exercise over its use.

The consequences of the imbalance of power in the market are not confined to the work situation. The ownership of the means of production provides the base for economic and political power in a society. Where ownership rests in a few private hands then the power is used to perpetuate the system of distribution which supports this state. The availability of opportunity, the distribution of rewards, the allocation of status and privileges and the dominant supporting ideology all reflect the basic power position and serve to preserve it. There is no escape from the realities of the conflict situation for those who are compelled to sell their labour power in order to subsist.

The conflict described above is caused by the structure of the society which is, in turn, derived from the social relations to the means of production. The means of production are privately owned and labour power is obtained through the open market. It follows that so long as these factors remain unchanged then so will the conflict situation. In other words, the necessary condition for the elimination of class conflict is the destruction of the relationship between the buyers and sellers of labour power. No amount of superstructural adaptation will achieve this end.

When conflict is viewed in this way then trade unionism is given a clear unambiguous meaning which is quite distinct from that derived from any other view of conflict. The conflict situation creates the need for employees to combine to protect themselves. Trade unionism, therefore, has structural determinants and is as permanent and ineradicable as conflict itself, given that the structure remains unchanged. There is another logically inevitable similarity. Class conflict permeates the whole of society and is not just an industrial phenomenon. In the same way trade unionism is a social as well as industrial phenomenon. Trade unions are, by implication, challenging the property relations whenever they challenge the distribution of the national product. They are challenging all the prerogatives which go with the ownership of the means of production, not simply the exercise of control over labour power in industry. The essential activities of unions are concentrated at the point of production because it is there that the impact of the dynamics of the system is greatest. But they are not confined to the work place. In other words, trade unionism is a dynamic social movement with implications for the system of capitalism which are far more profound than is generally recognized by the participants.

If trade unions are structurally determined then so must their methods be. [Strikes are an index of conflict and are a permanent feature of a capitalist system. Individual strikes can be resolved, as empirical evidence shows, but the phenomenon of strike action—the possibility of strikes recurring—must be accepted as an inevitable consequence of the nature of capitalism. If conflict is permanent, endemic, pervasive, then nothing which unions do can escape its influence. Collective bargaining appears not as a method for settling disputes between employers and employees which is based on the application of reason and argument but as an institutionalized form of conflict. Collective bargaining can never be abstracted from the power struggle no matter how impressive its apparatus for the rational settlement of disputes. The involvement of government in industrial relations is seen as a means to contain trade unions. Labour law is restrictive, disarming, sometimes oppressive. Unions are part of the process of transformation of capitalism and governments represent the interests which want to preserve the system. No matter what their short-run, day-to-day relationships may be their long-run interests inevitably conflict.

Those who assume the dominance of consensus qualities, who believe that there are no structural conflict-making divisions in society, adopt a wholly different approach to conflict and, in consequence, to trade unionism. Conflict cannot be endemic because consensus is assumed to be so. Conflict can only exist as an aberration from the norm of consensus and it is seen, therefore, as a temporary remedial phenomenon. Because there are no common structural determinants of conflict, conflict in different places or at different times does not have a common explanation. The causes of conflict can be as numerous as there are variables in a situation and the variables can be chosen and correlated as the analyst sees fit. This view of conflict has four main consequences for the interpretation of trade unionism.

First, there is no necessary causal connection between a situation of conflict and the growth of trade unionism, with the consequence that it is possible to separate trade unionism from conflict action and to envisage it operating without recourse to strike action. The causes of trade unionism, if examined at all, would be decided empirically and, as in the case of conflict, there would be almost unlimited scope for choosing variables.

Secondly, strike action, like conflict, is treated as a remedial phenomenon. In any event, strikes must be treated as temporary aberrations from the norm of unity. If the causes of strikes are treated then the norm must prevail. Given the assumption of consensus, of the existence of a common purpose, then it must be possible to envisage a completely strike-free economy as a permanent state.

Thirdly, a consequence of the analytical possibility of separating conflict from trade unionism is that collective bargaining can be seen in an entirely different context from strikes. The completely strike-free economy would be one where employers and employees settled their temporary differences amicably and rationally and devoid of duress. In analyses of the contemporary situation where the assumption of consensus is made, collective bargaining is treated as an alternative to strikes as a means of settling disputes.

Lastly, trade unionism is seen primarily as a workplace phenomenon, concerned only with wages, hours and conditions. It is not a social movement but a consequence of imperfect market conditions. The logic of this approach is to treat trade unionism as business unionism, the trade union equivalent of business organizations, concerned only with negotiating contracts. The notion of a union as a business organization both constricts the character of the service given to members and specifies the administration through which it should be provided. The day-to-day running of the organization need not concern the ordinary members for they should be interested only in the end result. The unions would have a technical task for which professional skills ought to be employed. Lay intervention would only interfere with the smooth running of the organization. Questions of internal democracy should not arise. In reality, however, trade unions depend in the main on membership participation and they endeavour to practise internal democracy. In this event the notion of a union as a business organization applies to ends alone while internal democracy is also seen as an end and not a means. When internal democracy is analysed in this context it assumes an importance over the functions and purposes of unions.

The effect of adopting one approach rather than another can be seen in the way trade unionism in general is interpreted as well as the manner in which particular incidents or methods in the history of trade unionism are emphasized and highlighted. Chapter 5 in this Part is an illustration of the effect of the assumption of permanent class conflict on the interpretation of the contemporary situation in Britain. Chapter 6, 'The Origins of Industrial Conciliation and Arbitration', is about an historical misinterpretation concerning the role of arbitrators in the 1860s and 1870s and the effect of arbitration in the same period which originates in *The History of Trade Unionism* by Sidney and Beatrice Webb and has been perpetuated by many subsequent writers about conciliation and arbitration, in particular by

E. H. Phelps Brown in his book *The Growth of British Industrial Relations* (Macmillan, 1959). As was stated in Part I, that which is not recorded by historians ceases to be history because it is not regarded as having any explanatory significance. Chapter 7 recalls a too readily forgotten incident. On a number of occasions since 1945 governments have sought solutions to industrial relations problems by initiating grandiose schemes such as a committee of experts like the Cohen Council in 1957 and the National Incomes Commission in 1962. Each time this is done the fate of earlier attempts is conveniently forgotten. Chapter 7 describes the National Industrial Conference, 1919–21, the most grandiose of all the schemes so far for settling industrial disputes.

The last two chapters in Part II concern the organization of non-manual workers. They raise a particularly important methodological question. It is maintained here that people who sell their labour are in the same conflict situation and are, in consequence, subject to pressures which cause them to take collective action. Put another way, the necessary condition for trade unionism is selling labour power so that *all* employees are potential trade unionists. This is so irrespective of the occupation, income, social background or any other characteristic of employees. Non-manual workers are just as much *potential* trade unionists as any other types of employees. It is clear, however, that all employees are not trade unionists and that, in Britain in particular, employees described as non-manual workers are much less organized than those described as manual workers. The question then is, what creates this situation? The issue is approached by making a distinction between the necessary and sufficient conditions for trade unionism. The sufficient conditions are those factors in an environment which determine the timing of the emergence of trade unionism, the forms it takes and the rate at which it develops. They only apply, however, given the presence of the necessary conditions. They include such factors as the degree of political freedom, social class attitudes to trade unionism, the type of work, the extent of factory production, the development of bureaucratic organization and the attitudes of employers. The approach of non-manual workers to collective action will be found by identifying and examining the sufficient conditions which apply in their particular cases. It will be seen, however, that the categories manual and non-manual, white-collar and blue-collar, have no analytical significance. Indeed nowadays non-manual workers are difficult to identify as an objective category. Their distinguishing characteristics, such as working by brain rather than by hand, working in clean clothes and in offices, receiving special fringe benefits, living in exclusive urban areas and receiving relatively high incomes, have all been altered, in many cases almost to the point of erasure, by the impact of machinery and the changing demand for different types of skills. The important question is not why are non-manual workers less organized than manual workers but why are people in some occupations slower to organize than in others?

5

Trade unions in contemporary capitalism

Trade unions are a generally accepted phenomenon in Britain. They have rights in law which can be regarded in some respects as privilege; they have established relations with the great majority of employers which are written into constitutional procedures for settling industrial disputes; they are accorded public and governmental recognition as political pressure groups so that they have access to government ministers and are asked for their views on a range of economic and industrial matters; their opinions are heard or read on the media of mass communications and they are formally involved in the political decision-making process through their membership of government advisory committees. Hardly ever is a Royal Commission or govern- ment advisory body established nowadays which does not include ~~INCORPO- RATION~~ trade union representation. In 1939 unions were represented on only twelve government committees, but since the advent of the Labour Government in 1945 the number has fluctuated roughly between sixty and eighty. Nowadays there are strong legitimate protests if unions are excluded from an important advisory committee.

The public and political stature of unions no longer depends upon the politics of the government. There was no substantial change in the status of unions when the Conservative Party displaced the Labour Party from office in 1951. The Conservative Government had no emotional bond with unions and did not feel as impelled to take cognizance of union opinions as did the Labour Government, yet the number of government committees on which unions were represented rose from sixty in 1949 to eighty-one in 1954. The change was not due to an increase in the number of committees formed but to a spread in union representation.

The integration of trade unions into the structure of society has been given meaning in occupational and social terms. A trade union official can now be drawn into all levels of public and private industrial management because of his knowledge and understanding of unions, and he is not necessarily excluded if he sympathizes with them. A close association with unions is not a disqualification for entry into hitherto exclusive social circles. A formal entry is made possible by the offers of government honours to union leaders. A trade union peer or knight or recipient of a lesser award is not a figure of curiosity. Indeed a government honours list which does not include the names of some union officials is itself a curiosity. Informally, in some social circles and some circumstances, union officials are people to be courted and flattered.

The non-legalistic integration of unions into society has proceeded in all capitalist countries but it has most probably gone further and deeper in Britain than elsewhere. In Britain the trade union movement is publicly acclaimed as an estate of the realm. The essential meaning of this integration is that unions now carry no revolutionary significance for the established political decision-makers in Britain and are seen as institutions which perform politically necessary and industrially useful functions. This situation raises important questions concerning the role of trade unions and its connection with their traditional aims and aspirations.

The paradox of trade unionism

Trade unionism is a universal phenomenon and is the collective act of protecting and improving living standards by people who sell their labour power against people who buy it. Clearly this protective, improving function can be performed in various ways, depending upon the precise nature of the environment in which unions find themselves, but before it can start certain necessary and sufficient conditions have to be present. The necessary conditions are the existence of a free market for labour in which it is possible for buyers to discriminate against, and therefore exercise power over, sellers, and enough political tolerance to permit potential opposition groups to arise. The sufficient conditions can be almost any factor which injects realism into the lives of people who sell their labour. In Britain in the eighteenth century the most significant sufficient condition was the excessive use of apprentices by employers; later the introduction of machinery. In the mid-twentieth century the main factor which impelled white-collar workers to organize was a fall in real incomes, and therefore status, through inflation. But in every case workers were responding to obvious well-formed forces. Trade unions from the very beginning were devised to protect their members from the exigencies of capitalism. They belonged essentially to capitalism because they grew out of the conditions it created.

This fact throws some light, but not all, on the present role of unions. Trade unions are patently not initiators. What they do is always in response to well-established forces such as rising prices, falling prices, unemployment, government action which influences living standards, and over which they have little or no control. They are not, and never have been, revolutionary bodies. They have never been in the vanguard of revolutionary change though they have been vehicles for change. In a number of revolutionary situations unions have formed the organized basis for mass industrial support once the movements for change have commenced. Where revolutions have started without the existence of unions then the unions have had to be created. In Russia before the October Revolution unions were largely the creation of a revolutionary political party. In the struggle for political independence in Ghana and Tanzania the nationalist parties had to ally themselves with unions to make political action apparently and decisively effective.

The fact alone, however, that unions originated as protective societies does not invalidate them as revolutionary, or even initiatory, bodies, unless there is something in their nature which inhibits quick movement. Two factors in concert inhibit quick movement. The first is that trade unionism is a mass act in that it depends for its effectiveness upon the widest possible basis of support. A union must include at least a substantial minority, but more often a majority, of its potential membership before it can command respect from an employer. Secondly, because a union is operating in a conflict situation in which serious adverse consequences might flow from a decision, every major act of policy must be based on the consent, tacit or overt, of a majority of its members. In other words, trade unions are relatively large-scale democratic organizations. Decisions which are acceptable to the majority of the members must necessarily resemble compromises of extreme possibilities and before the need to take a decision is obvious to the majority, the impact of the forces creating the need for a decision must be experienced by most of the people involved. Trade union decisions then are relatively slowly reached compromises. The speed at which a decision is reached is finally determined by the democratic processes within the union. The more serious a matter is, the wider and lengthier must the consultation with the members be. When such a decision is eventually reached the situation which gave rise to it may have changed, thus necessitating a revision of the decision. This is because organizational decisions should reflect actual situations correctly. Every organization, of course, acts in response to forces external to it. But some can anticipate the nature, intensity and direction of the forces and by the speed of their responses appear to initiate change. It is not fortuitous that revolutionary bodies practise what is called democratic centralism.

Trade unions have always been sluggish in their assessment of circumstances, even when their democratic processes were simple and direct. Their responses, however, have been considerably slowed down because as their organizations have grown democracy has become institutionalized. In 1962, 9 per cent of the 176 unions affiliated to the Trades Union Congress organized 71 per cent of the 8,315,332 members. More than 47 per cent of the total membership was in five unions. In these large unions there are rigid, formal bureaucratic structures because only with these can numerous geographically scattered members with diverse interests be serviced. Communications in these structures, however, are slow because every part of them has to be functionally related to and synchronized with every other part. It may take months for communications to pass from one end of the hierarchy to the other. There are also informal obstacles to quick movement. The ability to respond is in part a function of age. The longer the unions exist the more deeply they become tied by vested interests and tradition. In trade unions tradition is a significant determinant of motivation. Unfortunately traditions carry over from one set of circumstances to another. Attitudes evolved, say, during a long period of unemployment become traditional during a phase of full employment and inhibit responses which full employment makes necessary.

These disabilities would not matter if trade unions could satisfy their moderate aims of protection satisfactorily without revolutionary change. As it is, they cannot. It is not possible to state the precise part unions have played in determining the living standards of their members because so many variables are involved. Changes in the demand for labour have a swift impact on workers' living standards while improvements in technology have a longer term, and perhaps more substantial, effect. These and other variables cannot be isolated and controlled and assessed but it is possible to examine the general effectiveness of unions.

The protective function of unions means more than simply holding what is already possessed. It involves insulating workers from the uncertainty, the insecurity and the differentials which characterize capitalism, and this can only be done effectively by making positive demands for security against contingencies such as sickness and unemployment; by providing for that level of income which would act as a buffer against fluctuations in living costs; by narrowing differentials, including the differential between wages and profits, to remove any sense of injustice; and by providing physical amenities in work and out which would protect against excessive fatigue, discomfort and the like. The protective function is based on certain ethical considerations which have their origin in the exigencies of capitalism. The plight of individual employees *vis-à-vis* employers has given rise to a deep sense of solidarity. Protection must involve all in the group, or, depending on the circumstances, the class. Secondly, the injustices of differentials, particularly within a group, have created a desire for equality so that everyone in a group should not only be protected but treated equally.[1] There is a direct relationship between protection and the belief in equality because equality means removing friction-creating differences, not levelling everyone, irrespective of function, to the same standard. All of these basic trade union demands are made initially within the context of the existing distribution of income because trade unionists at large have been socialized to accept their economic and social ratings and to couch their demands, therefore, in 'reasonable' terms. But the logic of the implementation of the protection function is that there should be changes in the distribution of the national income in favour of trade unionists. The extent to which there have been changes is one measure of trade union effectiveness.

The full cost of protecting workers under capitalism is the price of labour. This price, to employers, is a production cost which can be manipulated. If it is regarded as excessive it can either be minimized by using more capital intensive methods or passed on to consumers through higher commodity prices. In each case the distributive process so works as to maintain the *status quo*. The switch to more capital intensive methods will displace labour, so that if the workers who remain in employment obtain gains they will be at the expense of those who have lost their jobs. But even if no labour is displaced there will be an argument about the distribution of the gains and the likelihood is that at the best from the workers' point of view it will follow the traditional pattern. This is because if a union is strong enough to obtain what an employer regards as a disproportionate share he will attempt, and in general succeed, in passing the cost to the consumer. A problem for unions is that they rarely know the gains from improved technology, so they are not able to make definite claims about their distribution anyway. If the commodity market is rising then it will be

---

[1] For a deeply analytical explanation of differentials see W. Baldamus, *Efficiency and Effort*, Tavistock Publications, 1961.

possible for employers to pass on the cost of all trade union demands to consumers simply by increasing prices. As trade unionists are consumers their real incomes remain as they were before the demands were made. Only if unions can increase the price of labour power on a falling commodity market, thus making it impossible for employers to pass the cost on, can they increase their share of the national income, and even then the increase is temporary because as soon as the market conditions improve employers can recoup their losses. It rarely happens that unions are able to increase the price of labour power when employers are finding it difficult to sell their commodities, because a deteriorating state of trade normally produces unemployment and this weakens the unions by making it difficult for workers to pay their union subscriptions and to be militant because they fear unemployment. It is an anomaly that unions are weakest when the possibility of gains is greatest, and are strongest when the possibility of gains is least. There are exceptions in occupations, firms or industries but in general, so long as unions work within the free price mechanism, their basic aims are frustrated. The share of wages in the national income has remained remarkably stable since the last quarter of the nineteenth century.[2] One estimate showed that the share was 41·4 per cent in 1880 and 41·8 per cent in 1935.[3] There were variations between these dates but not sharp ones. In 1913 the share of wages was 39·4 per cent and in 1931 it was 43·7 per cent. Another estimate showed that between 1870 and 1950 wages were never less than 36·6 per cent of the national income and never more than 42·6 per cent.[4] In the period 1946–50, when the money earnings of industrial workers rose by about one-third, the ratio of wages to profits remained roughly at the level of the interwar years. The main determinant of the share of wages was the market environment and unions had no control over this.

The point emerges, then, that although unions are incapable of initiating revolutionary change it is only through such change that they will achieve their basic aims. That is, if an effective means of protection cannot be applied under the present system then it is necessary to alter the systems fundamentally. A step, however, which altered the process of distribution would involve other changes. Unions would not achieve their ends directly but through the agency

---

[2] See J. M. Keynes, 'Relative movements of real wages and output', *Economic Journal*, xlix, 1939, 48–9; M. Kalecki, 'The distribution of the national income', in *Essays in the Theory of Economic Fluctuation*, Allen & Unwin, 1939, pp. 13–41; and E. H. Phelps Brown and P. E. Hart, 'The share of wages in the national income', *Economic Journal*, lxii, 1952, 253–77.

[3] Kalecki, *op. cit.*   [4] Phelps Brown and Hart, *op. cit.*

of a central government with planning authority. The relative shares in the national income could only be disturbed by interfering with the free price mechanism and thus by taking from unions their right to bargain over wages. In order, then, to escape from the restrictions and frustrations imposed by a capitalist society, unions would have to undergo a radical character transformation. There are important sociological reasons why this transformation is resisted.

Union leadership

Trade union officials provide leadership at all levels. Because of the inevitable oligarchic control in unions, leadership involves directing the organizations in all of their major activities and is, therefore, a role which must be analysed if the obstacles to the radical character transformation of unions are to be understood. The role of a union official is set so that the behaviour of any person who becomes an official is almost entirely predictable. The only significant variations which occur are those which exist within the hierarchy of roles in a union. If a person moves from being a local to a national official then different behaviour will be expected of him. The dominance of the role over the individual explains why the union behaviour of communist and anti-communist officials varies so little; why, in other words, there is continuity of activities despite marked changes in personnel. A new union leader might give greater meaning to his role because of his intellectual ability but if this results in a significant difference in the direction of union activities it will be because the environment of the union has also changed.

The behaviour of a union official is confined by various kinds of sanctions which have been created by social and administrative factors. The first set comprise the process of socialization whereby the role of union officials has been conditioned to be consistent with the norms and values of a capitalist society. The second set can be described as the bureaucratization of union organizations.

The process of socialization[5] was an inevitable one, for unions could not perpetually stand out against the system, fail to change it and yet continue to exist without taking on some of the values of the system itself. The consequence has been to make unions work with

[5] The term 'socialization' has two distinct meanings. The one current in socialist terminology refers to the state of industry in a socialist society after the initial stage of nationalization. The second meaning is a description of the process which starts with the 'training of individuals' to fulfil the roles which make up society (C. W. Mills and H. H. Gerth, *Character and Social Structure*, Routledge, 1954). Here the term is used in its second and sociological meaning.

and to some extent for the system. This is what the non-legalistic integration of trade unions into society is all about. The results of the process can be seen in many ways. A dominant trade union ethic is a belief in solidarity. This was forced on unions by their need for cohesion in a hostile environment, yet their practice of solidarity is disrupted by the way in which each individual union stoutly protects its own vested interests. The trade union movement reflects the competitive nature of British society through the competition of unions with each other over wages policies, members, and, in the case of craft unions, jobs. Trade unions have imbued capitalist values to the extent of becoming involved in the competitive process. The unions have welded themselves to the price mechanism through an uncritical belief in collective bargaining so that it would be difficult for any government, no matter how sympathetic towards trade union aspirations, to interfere with the wage bargaining process without evoking strong union protests and arousing their antipathy. The unions advocate limited forms of planning for other sections of the economy but insist that wage determination, the vital variable in the planning process, should remain free. Unions support the principle of equity and through the introduction of uniform rates for jobs attempt to apply it. Yet in collective bargaining they practise the most iniquitous form of wage determination.[6] Free collective bargaining is an institutionalized way of operating the play of market forces and their interaction with the subsidiary forces which make up the balance of industrial power. Workers, irrespective of their needs, are in a strong or weak bargaining position because of market forces. In the interwar years the coal miners, for instance, suffered privations because the export demand for coal declined; in the immediate post-Second World War period they obtained relatively high wages because the demand for coal increased; now that alternative sources of power are established the demand for coal is again decreasing, with the obvious depressing effect on miners' living standards. The treatment of the miners in the past has been iniquitous, as is that of the railway workers at present compared with motor production workers. The justification for allocating rewards according to market forces is crudely economic; it has no basis in equity.

The acceptance of free collective bargaining has led, too, to what can be called the myth of achievement. This is simply a situation where union officials are so preoccupied with the means of achievement that they create an illusion about the ends. Instead of being

[6] See Barbara Wootton, *The Social Foundations of Wage Policy*, Allen & Unwin, 1955.

directly concerned about the redistribution of income and devising a means to achieve this, they show satisfaction with fractional changes in money wage rates. In doing this they accept the expectations which employers have deemed suitable for them. These expectations are buttressed by disarming notions of compromise and fairmindedness. Any departure from what is equitable can be justified if the result can be construed as being fair, the meaning of which is set by the limits of voluntary concessions from employers. Nothing which is achieved through conflict is considered to be a fair result. The illusion of achievement was doubtless necessary to maintain trade union morale when actual achievements were consistently meagre and for this reason was present to some extent during the whole course of trade union development. But it became enlarged in the decade of trade union seduction from 1868 when employers, politicians and middle-class intellectuals persuaded union leaders that reason discussed over a table could solve questions of industrial conflict to the benefit of trade unionists. Reason, in fact, only prevails when it is consistent with the movement of market forces. Union leaders who accept its validity lose sight of the reality that they are in a conflict situation. But then this, too, is a consequence of socialization. There is an illusion about a harmony of industrial interests which also influences the role of union officials.

The sanctions on union leaders are of a prohibitive, prescriptive or permissive character and can be seen in attitudes to making 'unreasonable' demands, breaking negotiated agreements, refusals to compromise and 'irresponsibility' to society at large. There are also sanctions which are derived from the integration of unions into the political parliamentary democratic system. There have always been occasions when the objectives of unions demanded political action. At first the need was for legislation to protect women and children in industry, then to protect union funds, enforce industrial safety standards and establish minimum wage rates for workers in sweated industries. Now the need arises from the growth of the government as an employer and its frequent and decisive interventions in industry. Unions are forced into an intensive relationship with the government but are confronted by limitations on the political action they can take, which are set by a belief in political democracy in general and party politics in particular. The sanctions from this situation concern acts which challenge the authority of an elected government or usurp the party system. There is, in consequence, a general prohibition on industrial action for political ends; indeed on anything which savours of coercion of the government; and union leaders respect it. When union leaders during the General Strike realized they were challenging the authority of the government they backed down as quickly as they could. The unwillingness of the Trades Union Congress to support the London busmen in their 1958 strike indicated that most union leaders did not want even to appear to challenge the government. These restrictions can be extensive for there can be so many points of conflict between unions and the government and when they are expressed, the government invariably adopts a constitutional position which gives it automatic protection.[7]

Bureaucracy does not belong to any particular economic system but it is authoritarian, and is consistent, therefore, with the private ownership and control of the means of production. It has been associated with achievement and is a dominant feature of contemporary capitalism. It is understandable, though not necessarily justifiable, that unions should copy bureaucratic practices as far as their allegiances to democratic control permit. Whereas the socialization process has set limits to the uses to which the role of union leadership may be put, bureaucratization has prescribed limits to the role itself. It has combined all the roles involved in trade unions in a hierarchical structure with fixed layers of command and lines of communication, and has prescribed their duties. Formally, union officials must act towards each other and committees they serve according to regulations. Their informal relationships may differ from the formal ones but only in so far as this accords either with tradition or greater efficiency. The informal power of a general secretary is generally much greater than that provided for by his union constitution because he commands power as a specialist in addition to his formal authority. This is not usually disputed so long as the specialist power produces greater efficiency. But all the time he has to be guided by the formal limits to his activities.

Bureaucracy inevitably slows down movement, as was mentioned earlier, but it does not necessarily result in faulty movement. Faultiness is the product of an inability to respond to changing circumstances. There are two elements in bureaucratic organizations which make accurate and immediate responses to changes difficult. The first is the constitutional provision for action. Rules and regulations are difficult to change unless the need for change is intense and imperative. Unions, moreover, deliberately make constitution-changing difficult because alterations not associated with variations in circumstances can be a handicap to action. Secondly, it is possible for bureaucratic attitudes to develop which make a ritual of adherence to

[7] See V. L. Allen, *Trade Unions and the Government*, Longmans, 1960, ch. 17.

regulations. If circumstances alter but not the regulations, then people with these attitudes cannot cope with the situation.

Trade unions, then, have acquired aims which are legitimate within the context of a capitalist society. They are limited aims, concerning wages, hours of work and working conditions, which can be achieved without unduly disturbing the fabric of capitalism; without, indeed, unduly disturbing capitalists because it is possible to conceive of them being obtained through labour market pressures. These legitimate aims are pursued through institutionalized practices. So long as the environment of unions remains stable there need be no inconsistency between the aims and the practices; that is, the ordinary members may feel they are getting satisfaction. But if there are sharp environmental changes, equally sharp inconsistencies develop because institutionalized practices are relatively unresponsive to change. This is what has happened in Britain. Trade unions now are not capable by themselves of achieving satisfactorily even their limited aims.

The meaning of contemporary capitalism

There have been many journalistic and academic claims that contemporary capitalism differs essentially from the classical capitalism of the nineteenth century. These argue in general that economic class conflict no longer exists and that trade unions, in consequence, can have no serious, ineradicable differences with employers. One basis for the claims is that there has been a divorce between the ownership and control of industry and that, in consequence, managers who are employees control industry and do not adopt the same attitude towards profit-making, and therefore relations with other employees, as do employers. Using this assumption there has been much sociological treatment of the theme that conflict does not have an economic class basis but is created by the distribution of authority.[8] Others see contemporary capitalism as consisting only of frictions which can be removed by individual or small group adjustments because the system itself has an organic unity. These beliefs have underlain the creation of a vast apparatus of personnel management and the extension of education and training courses for managers, which in turn have tended to spread the notion that conflict is different now. Social class analysts have added their endorsement, too. Many sociologists have emphasized social class as if it had superseded economic class divisions.

[8] Cf. Ralf Dahrendorf, *Class and Class Conflict in Industrial Society*, Routledge, 1959.

They have generalized about the effect of increasing prosperity on social class positions, regarding these as relatively fluid and determined largely by the acquisition of material things. When the working class becomes more prosperous, it is often claimed, it moves on to middle-class or bourgeois-class values and ways of living. In its new class position it votes differently and adopts more conciliatory attitudes over industrial relations. The point about looking at class as a social phenomenon only is that it makes class divisions into relationship differences which are neither wholly explicit nor immovable. Conflicts, therefore, become individual or small group frictions and can be eliminated by piecemeal action.

These contentions concerning the nature of conflict stem more from a desire to preserve the *status quo* than from thorough and systematic analysis. As far as Britain is concerned, the divorce of ownership from control in industry is by no means as widespread as has been assumed.[9] But in any case it is difficult to substantiate the view that managers do not represent the value system of employers. Managers are employed to maximize profits; that in doing this they take other factors, such as stability, power and prestige, into account is not surprising, because employers undoubtedly do the same. There is no evidence, either from the existence of a managerial group or any other factor, to show that industry has organic unity. Piecemeal action in the form of higher wages, better working conditions and shorter hours has never removed conflict. Indeed the advocates of organic unity find it difficult to reconcile the industrial militancy of highly paid skilled workers and the spread of militancy to non-manual and professional workers with their contention. Social class is doubtless one of many variables which influence the collective behaviour of employees but there is no single direct correlation between social class positions and trade unionism, or even industrial militancy, as has been shown by the collective behaviour of doctors, nurses, teachers and bank clerks in recent years. But even if it could be shown that social class positions determined attitudes to collective action and that some classes found trade unionism either repugnant or unnecessary, it still has to be shown that contemporary capitalism has experienced a substantial movement between the classes or, more significantly, from the manual workers' group to higher status group. Social class analysis is so far unsatisfactory. More basic research needs to be done into it and more questions asked of it. Dubious correlations are made concerning the acquisition of material things and social class posi-

[9] P. Sargant Florence, *Ownership, Control and Success of Large Companies: an analysis of English industrial structure and policy, 1936–1951*, Sweet & Maxwell, 1961.

tions; and about class identification and actual class membership. It is not possible, then, to make precise statements about movement between classes.[10] It is fairly clear, however, that the acquisition of washing machines, refrigerators, television or cars, does not convert a person from the working-class to the middle-class value system. Prosperity to members of the working class means little more than that they can afford commodities and services they could not afford before. They continue to live in relatively unchanged communities and work situations. Some manual workers, under the influence of high wages and confusing statements about class, might identify themselves with the middle class. But an important thing about class is that, irrespective of what a person thinks, his position is determined by social attitudes towards him. Working-class families do not find it easy to gain acceptance in middle-class circles. The social class barriers in Britain are relatively rigid, even under contemporary capitalism. As the working class changes, for whatever reason, so do other classes and social distances remain unchanged.

Class which gives rise to trade unionism is a structural phenomenon and cannot be removed, or even altered, without structural alterations. There have been no such alterations in Britain; nor could there be without removing the essential features of capitalism. British society is still primarily based on the private ownership and control of industry motivated by profit; economic class divisions determined by relationships to the means of production remain undisturbed by the professionalization of management and economic prosperity. Nothing has happened, in consequence, to remove the conflict between the sellers and buyers of labour power, and, therefore, the *raison d'être* of trade unionism.

Capitalism today, however, differs from that in years before World War II in important, though not essential, respects for trade unions. The first is that it has learned from Keynesian economics how to tackle the problem of unemployment. There is a much greater likelihood now that full employment will be maintained. Full employment eases the problem of recruitment for trade unions largely because employed workers can afford to pay their union contributions. The size of the working population has barely changed since 1939 yet the number of trade unionists has risen from 6,274,000 to 9,872,000 in 1962. Trade unions are stronger because they are more extensively organized. But, as was mentioned earlier, it is a misplaced strength because full employment removes the fear of unemployment from the

[10] See David Lockwood, 'The new working class', *European Journal of Sociology*, i, no. 2, 1960, 248–59, for an illuminating article on this topic.

worker and strengthens his individual bargaining position so that he may feel that he does not always need the protection of his union. In so far as the individual worker wants union support he wants it promptly. Delay is not criticized when the issue is one of wage reduction, but when a wage increase is concerned it is a different matter.

The British collective bargaining system is centralized. It took on its form largely in the interwar years when workers were relatively helpless through unemployment and unions were weak from both unemployment and the General Strike. Employers on the other hand were dominant. In this situation national bargaining was necessary because without it there would not have been a sufficient balance of power to make bargaining possible. National bargaining, moreover, was preferred by workers, as were centralized unions, because they were weak at the workplace. Employers in most industries felt they could control and contain unions whether organized nationally or not but preferred nationally determined wage rates because they tended to equalize labour costs and assist in the elimination of price competition. Just as national collective bargaining became established, full employment changed its environment by switching the balance of power to the workplace. The centralized system was inappropriate, but it was not changed, so both workers and individual employers tended to disregard it. Workers used their own shop stewards' organizations either to negotiate directly with employers or to interpret national wage agreements. Sometimes the decisions of national bargaining were ignored because they did not correspond with reality. Shop stewards' organizations or local union branches then negotiated separate agreements. Individual employers did not hesitate to pay more than negotiated rates if this was the only way in which they could get and retain labour in a competitive market. Hence there has been a substantial amount of wage drift since the war. Trade union negotiated rates were often nothing more than fallback rates.

The inability of unions to respond to the full employment situation is to some extent reflected by the number of unofficial strikes. The vast majority of strikes are called and conducted without official union support. But the most significant indication is the spread and intensified activity of shop stewards' organizations. These bodies are not hampered in their movements by a bureaucratic hierarchy and, because they are located at the place of work, they are in close and immediate touch with the ordinary members. Shop stewards' organizations fulfil an essential democratic need. Their activities are not contrary to those of unions nor do they usurp the authority of unions, for they are making up for trade union deficiencies. They provide bases for flexible and spontaneous action and this is possible only because they are to a large extent formally independent of official union bodies. Any move to integrate them into the formal constitutions of unions would lead to frustration and eventually to the creation of new, independent bodies.

An interesting outcome of a prolonged full employment situation has been the development of refined, rather sophisticated techniques for handling labour problems. Personnel management departments have been created because employers cannot select and sort their labour forces under full employment conditions, as they did with unemployment. Inducement, persuasion and cajolery have taken the place of strict discipline. In some ways personnel managers supplement the work of shop stewards; between them they tackle and solve many of the minor grievances which arise continually in industry and in so doing help to protect the official union bodies from serious rank and file pressure.

In the post-Second World War period, trade unions have attracted much attention from the public and the government because of their supposed role as determinants of the general level of wages in an inflationary or potentially inflationary situation. Trade unions have large memberships for whom they negotiate wages, therefore it is assumed that they are responsible for the upward movement of money wages. This movement, however, is a product of a market situation where the demand for labour exceeds the supply and it would, indeed does, take place irrespective of union behaviour. Most unions do not know what the actual money earnings of their members are and certainly have no control over them. None the less, governments have placed the responsibility for wage advances with unions and unions have largely accepted it because it has drawn them into the field of national policies and has given them a public status. Since 1947 the trade union movement, represented by the Trades Union Congress, has been involved in a political game over wages with successive governments. The game has been played in all seriousness but it has been nonetheless a game in that any real attempt to solve the problems of inflation and perpetual balance of payments crises would have involved serious planning of the factors which cause wage movements and determine their relationship with prices. The game, however, in the early 1960s, began to test vital union attitudes over wage determination and to reveal unusual postures with regard to planning.

During the period of perpetual economic crises and Conservative Government between 1951 and 1964, the attitude of the government and employers towards economic planning was seriously modified. Planning, with the important proviso that it should support rather than interfere with private enterprise industry, became a respectable term. The approach to it was uncertain for it was not clear how to plan with effect without interfering with someone's rights. The government respected the rights of private industry because that was dictated by its doctrine and did not, therefore, want to direct resources into uses and felt impelled to respect the rights of trade unions because only in that way could it obtain their collaboration. It decided on using the mechanism of a national body representative of the major industrial interests and served by independent specialists and, in the summer of 1962, established the National Economic Development Council. It was intended that this council should, under the guidance of the Chancellor of the Exchequer, evolve national economic plans. To supplement its activities the National Incomes Commission was formed to collect evidence and express opinions upon the effect or possible effect of claims and collective decisions of trade unions and employers upon community interests as construed by the Commission. No provision was made for implementing the devised plans or recommendations. This was to be a matter for the government. The employers gave their immediate support and, after much debate and hesitation, the Trades Union Congress agreed to join the National Economic Development Council but to withold support from the National Incomes Commission. The Trades Union Congress wanted to test the sincerity of the government but it could not for long reject the prestige value of being part of a widely publicized national advisory committee on planning. On the other hand it rejected the very idea of the National Incomes Commission because it was

> an attempt from the top, outside industry, by people not responsible to working people who receive wages, to superimpose limitations, control, upon people in negotiations whose responsibility lies that way to their own members. . . . The whole idea of a super body at the top, NIC or TUC, imposing restrictions, limitations, upon the right of trade union representatives to represent their members is foreign to everything we stand for in this country.[11]

One of the main purposes of the National Economic Development Council was to find a way of ensuring that wages did not rise further than the rate of production. The TUC did not object to this provided the policy included incomes as a whole and on the understanding that it was involved in the formulation.

[11] George Woodcock, General Secretary of the TUC, at the 1963 Congress (*TUC Report*, 1963, p. 391).

The National Economic Development Council met approximately every month and published reports on the factors influencing economic growth in Britain but it had not, by the end of 1963, reached agreement on incomes and profits and, therefore, on wages. The dilemma of the TUC was that in its responsible public role it was compelled to support the notion that money incomes should be restrained to keep pace with the rate of production but that in its role as a higher representative organization, committed by tradition to pressing for higher wages, it had to oppose restraint. This dilemma was revealed clearly at the 1963 meeting of the Trades Union Congress and undoubtedly influenced the attitude of its representatives on the National Economic Development Council. It is inherent in the capitalist situation and, irrespective of what government is in power, will not be resolved voluntarily. Only alterations in the system can remove it. Until then, TUC vacillations about a wages policy will persist; short-term palliative measures might be accepted but traditional attitudes will return and prevail in the long run.

The Trades Union Congress is proud of its pragmatism. It expressly rejects any suggestion that there is any logical theory in its development but although it may not be consciously following a theory there is logic in the sequence of its responses to employers and the government. The logic is an acceptance of, but not necessarily a belief in, the concept of the corporate state.[12] Firstly, by its membership of the National Economic Development Council, the Trades Union Congress accepts the organic totality of nation and state. The second report of the Council, welcomed by the TUC because of its progressive nature,[13] gave meaning to the concept of organic totality when it stated:

> A successful growth programme involves the identification of government, management and the trade unions with an agreed objective. . . . Success in achieving a higher rate of growth will depend, to a large extent, on the way in which government, management and unions carry out their respective functions and on a new spirit of co-operation between them to make a reality of the agreed common objective.[14]

The general theory of the corporate state assumed a complete conciliation of class interests with workers and employers cooperating for the sake of increasing national production in much the same way as the National Economic Development Council envisages. But there are

[12] I am grateful to Mr John Hughes for the suggestion which led me to this analysis.
[13] *TUC Report*, 1963, p. 266.
[14] *Ministry of Labour Gazette*, May 1963, p. 197.

other points of similarity. The state stands above corporations and syndicates in the theory. The NEDC is a government creation, designed to further government notions about national interest. These notions, as in the corporate state theory, have no other ethical basis than to consolidate what already exists; that is to maintain the present distribution of income, to preserve the distributive process and to guarantee the rights of the private ownership of industry. The corporate state theory contains various philosophical threads amongst which are a belief in national power and the ability of 'great minds' to direct the destiny of the nations. In practice the 'great minds' consist largely of a collusion of the representatives of the dominant vested interests, though in Britain the idea is gaining currency that an élite sifted from intellectual and public life can apply its wisdom under the tutelage of the government to help direct the state; hence the Cohen Council in 1957, called the 'three wise men', and the National Incomes Commission with similar personnel.

The NEDC combines the two aspects of control by an élite. The strain of an élite theory has long been present in the conduct of industrial relations. In 1911, when Britain experienced large-scale national strikes for the first time, the Prime Minister, H. H. Asquith, established a special business court, called the Industrial Council, consisting of employers and union leaders, to deal with industrial disputes. The Council did not function for long. The National Industrial Conference set up by Lloyd George in 1919 to achieve industrial peace in an unsettled environment was a similar, though more widely based, organization. Though constituted differently and without the formal support of the government, the Mond-Turner talks in 1928 were of a similar character. Each reflected the belief of union leaders and employers in their ability, corporatively, to solve industrial problems. Ernest Bevin stated this explicitly when he supported the Mond-Turner talks. 'With whom can you meet to discuss unemployment?' he asked, 'Government Departments who do nothing? No, I would rather sit down with some considered policy on a problem of that character facing the capitalists themselves across the table. . . .'[15] The general secretary of the TUC, Mr George Woodcock, expressed a similar view at the 1963 meeting of the TUC.[16] The manifestations of the attitude of union leaders towards a corporate policy are not confined to their willingness to sit on the NEDC, though this is an important institutionalized expression of it. The existence of the NEDC and its industrial subsections could assist the government to contain a disruptive situation if a crisis occurred. It

[15] *TUC Report*, 1928, p. 250.   [16] *TUC Report*, 1963, pp. 390–3.

would only be necessary for the government to make membership of these bodies compulsory for the next step to be taken to a corporate state. The trade union movement then would have gone a long way towards disarming itself.

Finally, the capitalism of the post-Second World War period differs from that in earlier years by the rate at which industry is becoming capital-intensified. This process, which is changing the character of the labour force, is presenting trade unions with serious organizational problems. Lines of demarcation are fluid, sometimes disappearing altogether as new mechanized techniques are introduced. New skills, such as those of technologists, are emerging and demand recognition. Old skills, such as those of traditional maintenance engineers, are becoming re-established as processes become automated. And, of course, some old-established skills, as in weaving, shipbuilding and printing, are disappearing. These changes present issues which the trade union movement has always had, but with greater intensity.

The most important long-term change in the character of the labour force is the increasing proportion of employees in white-collar employment. In 1962 about one-quarter of the total labour force was in white-collar employment. Administrative, technical and clerical staff in 1948 constituted sixteen per cent of the labour force in manufacturing industries whereas in 1962 the percentage was 22·6. The fastest growing points in the economy were those with a high white-collar content.[17] Workers in the non-manual category are all potential trade union members but the majority have been insulated against trade unionism by a social image determined by middle-class values and privileged treatment from employers. White-collar workers were called staff, not hands, operators or workmen; they were paid salaries by the month, not wages by the hour, day or week; they received considerable fringe benefits without collective action; they were encouraged to identify their interests with employers and to regard trade unionism as a rather vulgar form of manual worker activity. Nonetheless, some non-manual workers formed unions because for various reasons they were compelled to recognize that they had common interests which could only be protected by collective action. The support these unions received depended upon the intensity with which economic pressures injected realism into the lives of non-manual workers and revealed that their social images were false ones The most prevalent of these pressures has been inflation which has devalued the real incomes of these relatively fixed income employees. It is this pressure which caused white-collar militancy in the 1950s

[17] PEP, 'Trade Unions in a changing society', *Planning*, June 1963, pp. 185–7.

and 1960s, as it did in the period immediately following the First World War. Another pressure has been the spread of mechanization to non-manual employment which has reduced the social distance between that and manual work.

Irrespective of what the trade union movement does, white-collar workers establish and extend trade unions as the pressures on them increase, for they know of no other form of protection. But the methods they use differ from the traditional union methods because they cannot dispense readily with the values which have led them in the past to denigrate crude industrial action. They are presented with a conflict between what is industrially expedient and that which is socially permissible. They employ collective bargaining and arbitration more frequently than manual workers as their sole means of protection. They are more concerned about their public reputations than manual workers. In consequence, they are prepared to collaborate with employers and to ignore economic class differences as far as they can. The movement by default of manual workers' unions to the idea of the corporate state is likely to be accentuated by a conscious movement by white-collar unions. There are political reasons too for such a movement. With few exceptions white-collar unions try to avoid political party alignments. Their members are conservative by conditioning, preferring to conform and be safe. More than any others in society, they develop the bureaucratic mentality, for they frequently operate within impersonal, hierarchial organizations. Their bureaucratic personality spills over into their political affairs so that they look for neat, ordered solutions to their problems. They can find these within a system of regulated capitalism. But they will only look for such solutions under conditions of crisis and these are likely to affect all sections of the community. What would happen in totality then to the trade union movement would depend upon the vigilance of organized socialist groups in the flexible, relatively unstructured, sections of the movement.

6

The origins of industrial conciliation and arbitration[1]

The relationship pattern

Trade unionism has always involved the settlement of industrial disputes by negotiations between workers' representatives and employers. On occasions in the eighteenth and first half of the nineteenth
centuries demands made by workers or employers were granted
without question by the other side; at other times the demands were
rejected out of hand and this was acquiesced in by the other side. In
between these extremes lay a number of possible outcomes. Demands
were sometimes conceded after strikes or lockouts or they were
moderated and then accepted. The precise outcome depended upon
the state of the labour market, and hence the degree of labour organization, and the cost position of the employers. These factors not only
varied over time but differed in their intensity between industries and
firms at any one point of time. The extreme situations occurred at
high and low levels of employment. In the competition for labour,
which a high level of employment implies, employers readily gave way
to collective demands but as commodity markets deteriorated and the
volume of production declined, they at first resisted claims which
would have increased labour costs and then deliberately set out to cut
wages, lengthen hours and intensify work. Workers commonly resisted initial attempts to reduce labour costs so that a spate of strikes and
lockouts ensued. At the onset of the depression in 1819 and at the first
suggestion of wage reductions the Lancashire miners, the North
Staffordshire potters and the Nottingham framework knitters all
responded by striking. The Glasgow cotton spinners resisted wage
cuts in 1837 as did the London building workers and miners and

[1] This paper was originally read to a meeting of the Labour History Group in
Leeds on 9 October 1963. I am grateful to Dr J. E. Williams who discussed the
subject of the paper with me throughout my work on it and who read and criticized
it in draft form.

textile workers in the Midlands and North in 1841 and the typographical workers in 1846. Frequently, however, these disputes resulted in compromise settlements which were superseded by other compromises as trade conditions got worse.

The ability of workers to engage in industrial action depended largely upon the condition of their union organizations. Union membership declined with the level of employment so that at the trough of a trade depression the ability of workers to resist was also at its lowest point. In the upward trade movement from the trough workers in various industrial groups tried to regain their former wages and initiated strike movements for this purpose. Building workers in Manchester took advantage of the brief improvement in trade in 1818 to strike for wage increases and were followed by dyers, cotton spinners, powerloom weavers and handloom weavers from various parts of Lancashire. A revival in trade in 1825 stimulated the long and bitter strike of Bradford woolcombers and weavers and a strike of clay potters in North Staffordshire. The National Association for the Protection of Labour and the General Union of Spinners both emerged from agitations for wage increases in 1829 as trade began to improve. In 1833 trade recovery resulted in widespread trade union activity, particularly among building workers. Strike action marked the movement away from depression after 1842. In these cases too compromise settlements were often reached until the point at which the willingness of employers to resist was at its weakest, namely when there was full or overfull employment.

In so far then as there was a pattern of industrial action up till 1860, it took this shape. The action had some marked characteristics. Notice of intended or desired changes was sometimes given in writing. Employers posted notices in their works, workers put notices in the press or submitted them by letter. Usually, date lines were given after which strikes or lockouts were enforced. In some cases workers gave notice of their intentions by striking. Wherever resistance to a demand was met there would be immediate strike or lockout action. In a few trades such as printing and bookbinding it was the practice for workers' representatives and employers to meet before industrial action was taken but usually discussions followed such action. In all trades, however, employers and workers' representatives met only when issues arose which threatened to disrupt production. They did not anticipate disruption.

After the French Revolution had lost its immediate significance for Britain industrial disputes were largely regarded as the private affairs of employers but occasionally it was suggested that employers should countenance a form of outside interference. The Government attempted to influence the determination of disputes through the Arbitration Act in 1824, after the repeal of the Combination Acts. The Act excluded the determination of wages unless the mutual consent of both parties was obtained; it made arbitration compulsory and contained penal provisions. The intention of its draughtsmen was to displace voluntary settlements. The Act was amended in 1837 and 1845 but it was never applied. There were advocates of a permanent system of arbitration along lines suggested by the French *conseils des prud'hommes* formed after 1806. William Felkin, the Nottingham lace manufacturer, was the most prominent early advocate. In 1834 he translated into English an account of the *conseils des prud'hommes* and ten years later read a paper on boards of conciliation before the British Association.[2] Under Felkin's influence the largest hosiery union petitioned Parliament in 1845 for the establishment of Courts of Conciliation and Arbitration.[3] The National Association for the Promotion of Social Science became a forum for advocates of conciliation and arbitration after its formation in 1857. The writer of a paper on the 1858 West Yorkshire coal strike, read at the 1859 meeting of the Association, suggested that Courts of Arbitration would be a fitting and proper mode of settling industrial disputes.[4] The subject gradually became a popular one for intellectual sympathizers of trade unions to argue.

The advocacy made little impression before 1860. The Glasgow and Risley textile employers and operatives established an annual conference in 1834 to revise prices for the ensuing year; in the same year an arbitration committee was formed by the Staffordshire potters; three boards of arbitration were formed in the 1850s, in the Macclesfield silk trade, the wooden shipbuilding industry, the London printing trade.[5] None of the experiments, however, was successful; all were shortlived for reasons associated with their immediate environments. In printing, for instance, a permanent joint Arbitration Committee was established in 1856. Three journeymen sat with three employers under the chairmanship of a barrister with a casting vote.

---

[2] W. H. G. Armytage, *A. J. Mundella 1825–1897. The Liberal Background to the Labour Movement*, Benn, 1951, p. 33.

[3] William Felkin, *A History of the Machine Wrought Hosiery and Lace Manufacture*, London 1867, p. 471.

[4] *Transactions of the National Association for the Promotion of Social Science*, 1859, p. 653.

[5] I. G. Sharp, *Industrial Conciliation and Arbitration in Great Britain*, Allen & Unwin, 1951, pp. 1–2.

The union and employers stated that the Committee would 'serve for the amicable settlement of all Disputes which may hereafter arise relative to the Prices to be charged and paid for Work, without incurring the expense, trouble and irritation consequent upon an appeal to a Court of Law'.[6] The Committee settled minor differences satisfactorily but the first important dispute, submitted nine months after the Committee's formation, had to be solved by litigation.[7] The Committee did not survive this failure. Then in 1860 a standing committee for regulating the relations between employers and workers in the Nottingham hosiery trade was formed. This had an immediate public impact but nothing else like it was formed until 1864 when an arbitration board for the building trades in Wolverhampton was established.

Thereafter the number of conciliation and arbitration bodies increased. The Nottingham Chamber of Commerce convened a board for the lace trade in 1867; by the following year standing committees of one kind or another were operating in the hosiery trade in Leicester, the Staffordshire pottery trade, the glass bottle industry, and the building industry in Leeds, Manchester, Coventry and Worcester. The Board of Arbitration and Conciliation for the Manufactured Iron Trade of the North of England was formed in 1869. The number of industries covered by joint committees or boards increased in the first half of the 1870s. In addition arbitration, without the existence of standing provisions, became popular. A recognized group of arbitrators emerged consisting largely of A. J. Mundella, MP, Judge Rupert Kettle, Thomas Hughes, QC, Henry Crompton, Lloyd Jones and a small group of lesser known men, mainly barristers. These sometimes intervened on their own initiative; at other times they were invited to intervene. Such was the climate of opinion about arbitration that almost any public figure could offer his services as an arbitrator without offending the parties involved. In 1874 the Bishop of Manchester arbitrated in a Manchester building dispute, and heard the parties in his residence.[8] During a six weeks' strike in Dundee in 1875 a local solicitor intervened and brought the parties together.[9] By 1875 there was barely a trade where trade unions existed which did not have either a standing joint committee of employers and workmen to settle disputes, with provision for arbitration, or the experience of settling disputes through arbitration on an *ad hoc* basis. There was, as

[6] Ellic Howe, ed., *The London Compositor, 1785–1900*, Oxford, Bibliographical Society, 1947, p. 266.
[7] *Ibid.*, p. 248.
[8] *Capital and Labour*, April 1874, p. 106.
[9] *Ibid.*, September 1875, p. 496.

the editor of *Capital and Labour* pointed out in October 1875, an 'arbitration craze'.[10] To round the craze off a National Conciliation League was formed in December 1875, to foster the principle of arbitration.

There were boards of arbitration and conciliation, of arbitration alone and conciliation alone but regardless of the nomenclature they frequently functioned as joint negotiating committees consisting of equal numbers of employers and workers' representatives. They had written constitutions with provisions to specify their composition, regulate the timing of their meetings and to stipulate their powers. Thus they constituted a systematic, orderly method for dealing with industrial disputes which formed the framework for a system of collective bargaining. Mostly provisions were made for removing deadlock; a chairman was given a casting vote, or a referee was provided for, or assessors from each side sat with an independent arbitrator. It was not necessary, however, for a constitution of a board to contain arbitration provisions for arbitration to be used. Whilst the institution of collective bargaining procedures was a radical departure from past practices, the acceptance of arbitration by employers was even more remarkable for it was an acknowledgement that independent persons could sit in judgement on what hitherto had been regarded as the private preserve of employers. Why in the two decades following 1860 did these changes occur?

The necessary conditions

The necessary conditions for the existence of both conciliation and arbitration were present before 1860. Both trade unions and employers in some trades were sufficiently well organized and in charge of their affairs to be able to meet and reach decisions about their relationship and to enforce those decisions. Trade unions in some trades, such as engineering, printing, bookbinding and building, were well-established and relatively effectively organized. The fact that most unions were not centrally organized was not important for action could still be taken at a district or local level. In their respective spheres of influence union officials were capable of negotiating regularly on behalf of their members for that indeed is what they did but in an *ad hoc* manner. There was no ideological reason in the way of their wanting to establish regular relationships with employers. An increasing number in the 1840s and 1850s were becoming full-time and desired to make their positions permanent. They tried to

[10] *Ibid.*, 27 October 1875, p. 621.

centralize union affairs and this involved curtailing the strike activities of branches. The accumulation of union funds was also dependent upon a reduction in local strikes. Any move, therefore, which assisted union officials in this direction would have been welcomed. As for employers, there were no institutional reasons in the way either of their membership of standing joint committees or of their accepting arbitration. There was relatively little permanent collusion between employers but they were capable of acting together as they had shown through the enforcement of numerous lockouts as retaliatory measures. Some employers were sufficiently large to be able to act unilaterally over negotiating machinery. Nor was trade union recognition a problem.

It is not possible to estimate the extent to which unions were recognized by employers in the two decades prior to 1860 but in the majority of trades where unions were strong enough to engage in disputes at some stage they usually had to be given *de facto* recognition by employers. Employers, however, resisted conceding permanent recognition to trade unions which the creation of standing conciliation machinery would have involved. There was a strong reluctance to regard unions as established sections of industry—they were treated always as if they could be suppressed either by the lockout and the document or by law and, in the main, employers behaved as if they were anticipating suppression. The degree of recognition accorded to unions depended upon their ability to force their attention upon employers; that is upon their actual or potential strike power in relation to the market position of the employers. Because of frequent and intensive changes in the state of trade and level of employment the power of unions varied too so that an employer's assessment of a union was never constant for long; nor, therefore, was his desire to maintain conciliatory relations with it. The attitude of employers towards arbitration was typified by the reaction of the Preston textile employers in 1854, when, during a trade dispute, a group of middle-class residents offered to mediate. Wages, the employers asserted, had to be left to the 'free operation of supply and demand'. To accept mediation, they added, would be to acknowledge 'a principle, most dangerous and mischievous in its tendency—a principle alike subversive of the rights of the working man in the disposal of his labour, and of the rights of the master in the employment of his capital'.[11]

Both attitudes persisted throughout the nineteenth century and

[11] The National Association for the Promotion of Social Science, *Trade's Societies and Strikes*, 1860, p. 245.

into the twentieth. Permanent negotiating machinery was not widely established until after the First World War; and as late as 1897 an employer informed the Government that his acceptance of a Board of Trade mediator would 'establish a precedent for outside interference with the management of my private affairs'.[12] But from 1860 the attitudes of some employers altered sufficiently to allow for the growth of permanent machinery and arbitration provisions.

A common explanation by contemporary participants and observers of the rise of conciliation and arbitration was that after decades of bitter conflict reason was being applied to industrial relations. Prior to 1860, wrote Henry Crompton in 1876,

> the history of the relations between employers and employed in the [hosiery] trade is that of war. If the worst aspects of this war, the terrible riots, the murders, arsons, and machine-breakings of the early part of the century, had disappeared, there was still hatred and suspicion by the operatives towards their masters, who in turn entertained feelings of animosity against the men . . . the change has been from war to peace. Confidence and good will have replaced suspicion and open hostility.[13]

A. J. Mundella, in 1868, stated that the 'want of some connecting link betwixt masters and workmen—some arrangement for the friendly bargain and sale of labour—has resulted in those dreadful strikes and lock-outs which have disgraced our age and country'.[14] In a debate on the merits of conciliation and arbitration at the National Association for the Promotion of Social Science in 1868 opinion almost unanimously regarded conciliation and arbitration as means of removing industrial conflict.[15] This contention appeared to be substantiated by the reduction in the number of official strikes in trades where conciliation and arbitration were practised. In the mid-1870s the employer members of the North of England iron trades board stated that 'the Board has been in operation since 1869, and during the whole of the intervening period the general district wage regulations have been settled without resort to strikes or lockouts'.[16] Similar claims were made for the Nottingham hosiery trade, the Northeastern coalmining industry, and the Midland building industry.[17]

[12] Lord Penrhyn to the President of the Board of Trade; see V. L. Allen, *Trade Unions and the Government*, Longmans, 1960, p. 52.
[13] Henry Crompton, *Industrial Conciliation*, H. S. King, 1876, pp. 33–4 and 48.
[14] *Transactions of the National Association for the Promotion of Social Science*, 1868, p. 525.
[15] *Ibid.*, pp. 579–92.
[16] Crompton, *op. cit.*, p. 59.
[17] E. H. Phelps Brown reiterates these claims in *The Growth of British Industrial Relations*, Macmillan, 1959, p. 126.

Common characteristics

The circumstances surrounding the establishment of a number of boards in the 1860s possessed common characteristics. The Nottingham hosiery trade was in a state of stagnation for about thirty years until the 1850s when technological improvements were introduced. During that period the hosiery workers were 'forced to acquiesce in whatever conditions might be offered'.[18] In the late 1850s there was renewed activity by the hosiery unions which endeavoured to exploit the expanding trade and increasing demand for labour. The most prosperous section of the trade was machine production and a widening disparity between the earnings of machine and hand workers occurred.[19] The hand workers, therefore, had most reason to be disgruntled; they did not receive automatic benefits from a favourable market situation so they called a number of strikes. In 1860 there were three strikes in the wide-frame branch of the trade, one of which lasted for eleven weeks. Such was the demand for hosiery, however, that the manufacturers depended upon production in all the branches of the trade to satisfy it. The strikes prevented the manufacturers from meeting 'the heavy demands of the American trade',[20] but at the same time they were not prepared to grant wage increases. As Felkin put it, 'the workmen struck for an advance of wages which the employers believed it would be impolitic to grant'.[21] The strikers were supported by workers in employment so the dispute concerned the whole of the trade and some employers wanted to retaliate by using the lockout. They could have done so uniformly because, in 1860, they had united in both a Hosiers' Association and the Nottingham Chamber of Commerce.

Thus in a situation where both the traditional lockout and the continuation of the strike were economically undesirable *any* course which held down labour costs without interrupting production was to be preferred. Given the existence of employers' and workers' organizations, a rational way seemed to be to obtain the support of workers for steps to make the industry competitive with continental producers —that is to withold from making excessive demands or from stopping production. This way was pointed to by A. J. Mundella, a manufacturer, who supported the ideas of Felkin. He advised his fellow employers to meet the operatives in conference.[22] The advice was

---

[18] F. A. Wells, *The British Hosiery Trade*, Allen & Unwin, 1935, p. 160.
[19] Cf. Roy Church, 'Technological change and the Hosiery Board', *Yorkshire Bulletin of Economic and Social Research*, XV, no. 1, May 1963, p. 53.
[20] Wells, p. 160.   [21] Felkin, p. 484   [22] Armytage, p. 32.

accepted and on 21 September a joint statement was issued which stated that: 'It is further agreed, that in order to prevent a recurrence of strikes which have been so disastrous to employers and employed, a Board of Arbitration be at once formed . . .[23]

Mundella's case for conciliation was in effect an argument for moderation. He spoke of the need to consider the interests of the trade and maintained that because of competition from Germany it was impossible for the trade to pay higher wages. He even offered to pay the passage for a workers' delegation to Germany to investigate the extent of German competition. This appeal for reason took place against the background of an expanding market and a high level of employment.

In Nottingham at the same time, the lace trade was also experiencing continental competition, mainly from France, but the market was not expanding, with the consequence that the Nottingham trade was contracting.[24] The lace manufacturers, like the hosiers, wanted to cut their labour costs, and because the labour market favoured buyers they were in a position to do so unilaterally. They imposed wage cuts and locked out the employees who would not accept them for three months, endeavouring in the process to break up the unions.[25] The Nottingham hosiery and lace manufacturers both belonged to the Nottingham Chamber of Commerce which had been formed to counter the effects of foreign competition, yet their responses were entirely different. The Chamber of Commerce supported conciliation and arbitration in hosiery but refrained from intervening in the lace trade. The main variable in the situation was the level of employment and indirectly the strength of the trade unions. The variable differed in its impact in the two trades and evoked opposite responses. When, however, the lace trade was moving out of a state of depression after the mid-1860s and the employment situation was becoming more difficult for employers, they both formed their own association and in 1867 established a Board of Arbitration for the Nottingham Machine-Lace Trade. The Chamber of Commerce undertook the task of constituting the Board when Mundella was its president. A factor which undoubtedly influenced the lace manufacturers was the apparent success of the Hosiery Board in quietening the unions.

A. J. Mundella was joined at an early stage in his self-appointed task of propagating the idea of conciliation and arbitration by Rupert

[23] *Nottingham Review*, 21 September 1860, p 5.

[24] In the three years ending June 1860, fifty-seven lace houses went bankrupt; see Norman H. Cuthbert, *The Lace Makers' Society*, Nottingham, Amalgamated Society of Operative Lacemakers, 1960, p. 41n.

[25] *Ibid.*, p. 42.

Kettle, Judge of the Wolverhampton County Court. Kettle concentrated on the Midlands area and had most effect in the building trade. In 1864 he participated in a court of arbitration for carpenters and joiners in Wolverhampton. The situation in all essentials was similar to that which existed in the hosiery trade. From 1861 to 1863 the number of houses built each year rose from 45,200 to 64,400.[26] The number remained high, at 60,900 in 1864, then it fell sharply. In 1863 and 1864 there was, therefore, a high demand for labour and the building unions used the occasion to strike for higher wages. In 1864 one strike in Wolverhampton lasted about seventeen weeks. It ended with an uneasy settlement which the Mayor of Wolverhampton thought would be followed by another strike so he called a public meeting. From this meeting an arbitration court with Judge Kettle as its chairman was formed. The building workers, instead of exploiting this market situation, were prevailed upon 'to take a gradual rise in wages'.[27] Thus the experience of the hosiery board was repeated. The Working Men's Club, of which Kettle was president, asked him to assist with establishing conciliation and arbitration courts in other towns and as a result the building industry in Coventry, Worcester, Leeds, Manchester and Salford had courts by 1868. But these too were established in a rising market for labour for the industry moved out of its depression after 1864. When the Royal Commission on Trade Unions sat in 1867–68 conciliation and arbitration were seriously examined on the basis of papers by Mundella and Kettle.

The boards were also a subject for discussion by trade unions. At the conference of the United Kingdom Alliance of Organized Trades in Sheffield in 1866 George Odger raised the subject and condemned strike action. The conference advocated the establishment of councils of arbitration and conciliation. Both Mundella and Kettle pressed their advocacy to the point of offering their services as mediators or arbitrators in disputes. One such occasion occurred in 1868 in South Lancashire when the coal miners struck against an employer's attempt to impose a wage reduction of 15 per cent.[28] The strike lasted from March until May and was marked by almost continual violence because of the determined use of blacklegs. After about a month A. J. Mundella wrote in his capacity as president of the Nottingham Chamber of Commerce to the Mayor of Wigan suggesting that he should give 'a lecture advocating the establishment of a Court of

[26] B. R. Mitchell and Phyllis Deane, *Abstract of British Historical Statistics*, Cambridge University Press, 1962, p. 239.
[27] *Transactions of the National Association for the Promotion of Social Science*, 1868, p. 577.
[28] *The Times*, 2 May 1868.

Arbitration and Conciliation in Wigan'. The court, he suggested, should consist of six employers, six employees and a chairman.[29] The coal owners were not interested in arbitration and Mundella refused to intervene until they were. Early in May, when both parties and the civic authority were exhausted, the employers agreed to arbitration and, with Mundella's help, an agreement was reached. The reduction the employers wanted at the beginning of the strike, namely 15 per cent, was enforced, but there was to be no victimization. It was also agreed that 'as soon as the strike is at an end, the agitation subsided, the employers will seriously take into consideration the practicability of establishing a Board of Arbitration and Conciliation'.[30] The workers returned to work but no board was established; their only gain from the intervention was the assurance that there would be no victimization. Elsewhere in the coal industry there was no economic reason to compel coal owners to accept arbitration. In South Derbyshire a lockout lasted for more than a year because the employers refused to submit their case to arbitration.[31]

A few employers were converted to the idea of conciliation irrespective of economic conditions. One such man was David Dale, the Darlington ironmaster. Dale attended meetings of the Associated Chamber of Commerce from 1865 at which he heard papers read on conciliation boards. He was particularly impressed by Mundella's contribution and decided that a board might be useful in the iron trade.[32] In March 1867, Dale circularized each member of the Iron Manufacturer's Association with a letter asking them to consider the formation of a 'standing local committee' of employers and men to discuss 'questions affecting their mutual relations', but most were not interested.[33] John Kane, the general secretary of the Association of Ironworkers, had pressed for arbitration during a six month lockout in 1866, but the employers had refused. And in December 1867 they had turned down his request for a general conference of employers and workers. The American demand for rails was low in those years and the price of rolled bars was falling. The employers were in a position to enforce wage reductions in 1866 and virtually to destroy the three-year-old Association of Ironworkers. In 1869 the demand for iron increased, the level of employment rose, and employers faced the prospect of

[29] *Ibid.*, 18 April 1868.   [30] *Ibid.*, 5 May 1868.
[31] *Ibid.*, 16 March 1868; also J. E. Williams, *The Derbyshire Miners*, Allen & Unwin, 1962, pp. 115–17.
[32] Cf. A. J. Odber, 'The Origins of industrial peace: the manufactured iron trade of the North of England', in *Oxford Economic Papers*, iii, no. 2, June 1951.
[33] *Ibid.*, p. 207.

demands for wage increases with the possibility of strikes if they were not conceded. In this situation, on 22 March 1869, the Board of Arbitration and Conciliation for the Manufactured Iron Trade of the North of England was formed.

The ironmasters not only wanted to avoid strikes because of prosperity they saw ahead, but because of their high cost to the employers. The iron industry was highly capitalized and even short strikes were expensive. The coal industry was in a wholly different position. Apart from the problem of keeping the pits clear of water strike action involved little technical cost, so there was no incentive to avoid strikes on this score. Because coal stocks were bulky coal owners sometimes welcomed strikes as a means of clearing them away, and, in the process, of forcing coal prices up. Wages fluctuated considerably. Labour costs were dominant in total costs so employers endeavoured to reduce them immediately the market situation changed adversely for them, but because they found it relatively simple to pass increasing costs on to consumers during a period of prosperity, partly because they faced relatively little foreign competition, they did not then strongly resist demands for wage increases. The coalfields, however, differed from each other in the ease of coal-getting, in their market situations and in their labour requirements, and the owners in them reacted differently to union and external pressures for conciliation and arbitration boards.

A. J. Mundella believed that the coal-owners should have established boards in 1869 when trade was bad.

> My only desire [he wrote], 'is that employers will have the sense to adopt what is good in my plan and to seize the present state of trade as a favourable opportunity of doing it; otherwise I fear, when trade revives, they will reap the bitter fruits of their present obstinacy and folly. . . . I fear Normansell and all his societies will be involved in temporary ruin, and when prosperity returns they will not be in so tractable a frame of mind as at present.'[34]

The coal-owners did not seize the opportunity. The unions in any event were weak at that time. In addition the union leaders did not change their minds about the boards; they consistently advocated them through good and bad trade. During the coal boom years from 1871 to 1874 the unions expanded and accumulated funds which some of the leaders wanted to preserve at all costs. John Normansell of the South Yorkshire Miners, Thomas Burt of the Northumberland Miners and William Crawford of the Durham Miners' Association knew sufficient about the impact of boards to realize that they reduced the

[34] Quoted by Williams, p. 140.

incidence of official strike action, and therefore, the financial responsibilities of unions.

All the prominent union leaders in the mines supported conciliation and arbitration but, depending on the coalfields they operated in, they faced two types of reaction from employers. The owners in the old established fields of Northumberland and Durham formed joint committees to discuss local matters but preferred to refer disputes to arbitration on an *ad hoc* basis.[35] A permanent board was formed in South Yorkshire but here too as well as in West Yorkshire single arbitrators were used.[36] On the other side of the Pennines, in Lancashire, North Wales, South Wales and South Staffordshire, the coal-owners refused to form joint committees and bitterly opposed arbitration of any form. The South Wales coal-owners considered it was onesided and favoured the men; in addition they disliked it because it involved acceptance of trade unions. Towards the end of 1874 and in 1875 the owners in these fields accepted arbitration but then only after long and bitter disputes. The Scottish coal-owners had one conference with the miners' representatives in 1873 and then did not meet again until the end of the century.[37] The South-west Lancashire coal-owners rejected arbitration because they did not believe their disputes should 'be settled by men with no interest in the trade'.[38] In South Staffordshire a strike against a wage cut lasted for sixteen weeks before the owners were prevailed upon to accept the mediation of the Mayor of Birmingham, Joseph Chamberlain. The Amalgamated Association of Miners, which organized the miners in these fields, adopted a policy of arbitration in all cases where employers sought wage cuts in 1874 but promised support should arbitration be refused.[39] The intensity of the employers' reaction can be seen from the fact that during 1873, 1874 and 1875 the union was virtually destroyed by the constant strain of strikes and lockouts.[40]

[35] Cf. E. Welbourne, *The Miners' Unions of Northumberland and Durham*, Cambridge University Press, 1923. After the strike against the yearly bond in 1869 in Durham there were no large strikes or lockouts which officially involved the unions in Northumberland and Durham until the late 1870s.

[36] South Yorkshire had more troubles than the North-east coalfields. Neither the miners nor the coal-owners operated arbitration so consistently and in 1874 there was a lockout of 23,000 miners over a wage reduction. But even so, Yorkshire was an area of industrial peace compared with the coalfields on the other side of the Pennines.

[37] R. Page Arnot, *A History of the Scottish Miners*, Allen & Unwin, 1956, p. 54.

[38] *Capital and Labour*, 8 April 1874.

[39] *Ibid.*, 11 March 1874, p. 39.

[40] Cf. G. D. H. Cole, 'Some notes on British trade unionism in the third quarter of the nineteenth century', *International Review for Social History*, ii, 1937, 1–23. In addition to a large number of local strikes, the Amalgamated Association of

Workers' reaction

The workers who were convinced by the eloquence and reasonableness of the middle-class intellectual advocates of conciliation and arbitration to act moderately during a rising market were quickly disillusioned when trade began to slacken off and employers wanted wage cuts. Conciliation worked only where the union leaders were willing to endorse the wage reductions suggested by employers and then it was only operative at the top negotiating level. William Crawford, who accepted a wage reduction of 10 per cent for the Durham miners in May 1874, had to contend with unofficial strikes by colliery mechanics.[41] When, early in 1874, the Scottish coal-owners demanded a wage reduction of 20 per cent, Alexander Macdonald advised the miners to accept it. There were vociferous protests.[42] Unofficial strikes were frequently called against adverse arbitration awards; indeed this period saw the beginning of unofficial strike action. When in October 1875, an arbitration award granted the North Wales coalowners the reduction of 15 per cent they demanded, the miners struck work and submitted a demand for a 20 per cent wage increase.[43] A breakaway union of colliery mechanics was formed in the Northumberland coalfield because of an adverse award in April 1875. The depression after 1873 broke down effective conciliation and arbitration in the Nottingham lace trade. 'The capitulation of the Levers Lace Trade Society in the face of repeated reductions resulted in the formation of a breakaway union resolved to ignore the decisions of the Board of Arbitration.'[44] Later, in December 1873, the whole of the union struck against a wage award. Mundella's hosiery board met

Miners was rarely left without a major strike or lockout to finance. It grew out of a six weeks' strike in South Lancashire in 1868 (*The Times*, 16 March 1868 and various dates till 5 May 1868). A thirteen months' strike for union recognition in Burnley was a constant drain (*The Times*, 8 October 1873; *Capital and Labour*, 6 May 1874, p. 229 and 26 August 1874, p. 612). In 1873 there was a lockout for three months in South Wales (*The Times* for various dates between 7 January and 19 March 1873). In the same year there was a lockout in North Warwickshire (*The Times*, 7 January 1873). In 1874 there was a four months' strike in South Staffordshire (*The Times*, 11 July 1874), a seven weeks' strike in South-west Lancashire (*The Times*, 6 October and 10 November 1874), and a seven weeks' strike in the Forest of Dean (*The Times*, 1 January 1875). 1875 was dominated by a five months' strike in South Wales (*The Times*, 29 December 1874; 2 January 1875 and various dates to 28 and 29 May 1875). By the summer of 1875 the union was virtually insolvent. It merged with the Miners' National Association in August 1875.

[41] E. Welbourne, p. 160.
[42] A. J. Youngson Brown, 'Trade union policy in the Scots coalfields, 1855–1885', *Economic History Review*, VI, no. 1, 1958, 42–4.
[43] *Capital and Labour*, 13 October 1875.
[44] Cuthbert, p. 45.

serious difficulties as early as 1871 when an unpopular award caused a rift between the handframe workers and machine operatives.[45] No industry which used arbitration was able to use it successfully to enforce wage cuts. The North of England Arbitration Board had to contend with unofficial strikes in 1875. The Board fined the puddlers at a Stockton works for taking unofficial action in April 1875;[46] on other occasions strikers were simply admonished. The strikes were accompanied by the denigration of union officials associated with the Board.

Where employers could not get the wage reductions they required they submitted successive demands. For instance in February 1874 the Oldham and Ashton-under-Lyme coal-owners asked for a 15 per cent wage reduction and were awarded 10 per cent. The next month the employers gave notice of a further 5 per cent decrease.[47] Arbitration did not noticeably slow down the tempo of wage reductions. Coal-owners in Somerset asked for 10 per cent wage reduction in April 1874; the workers asked for arbitration and while this was pending the employers demanded another 15 per cent reduction. The arbitrator, Judge Kettle, awarded a $23\frac{1}{2}$ per cent reduction.[48] When arbitration acted as an obstruction it was sidetracked. Thus the Hosiery Board was completely inactive for about three years following the breakdown of trade due to the American civil war. It was as R. Fothergill, MP, the chairman of the South Wales Coal-owners Association, stated before the long lockout in 1875, that 'no arbitrator could say that a master should carry on his business at a loss'.[49]

Consequences for trade unions

The development of conciliation and arbitration had important consequences for trade unionism. Mundella's Hosiery Board was concerned with conciliation. The chairman of the Board, which had an equal number of representatives from each side of industry, had a casting vote, but it was rarely used. Mundella was the chairman until 1870 and as it was considered undesirable for an employer to have the

[45] Church, 'Technological change . . .', p. 58.
[46] *Capital and Labour*, 5 May 1875, p. 195.
[47] *Ibid.*, 4 March 1874, p. 85.
[48] *Ibid.*, 6 May 1874, p. 224.
[49] *Ibid.*, 17 March 1875, p. 55. A similar view was expressed by Thomas Ellison, Judge of the Sheffield County Court, in 1879 when he arbitrated in a Yorkshire mining dispute. He awarded that wages should not be reduced, 'provided always that this award is not intended, and shall not be construed, to restrict or in any way interfere with the right of the owners to close at their discretion all or any of the collieries within the said area . . .'. (Williams, p. 163).

decisive vote in case of deadlock the Board's constitution was changed to give the casting vote to an independent referee.[50] The Nottingham Lace Board which was largely modelled on the Hosiery Board provided for the use of an independent referee from the outset.[51] The boards set up by Judge Kettle were essentially arbitration boards. They could conciliate but they specifically provided for decision-making by an umpire and his decision was binding on the parties.

There was much discussion at the Royal Commission on Trade Unions and at the meetings of the National Association for the Advancement of Social Science about the relative merits of the types. Opinion favoured conciliation but it was Kettle's system which spread. By the early 1870s many disputes were decided by referring them to independent arbitrators. The practice in the North-eastern coalfields was to appoint two arbitrators or assessors from each side and an independent umpire. When trade unionists voted for arbitration, as they did in all the miners' unions at various times, and when the employers resisted it on the grounds that outsiders should not interfere, arbitration meant decision-making by a person not connected with the industry.

When unions and employers opposed each other in strikes or lockouts each side had its own criteria for deciding what amounts should or should not be accepted or granted, but they were not discussed and a compromise could in fact be reached by using two entirely different criteria. Once conciliation was practised, the criteria had to be made explicit, though even here amounts could be agreed upon without reference to standards. Arguments about criteria on conciliation boards did take place but the real discussion occurred in arbitration cases for single arbitrators had to discover criteria which were acceptable to both sides. This discussion took place in public.

The question was by what standard should wages move up and down? According to changes in the cost of living? Changes in the level of profits, costs of production, selling prices and if so at what point of production, or according to the inexorable laws of supply and demand? The discussion was conducted by intellectual arbitrators with contributions from both sides, though the contribution from the unions was strongly influenced by the views of the arbitrators themselves. The discussion was hampered by a lack of statistics concerning costs and profits. There was rank and file trade union pressure for the criterion to be the cost of living or a 'reasonable minimum of comfort'.

[50] Church, p. 58, and Crompton, p. 37.
[51] Cuthbert, p. 43.

In March 1874 a public meeting of engineers, smiths, and boiler-makers complained that 'the present rate of wages is not commensurable with the expenditure of living'.[52] The Durham miners in 1874 contended in an arbitration case before Russell Gurney, the recorder of London, that wages should provide a 'reasonable minimum of comfort', but the coal-owners refused to admit that the high cost of living was a valid reason for withstanding a wage reduction.[53] The employers, too, refused to allow profits to be regarded as the standard; in any event they kept quiet about their profits. They used rising costs to justify a wage reduction,[54] but refused to allow costs to be a consistent criterion. The only standard the employers allowed was the movement of selling prices.

Other sections of the industry went through similar experiences so that by 1875 wages were by and large determined by movements of selling prices. The Board of Arbitration and Conciliation for iron-workers in Staffordshire fixed wages according to the selling price of bar iron. The question then arose that if there was a ready made criterion for determining wages then arbitration was not only costly, it was unnecessary. An arbitrator in a Durham coal dispute made this point in 1876 when he said he hoped 'some self-adjusting principle may be discovered for regulating wages, one more simple, ready and less expensive than arbitration'.[55] A sliding scale agreement which related wages to selling prices and which considered the subsistence aspect of wages only by containing upper and lower limits was accepted by iron workers early in 1875. Later, similar agreements became common in the coalfields.

The consequence for trade unionism was that with an automatic means of regulating wages, trade unions became, or so it seemed at the time, largely unnecessary. After the introduction of the sliding scale in the South Wales coalfield, trade unionism died for about two decades; in the Forest of Dean miners simply contracted out of the union because they thought it was unnecessary. The introduction of sliding scale agreements was one of the factors which caused the membership of the Association of Ironworkers to decline from 35,000 in 1873 to 1,400 in 1879.

[52] *Capital and Labour*, 18 March 1874, p. 63.
[53] Welbourne, p. 166. When Thomas Ellison made his award in the 1879 Yorkshire mining dispute he admitted 'that the wages now received by the miners are barely sufficient to afford a decent maintenance of themselves and families' and awarded accordingly. He went on, however, to concede to the employers the right to break the award if it proved too costly (Williams, p. 163).
[54] For example coal-owners considered that miners should bear part of the cost of administering the 1872 Mines Regulation Act.
[55] *Capital and Labour*, 23 February 1876, p. 140.

Conclusion

In conclusion, formal arbitration and conciliation machinery, then sliding scale agreements, occurred in the newly expanding industries. The traditional crafts were largely governed by working rules and regulations on which the unions permitted no scope for arbitration. Neither the Operative Stonemasons' Society nor the Boiler Makers Society, for instance, would countenance arbitration. And it was only on occasions that arbitration occurred in the engineering industry. It was not possible, moreover, in many crafts to find a simple and acceptable criterion for determining wages; certainly selling prices could not always be used. Also the crafts were often dominated by employers who were difficult to organize. In Sheffield, for example, the industrial structure was dominated by many anachronistic features. The employers ranged from small masters to large integrated joint stock companies and it was difficult to achieve cohesion among them. Local arbitration boards were proposed by the Sheffield engineering unions in 1867, 1875, 1883, 1887, but, despite the active interest of the Sheffield MP, A. J. Mundella, the proposals all came to nothing.[56] Where conciliation and arbitration were employed and were succeeded by sliding scale agreements, trade unionism was contained and disarmed at a significant stage of its growth. To this extent the advocates of the formal institutional treatment of industrial disputes succeeded where the document, lockouts and repressive legislation had failed.

[56] Sidney Pollard, *History of Labour in Sheffield*, Liverpool University Press, 1959, p. 134.

7

The National Industrial Conference, 1919–1921

The Government, early in 1919, beset with its industrial troubles, with strikes and threats of bigger strikes, apprehensive about unemployment, disturbed by protests over the pace of demobilization, and, despite its large majority in the House of Commons, unsure of its position in the country, was in urgent need of a means to provide a respite from industrial unrest. The means was sought through an imposing National Industrial Conference of employers and trade union representatives. It is not clear whose idea this was. The suggestion was made by the National Alliance of Employers and Employed[1] and the Federation of British Industries and was reported in the press on 14 February.[2] On the previous day, however, the general secretary of the Trades Union Congress had reported to his Parliamentary Committee that the Ministry of Labour was proposing to arrange such a conference and asked it to nominate representatives.[3] In any case the Government made its decision and within a few days of the first public suggestion that a national representative conference should be held had announced its proposals for the conference. Within that short time it had been rumoured that a 'Labour Parliament' was being set up with a 'Cabinet' of masters and men, or that a super Whitley Council was being established to make decisions on wages and related questions.[4] Nothing of the kind was contained in the Government proposals. Indeed the Government had no plan, though doubtless it had hopes. Trade union leaders received the

---

[1] The National Alliance of Employers and Employed was formed in the autumn of 1916 to harmonize relations between capital and labour. It established joint committees in industrial centres and organized conferences throughout the country to propagate its ideas. Its vice-chairman in 1919 was Arthur Pugh, secretary of the Iron and Steel Trades Confederation. The TUC was asked to affiliate to it but refused finally on 11 June 1919.

[2] Cf. *The Times*, 14 February 1919.

[3] Minutes of the Parliamentary Committee of the TUC, 13 February 1919.

[4] *The Times*, 18 February 1919.

proposals with responses which varied between cautious approval and scepticism.

The Government's haste was encouraged by industrial events. On 13 February the Miners' Federation in conference decided to ballot its members on the decision of striking to enforce a list of demands. On the same day the House of Commons debated a motion deploring the Government's lack of policy for dealing with the causes of the current industrial disputes. The National Union of Railwaymen and the National Transport Workers' Federation each had industrial claims pending over which they were willing to strike. And there was a possibility that the unions in the Triple Industrial Alliance would join forces in a combined industrial offensive.

By the time the National Industrial Conference met on 27 February 1919, the most important industrial movements had been halted, temporarily at least. The Miners' Federation had agreed to be represented on the Coal Commission under the chairmanship of Mr Justice Sankey, and had postponed taking strike action from 15 to 22 March on the assurance that an interim report from the Commission would be available by the 20th. The Triple Alliance had deferred making any momentous decision.

The Conference was attended by about 800 people. The Minister of Labour, Sir Robert Horne, acted as chairman; the Prime Minister, D. Lloyd George, was present, as were the most prominent employers' representatives and trade union leaders.[5] G. H. Stuart-Bunning, chairman of the Parliamentary Committee, represented the Trades Union Congress; J. H. Thomas spoke on behalf of the Triple Alliance and Arthur Henderson, secretary of the Labour Party, was there on behalf of the Friendly Society of Ironfounders. Sir Robert Horne opened the Conference with a long speech in which he described the conditions he thought were responsible for some of the unrest in industry; then he spoke of unemployment, hours of work, wages, the prevention of strikes, and war pledges; these issues were discussed by the Conference. The delegates were there without mandates to take action, but it was clear that the Conference would achieve nothing unless plans were laid for its continuance. Delegates said their pieces. The most prominent employers' representative, Sir Allan Smith (representing the Engineering and Shipbuilding Employers' Federation), deprecated the intervention of the Government in industrial relations, but pressed that the Conference should get down to work by appointing a small committee to prepare a report. This suggestion

[5] Invitations had been extended to members of the newly created Joint Industrial Councils as well as trade unions and employers' associations.

was amplified later by Arthur Henderson in a motion which called for the appointment of a Joint Committee, consisting of equal numbers of employers and workers, with a chairman appointed by the Government to consider:

1. Questions relating to hours, wages and general conditions of employment.
2. Unemployment and its prevention.
3. The best methods of promoting cooperation between Capital and Labour.

The motion was amended slightly by the Prime Minister who made the closing speech, and accepted by the Conference. The feeling of the Conference was amicable; the tenor was moderation. There were a few critics but these were dismissed as irresponsible.[6] The Conference divided into employers' and workers' groups and each group elected its representatives on to a National Industrial Conference Provisional Joint Committee.

The representative nature of the Conference was seriously impaired by the refusal of the miners, railwaymen and transport workers who comprised the Triple Alliance, and the Amalgamated Society of Engineers, to take any part in it after its first meeting. The Dockers' Union was highly critical of the Conference. It stated that the dockers' representatives were at the first Conference but the Central Office of the union had no intimation that they had been invited nor had the executive of the union been given an opportunity to discuss the purpose of the Conference.[7] It went on to state that 'it was evident that every precaution was taken by the Government to prevent united effort on the part of Labour in submitting constructive proposals'. The Labour participants who favoured the project came in for heavy criticism. The decision of the Triple Alliance unions to remain aloof from the National Industrial Conference was approved by the National Transport Workers' Federation and the National Union of Railwaymen at their annual meetings. The latter body stated that 'no useful purpose is served by collusion with the employers through the Government to maintain the existing order of society'.[8]

Meanwhile, the Joint Committee, undeterred by criticisms, engaged in discussions over a number of matters raised by Sir Robert Horne. At the first Conference the Minister of Labour had stated that the Government would not be averse to introducing legislation

[6] Ernest Bevin was the most vocal critic. He said that those who represented the Triple Alliance would have to think again about the Conference.

[7] *The Dockers' Record*, February 1919.

[8] *Railway Review*, 27 June 1919.

to fix hours or a minimum wage. The Joint Committee took him at his word and submitted a Report containing a number of proposals to a full Conference on 4 April. Briefly, it proposed that a maximum normal working week should be established by an Act of Parliament, subject to certain agreed exceptions, and that systematic overtime should be discouraged; that there should be a legal enactment of the principle of national minimum time rates of wages; that the Wages (Temporary Regulation) Act 1918 should be continued for a further period of six months from 21 May 1919; that trade conferences should be held to decide whether to add war advances and bonuses to time rates or piece rates, or to treat them separately. A proposal was also made to establish a permanent National Industrial Council consisting of 400 members equally representative of employers' organizations and trade unions. It was suggested that the permanent Council should be recognized by the Government 'as the official consultative authority to the Government upon industrial relations'.[9]

The Prime Minister was unable to attend the full Conference on 4 April but Sir Robert Horne was there and he read a letter from Mr Lloyd George in which he stated that if 'the recommendations of the Committee receive the approval of the Conference the Government will give them their immediate and sympathetic consideration'. Sir Robert Horne called the Report 'the most momentous document which had been presented to the country in a long number of years'. It was accepted by the National Industrial Conference without dissent. It was also decided to keep the provisional joint committee in being until the permanent National Industrial Council had been established.

The note of urgency which was conspicuous in the first Government overtures to the National Industrial Conference was soon dropped. It was not until 1 May 1919 that the Joint Committee was called to hear the Government's attitude to the Report in greater detail. Again Sir Robert Horne apologized for the absence of the Prime Minister and read from him the following letter:

[9] *Report of Provisional Joint Committee. Presented to Meeting of Industrial Conference*, *4 April 1919*, Cmd 139. Proposals were also made for the prevention of unemployment and the maintenance of unemployed workers. Appended to the Report was a trade union memorandum on the causes of industrial unrest. It was in effect a statement of Socialist policy. It concluded that 'The fundamental causes of Labour unrest are to be found rather in the growing determination of Labour to challenge the whole existing structure of capitalist industry than in any of the more special and smaller grievances which come to the surface at any particular time.' This memorandum was in strange contrast to the endeavours of trade union representatives on the Joint Committee which were aimed at reaching a *modus vivendi* with capitalists.

Gentlemen, I have read your report very carefully, and deeply regret that I am unable to meet you in person in order to thank you for the very valuable piece of work which you have done.

On the Continent, as I have good reason to know, your work is being closely watched. Foreign countries are looking to Great Britain to give them a lead in the foundation of a new and better industrial order, and this report marks the beginning of such a foundation.

Though I cannot commit myself to every detail, as many of them are complex and technical, I may say at once that I fully accept in principle your recommendations as to the fixing of maximum hours and minimum rates of wages. As regards hours, a Bill is now being drafted to give effect to your recommendations, and will, I hope, be introduced at a very early date. I think you will find that it fully carries out the principles set forth in your report, though, as you have recognized, elasticity must be provided in order to meet the special circumstances of particular industries.

There are certain industries, such as agriculture, in which seasonal and other conditions necessitate special consideration; and some cases, such as those of seamen and domestic servants, in which it would be impossible to enforce a week of 48 hours; but I agree that the Act should otherwise apply to all industries in which a legal limitation of hours is practicable, and that, where exceptions are necessary, they should be applied for by those concerned through the machinery which you have suggested in your report.

As regards wages, I accept the principle that minimum rates of wages should in all industries be made applicable by law. The question of the best method of doing this, however, is complex and full of difficulties, and I do not think it would be possible to frame legislation until a scheme for carrying out the principle of minimum rates has been fully worked out. I therefore gladly accept your suggestion that the Government should, in the first place, set up a Commission with wide terms of reference to report on the whole matter. As regards the extension of the Wages (Temporary Regulation) Act, a Bill has been prepared for this purpose and has been introduced.

In regard to unemployment, I understand that your Committee was unable to make any definite recommendation as to how the present provision against unemployment should be extended, though they were unanimous in thinking extension necessary. In view of the short time at your disposal, I do not think that the Committee could be blamed for this, but the question of unemployment is one of the most urgent and important of the problems confronting us, and until it is satisfactorily solved I do not feel that we shall have really effected one of the most vital improvements in our social conditions. I therefore hope that this is the first question to which the National Industrial Council will address itself.

I cordially welcome your proposal to set up a National Council, and hope that you will take steps to bring it into being as quickly as possible,

Dir

as I am sure that it will be of great value in assisting the Government to improve industrial conditions.

Yours faithfully,

D. LLOYD GEORGE.[10]

The Joint Committee adjourned until 29 May when Sir Robert Horne appeared before it with draft Bills to establish minimum wages and maximum hours. At this point he apologized for what seemed to outsiders to be a suspiciously dilatory approach.

> I am sorry, [he said] for the interval which has elapsed, because I am afraid it has been the cause of some suspicion growing up in the minds of some people in the country that the Government was not dealing with this matter as expeditiously as it might have done, and I see from the public press that suggestions have been made from certain quarters . . . that indeed the whole theory of the Industrial Conference was designed to save the face of the Government at a difficult point of time, and that, after having served its uses, it was to be left gradually to drop into the limbo of forgetfulness.[11]

Horne naturally denied this assertion. He was, he said, much too young a hand in politics to play such a game.

It is not possible to say how widespread was this feeling about the Government's motives. Certainly some trade union leaders in the Triple Alliance unions subscribed to it. Harry Gosling committed himself to it during his presidential address to the National Transport Workers' Federation. He said that they would support Whitley Councils 'but any effort like the Government's Industrial Council—which in the opinion of your Executive was only a temporary expedient to checkmate the workers' demands then fructifying—we shall not associate ourselves with. In this matter we are loyal to the spirit and purpose of the constitution of the Triple Industrial Alliance.'[12] The same opinion was later expressed by the Labour historian, G. D. H. Cole, who acted as the secretary of the workers' side of the Joint Committee.[13]

The trade union participants in the National Industrial Conference were certainly becoming impatient with the Government and suspicious of its intentions. The Government wanted the permanent

[10] Minutes of Proceedings of the National Industrial Conference Provisional Joint Committee, 1 May 1919.

[11] Minutes of Proceedings of the National Industrial Conference Provisional Joint Committee, 29 May 1919.

[12] National Transport Workers' Federation. *Report of the Ninth Annual General Council Meeting, 5th and 6th June, 1919*, p. 16.

[13] G. D. H. Cole, *A Short History of the British Working Class Movement*, pp. 389–90, Allen & Unwin, 1948 rev. edn.

National Industrial Council to be established quickly, but the trade union representatives and to a lesser extent the employers' representatives wanted it delayed until the Government had shown its hand by legislating for minimum wages and maximum hours. The Council was virtually being made the price of a bargain between the Joint Committee and the Government.[14] The trade unions needed a bargaining counter, for the content of the Bills presented by Horne met neither trade union requirements nor the compromise set out in the Joint Committee Report. At a Joint Committee meeting on 13 June 1919, Arthur Henderson said circumstances had changed since February, and 'the attitudes of certain people towards the work that we were asked to do has also changed. . . . I shall refuse to accept further responsibility, and . . . I shall intimate to the public the reason why I refused to accept responsibility unless we are going to give effect to the Report, and nothing but the Report.' The employers expressed their discontent more vehemently. Sir Allan Smith said that the Government was asking for trouble and would get it; and that 'either effective action shall be taken on the lines of the Report, or that we are unable to proceed any further'.[15] Both sides were convinced that the Government had gone back on the early assurances it had given.

After Sir Robert Horne had presented his two Bills the discussions at each of the subsequent meetings of the Joint Committee were preoccupied with the Hours Bill. Horne said at the meeting on 29 May 1919 that the trade union side of the Joint Committee had told him 'they viewed with alarm the report that certain trades are to be exempted from the terms of the (Hours) Bill . . . and reaffirmed the decision of the Joint Committee that the Act must apply generally to all employed persons'.[16] In particular the trade unionists objected to the exclusion of agriculture. Discussions over this went on for months without the matter being resolved.[17] Then on 17 June 1920—just over a year after the drafts of the Bills had been seen—a new Minister of Labour, Dr T. J. Macnamara, came to the Joint Committee with a redrafted Hours Bill. It was Macnamara's own Bill and it deviated appreciably from the Report of the Joint Committee.

This action showed a complete disregard for the purpose of the

[14] *The Times*, 3 June 1919.
[15] Minutes of Proceedings of the National Industrial Conference Provisional Joint Committee, 13 June 1919.
[16] *Ibid.*, 29 May 1919.
[17] Quite early in the discussion, in autumn 1919, the Government acted unilaterally and introduced its own drafts of the Hours and Wages Bills into the House of Commons. These were only given a first reading.

National Industrial Conference. The Government had clearly shown its hand. It was not concerned about implementing the recommendations in the Report. The portended labour crisis had not materialized. Dr Macnamara was questioned about the Bill. He was asked whether the Government would introduce it into the House of Commons even if the Joint Committee disagreed with its terms. He replied that the Government would proceed with it in any event.[18] The Government was sounding the end of the National Industrial Conference. At the next meeting of the Joint Committee on 28 June 1920 the employers, again the more outspoken, stated that the redrafted Bill was not within the terms of their mandate from the National Industrial Conference; they could neither consider it nor act in regard to it. Sir Allan Smith contended that the action of the Minister of Labour had terminated the function of the Joint Committee.[19]

The sentiments of the employers were expressed in a motion they submitted to the Joint Committee. The trade union members, clearly the only ones who wanted the National Industrial Conference to continue in being, asked for an adjournment so they could consider it. During the adjournment, which lasted for more than a year, they discussed the matter among themselves and corresponded about it with the Minister of Labour. During that time, too, the Minister of Labour had told the House of Commons that the Government could not proceed with the Minimum Wage Commission Bill due to the pressure of other legislation.[20] When the Joint Committee eventually met on 19 July 1921, at the request of the trade union side, it decided to resign and bring the National Industrial Conference formally to an end. The Prime Minister showed no concern. He did not even request to speak to the Joint Committee, though he had been eager enough to do so during the crisis of 1919. He simply wrote, through the Minister of Labour, regretting that the Provisional Joint Committee was not fully representative of the important industries of the country—of the miners, the railwaymen, the transport workers and the engineers; and regretting that it had not been possible to give legislative effect to all the recommendations of the Joint Committee.[21] It was more than coincidental that those two statements were made together for if the representatives of the important industries had been present on the Joint Committee the result might have been much different. It seemed their absence was a matter for rejoicing by the Government and not regret.

[18] Minutes of Proceedings of the National Industrial Conference Provisional Joint Committee, 17 June 1920.
[19] *Ibid.*, 28 June 1920.   [20] 17 February 1921.   [21] In a letter dated 2 August 1921.

8

White-collar revolt

It has been generally believed that militant trade unionism with its methods crudely forged out of force could never be used by white-collar workers and, in any case, was unnecessary for the protection of their economic wellbeing. It was felt that they could solve the problems they had with employers through their own individual efforts but if it should become necessary for them to act collectively then they would do so with dignity and refinement as befitted intelligent men. Not for them the methods of steel-workers, dockers and miners.

Recently, however, we have witnessed the spectacle of school teachers going on strike; of solicitors working to rule; of scientists parading their grievances through the streets of London; of insurance men lobbying the House of Lords; of chemists threatening to leave the National Health Service; of a vicar suggesting a trade union for clergymen. How do we explain this divergence between the accepted image of white-collar workers and their recent behaviour? Is it a temporary phenomenon or does it indicate a revolution in attitude?

It is neither. It is not new for white-collar workers to act collectively. A National Union of Elementary Teachers was formed as long ago as 1870. Clerks formed a union in 1897; local government officials in 1905; many civil service departmental unions were in existence before the First World War, and even the bank clerks, the élite of clerks, formed a union in 1917 and were 50 per cent organized by 1921. Nor is it the first time they have used militant methods. All were particularly aggressive after the First World War. There were strikes among bank clerks in Ireland, insurance agents in Scotland, and school teachers in England and Wales. Various other groups threatened strike action. Civil servants demonstrated in their masses against the Government.

Since the Second World War a number of industrial protests have been made. In 1950 doctors decided to leave the National Health Service but afterwards changed their minds, and in 1957 health service workers imposed a ban on overtime; on various occasions clerks in the motor industry have gone on strike.

But there is a difference between now and the earlier demonstrations. It is one of size and diversity. More white-collar workers from a wider range of occupations than ever before are willing to use the methods of militant unionism to redress their grievances. It seems reasonable that they should do so. They are, after all, members of a permanent employed class in exactly the same way as manual workers. They sell their labour power in a market which, on the one hand, has many sellers struggling to obtain the highest price for their labour power and, on the other, few buyers who are seeking to buy at the lowest cost possible. As individuals they suffer from being in a position of market inferiority.

But this clearly is an inadequate explanation, for despite their market similarity white-collar and manual workers on the whole have responded differently to economic pressures. Whereas approximately 60 per cent of the manual workers in Britain belong to trade unions, only about 21 per cent of the white-collar workers do so. All told almost two-thirds of the unorganized employees in Britain are in white-collar employment. What accounts for this?

Some social scientists seek an explanation in terms of the different conditions under which these two groups work. It is said that because the white-collar workers have often had higher earnings, greater security in their jobs, more congenial working hours and cleaner working conditions, than the manual workers; because they have not had to work tiresomely in factories and soil their hands; because they have been able to wear their everyday street clothes at work, they have not felt the same need to protest collectively.

This explanation presupposes a correlation between material well-being and industrial contentment which does not exist. It is incorrect to assume that the better off a man is the more complacent he is likely to be about his work situation. The whole weight of historical and contemporary research disputes this. The highest paid manual workers have always been among the most militant of their group, and it has been the doctors and school teachers, not the lowly paid clerks in dingy back-street offices, who have displayed the greatest collective aggressiveness. There is not an indirect proportionate relationship between militancy and earnings. A person earning £2000 a year may be no less dependent on his employer than one earning only £10 a week. The extent of his dependence is determined by the availability of other jobs. He may have to be given three months' notice of dismissal but the fact of dismissal is not made more palatable by that. The point is that a teacher or an administrator does not compare his industrial situation with that of a labourer or a porter in order to assess his satisfaction with it. He compares it with that of men with similar economic and social opportunities in different occupations. This provides vast scope for disgruntlement. We must look beyond the work situation for an explanation of the collective behaviour of white-collar workers.

Striving for prestige

A prime distinguishing mark of those in white-collar employment has been their striving for prestige. This has always been so. They have possessed social aspirations but have had limited means for achieving them. Unlike the members of the upper class they could not claim prestige as their birthright; nor could they, like the captains of industry, base it on power and authority. So they sought it in the only way left open to them—by concentrating on social differences; by relating prestige to appearances. Already they were separated from the manual group by the stigma attached to dirty work, and they sought to consolidate this separation by segregating themselves both physically and socially from manual workers. They were successful. The separation became a part of our social structure. It was embodied in the educational system and epitomized in the distinctions between elementary education on the one hand and grammar and bought education, often of a low standard, on the other. Its encouragement became a commercial proposition. Social pretensions were exploited for profit.

Prestige became linked with the ownership of particular commodities: with houses and cars; later with washing machines, then refrigerators. Products for the families of white-collar workers were designed to appeal to the socially aspiring; they were *de luxe* working-class editions but they were accepted and they made higher profits. Out of this situation developed the fetish of competitive consumption, making it necessary for one group always to keep ahead of the other in the range and quality of the goods it consumed. White-collar employment became associated with a way of life; with privately owned houses sitting in their tidy gardens; each as private and tidy as the other, glowing with respectability and oozing with smugness; with annual holidays, not outings; with wives who did not go out to work.

The social insularity of white-collar workers was fostered by the privileged treatment they received from employers. White-collar workers were called staff, not hands, operators, or workmen; they were paid salaries, not wages, and were paid by the month, not by the hour, the day, or the week; they received a high degree of formal job security, superannuation, holidays with pay, sickness benefits, social and sports amenities—most of which were denied to manual workers. The staff were encouraged to identify their interests with those of the employers and to regard themselves as having a personal relationship with them. To emphasize this, white-collar workers were paid at individual rates, and so completely did they accept it that they rarely revealed their salaries to each other. They were encouraged to regard trade union representation as being an intrusion into a highly personal affair. In general, manual and white-collar workers were discouraged from mixing at work. Their starting and finishing times were often different. Sometimes they were provided with their own entrances. The separation of staff from workmen was built into the structures of industrial organizations as if the two represented different castes.

The false image

As a result of working in a protected and controlled industrial environment and under the influence of vivid external pressures, white-collar workers became involved in a great social pretence. They formed an image of themselves which bore little resemblance to economic realities. They saw themselves as individuals, superior to manual workers and able to progress through society unaided and without protection. They recognized no common interests. This image acted as a barrier to collective action.

But there have always been some white-collar workers who, for a variety of reasons, many of them personal, felt so aggrieved by their treatment at work that no amount of pressure or influence could distract or deceive them. These people constituted those minorities who formed trade unions. The support they received depended upon the extent to which the predominant social image was modified. Some modifications have now occurred, and the factors which have caused them have been relative changes in real incomes, the advent of full employment and the spread of mechanization into manual and non-manual operations.

The effects of relative changes in real incomes are the most obvious. Because the status of white-collar workers has depended largely upon their ability to engage in selective consumption, anything which has reduced their purchasing power has had implications for status. Two factors have been at work here. The early respectability of white-collar jobs induced many socially aspiring parents to direct their children into them, so that the supply of entrants exceeded the demand. The result was that money earnings were depressed in relation to the earnings of others. White-collar workers have also suffered substantial reductions in their real incomes during periods of inflation compared with manual workers. This is because their money incomes are less responsive to price changes than those of manual workers.

The inflation after 1918 shocked many white-collar workers into taking collective action as it did after the Second World War, though then it was neither so sharp nor so shocking. Since 1945, however, price rises have been consistent and persistent. They have eaten into the real incomes of relatively fixed-income people and have brought about a substantial redistribution of money incomes as between white-collar and manual workers. In addition this period has been marked by a secular rise in living standards, making it possible for a wider range of people than ever before to engage in selective consumption. House ownership and the possession of cars, washing machines, refrigerators and holidays abroad now characterize the lives of some manual workers more than some white-collar workers. When there is an overlap to any considerable extent the prestige value of the commodities concerned is lost. White-collar workers, in the main, have not had the means to escape from this by shifting their consumption to commodities beyond the reach of manual workers.

Reduced privilege

Full employment has acted on the work situation of white-collar workers in much the same way as inflation has acted on their social position. It has reduced the element of privilege. When labour is scarce most workers have a relatively high degree of security in their jobs irrespective of the formal provisions for it. Inroads have been made into other privileges too, as employers have been compelled by the labour situation and union pressure to concede to manual workers' fringe benefits concerning holidays, pensions, and sickness. White-collar workers may still receive bigger and better benefits but they do not amount to privilege.

The spread of mechanization has also altered the image and so reduced the social distance between white-collar and manual workers. Work in offices nowadays often involves the operation of light machines such as calculating machines, dictaphones, and computers, which so dilute the tasks that many of them can be done by what might be called semiskilled non-manual labourers. The mechanization of the production processes has had opposite effects. It has moved from the stage of diluting craft skills to the point where machines operate machines, thus removing the elements of toil and dirt from work. Manual workers are increasingly able to wear light shoes and a tidy suit for work.

The factors I have mentioned function in an environment where there is an increasing number of opportunities for the traditional white-collar work. In the last decade the percentage of the total in civil employment which is engaged in such work has risen from 43 to about 50. This increase, coupled with the gradual spread of educational opportunities, has made it possible for the children of manual workers to enter non-manual employment relatively easily. It is no longer a social achievement to make this transition, nor is it such a pronounced social aspiration to want to do so.

Although all white-collar workers have felt the impact of inflation, full employment, and mechanization, some have felt it more than others. Public employees have been most affected by inflation and those in manufacturing industry least. The consequences of mechanization have been experienced most by workers in commerce and finance. Sometimes the incidence has varied within groups, as in the case of teachers where those on the basic scale suffer most from the Government's pay pause policy.

It is clear, then, that white-collar workers are increasingly practising trade unionism because they know they are losing their status and recognize that the causes are institutional ones. They are being compelled to scrutinize their objective relationships with employers and with each other. But this process has been going on for some time, so why the, seemingly, sudden outburst of militancy? The answer is that the conditions I have described are necessary for the rise of trade unionism but are not sufficient in themselves to determine its motion and intensity. Other things have to happen to shock, jolt, or prompt workers into phases of action. These other things are of a philosophical as well as a sociological nature, and for this reason they cannot readily be discerned and most certainly they cannot be anticipated. In the case of the phase of militancy in 1961 it seems that it was the Government's interference with the collective bargaining machinery of certain groups which was the jolting factor, but it could have been a feeling of tension or frustration unrelated to industrial affairs. But, whatever it was, it did not have the power to create an unhesitant urge to take industrial action. Nor could it have that power.

The only militant methods white-collar workers know about are those they have denigrated and deplored in the past. Because they cannot uproot nor readily pass over the values which had determined their attitudes, they are confronted by a conflict between what is industrially expedient and that which is socially permissible. The consequence is one of utter confusion, marked by much talk, much dither and hesitation, many second thoughts, and an eager search for more palatable ways of redressing industrial grievances. The conflict is worsened by the essential nature of the work engaged in by so many white-collar workers. They have no desire to harm patients, children, or the public, yet they know that their protests will undoubtedly fail unless they do. Because they feel so deeply about this they rarely practise solidarity in the manual workers' sense. Opinions are often sharply divided about what should be done. All the time, moreover, they have an eye on public opinion. They want to avoid appearing offensive, aggressive, or inconsiderate; they want to preserve as much of their social image as possible.

Because so many white-collar workers are government employees or are financed in part by the Government, they are frequently found making political protests when they are aggrieved. They lobby the House of Commons or canvass individual Members of Parliament. They use constitutional methods which are sometimes quite effective. For example, both civil servants and school teachers secured the defeat of the Government in the early 1920s through careful but vigorous political engineering.

With few exceptions all white-collar groups try to avoid political party alignments, whether in parliament or out of it. In this respect they reflect the dominant political attitude of white-collar workers in general. These workers, in Britain, are the political successors to the small, independent businessmen of the nineteenth century, but they possess neither their coherence nor clearcut political objectives. They do not comprise a well-informed political body which acts as a pivot or stabilizer between the interests of organized labour and capital. They are not Populists or Poujadists. Though their origin is liberal, by conditioning they are conservative, preferring to conform and be safe. In the main they emerge from their political cocoons only during inflations. When slumps have set in they retreat back into their security.

Although white-collar workers do not neatly pivot the interests of labour and capital, they do lie between them, contained on one side by a hostility towards the aspirations of organized labour and on the other by a suspicion of big business interests. The hostility presents a barrier to assimilation within the Labour movement which might persist long after white-collar workers have realized the need for collective action. French experience has shown that it is quite possible for white-collar groups to combine industrial aggressiveness with political conservatism. It is likely to be a long time before white-collar workers identify themselves with the political left, for not only must a substantial erosion of their social image take place but the effects of many years of propaganda about the administrative ineptness of Labour Governments must be wiped out.

In times of dissatisfaction white-collar workers, I believe, are more likely to adopt a negative than a positive political approach; that is, they would abstain from supporting the Conservative Party rather than vote Labour and they would not support the Liberal Party because, though it has many social qualities which appeal to them, it fails in the important respect that it does not present them with an efficient solution to their problems. In times of general crisis, however, there is little doubt that they would prefer a conservative authoritarian solution to their problems.

More than any other groups in society, white-collar workers operate within large, impersonal, hierarchical organizations. Their occupational activities are confined by rules which are obeyed unemotionally in the interests of efficiency. Through this environment they develop a bureaucratic personality which spills over into political affairs. They like neat, ordered, efficient solutions irrespective of wider implications. More than this: many of them, at heart, are impatient with parliamentary democracy. As public servants they see it at work and they dislike its gross inefficiency. The combined effect of these factors has led white-collar workers in other countries to support social movements which, like nazism, fascism, and de Gaullism, are nationalistic, authoritarian, and critical of parliamentary democracy. There seems little reason to suppose that in comparable situations they would act differently here.

9

The growth of trade unionism in banking, 1914–1927[1]

This chapter is concerned with a period during which trade unionism in banking first appeared, spread and then declined. It shows why trade unionism occurred at all in banking and why it occurred when it did, and reveals the factors which influenced the collective behaviour of bank workers. It enables us to compare, in general terms, the union activities of different groups of non-manual workers.

Banking conditions, before 1914, encouraged a belief in economic individualism. There were very few bank salary scales which provided for automatic increases after clerks had reached the age of thirty years. A clerk after that age who wanted to increase his remuneration, depended either on promotion or on obtaining a bonus for extra responsibility. Both promotion and bonus were controlled or strongly influenced by branch managers. Thus the future of a bank clerk largely depended upon his creating and maintaining a favourable personal relationship with his manager, or, if the bank were small, with his employer.

The bank employers consciously tried to create an aura of exclusiveness around bank employment. They recruited their staffs mainly from the public schools on personal recommendations and gave preference to the sons of professional men. As there were usually waiting lists for posts, the banks were able to choose their staffs with discrimination.

Bank workers regarded themselves as the aristocrats of clerks. They had no contact in their work with manual workers or even with other clerks. In their local communities they often enjoyed a status comparable to that accorded to professional men and they main-

[1] This chapter was written in collaboration with Sheila Williams. We wish to thank the officials of the National Union of Bank Employees for permission to consult material in their files. This chapter is concerned only with the trade union activities of bank clerks in England and Wales. In Scotland and Ireland quite distinct activities took place.

tained a standard of living which enabled them to give the necessary appearance of privilege to that status.

The formation of the Bank Officers' Guild[2]

The first attempt to form a union was made in 1914. Appeals for support appeared in the London and provincial press and in 1915 a National Association of Bank Clerks was registered. Support for the union was slight and it ceased to function in the same year. Then the working conditions of bank workers began to show a marked deterioration. The younger clerks joined the armed services and bank recruitment was suspended. A greater volume of work and increased responsibility had to be borne by the remaining clerks, without either an increase in pay or an improvement in status. At the same time Britain experienced a spell of inflation against which bank clerks had no protection. While organized workers succeeded in obtaining wage increases to counteract rapid price rises, bank clerks were given inadequate war bonuses at the discretion of the banks.[3]

The war speeded up the process of concentration in banking control. Private banks were absorbed by joint stock banks and joint stock banks amalgamated with each other. Between 1891 and 1918 the number of private banks decreased from thirty-seven to six.[4] The number of joint stock banks in England and Wales fell from forty-three in 1913 to twenty-six in 1918 while the total number of branches increased from 5797 to 6501.[5] The degree of concentration was greater than these figures indicate because the branches were concentrated in a small number of large banks and some banks had controlling interests in others. Even in 1909 about five banks had done half of the banking business.[6] The banks had become much more impersonal places in which to work. The determination of such matters as promotion policy and salary scales had moved into the hands of people with whom the ordinary clerk had no contact and on whom, in any case, he could make no impression with his individual demands.

[2] See David Lockwood, *The Blackcoated Worker*, Allen & Unwin, 1958, pp. 176–84, for a brief history of trade unionism in banking.

[3] War bonuses of about 20 per cent were handed out by some banks at the end of the war (see *The Bank Officer*, October and November 1919). Prices rose by 220 per cent during the war period, while weekly wage rates increased by 179 per cent, A. C. Pigou (*Aspects of British Economic History*, p. 230).

[4] J. E. Goodbar, *Managing the People's Money*, p. 306.

[5] League of Nations, *Memorandum on Commercial Banks, 1913–1929*, 1931, pp. 280 ff.

[6] Goodbar, p. 304.

A second attempt to form a union was made when a group of bank clerks who had been concerned with the first venture met in Sheffield in December 1917. They appointed a provisional committee to work out a scheme and inserted notices in provincial daily newspapers. To inquiriers they sent an explanatory letter making it clear that they intended to establish a conciliatory guild and not a militant trade union. They had a favourable response. Branches were formed in various provincial cities and in August 1918 a London branch was set up to which the head office was transferred from Sheffield about two months later.

The Guild grew relatively slowly until bank clerks in the armed forces had been demobilized. These men had been through new and revealing social experiences. They had mixed with members of all social classes and had exchanged ideas with them. When they returned to bank employment they were prepared to recognize collective action as a socially legitimate and necessary means of redressing their grievances. They joined the Bank Officers' Guild.

At Easter 1919 the first national conference of branch representatives was held to elect officials, a provisional national committee, and to consider a proposed constitution. A mass meeting was held in London in May 1919, at which a bank clerks' charter was outlined. The first issue of the Guild's journal, *The Bank Officer*, appeared in August 1919, and in October about 100 delegates met at the first annual general meeting of the Bank Officers' Guild. At this meeting various decisions concerned with the establishment of an organization were taken, including one to register the Guild as a trade union. The enthusiasm for the Guild was expressed in its rapidly increasing membership. In October 1919 the membership was estimated to be 10,000. By December 1920 the Guild had organized 27,000 of the 60,000 bank clerks in the country.

The organization of the Guild

The Guild catered for any member of the clerical or managerial staff whether employed or retired with a pension, of any bank or trustee savings bank with an office in the United Kingdom.[7] There were many discussions about whether it should include women, temporary staff and messengers. It was generally agreed that all the clerical staff should be organized, but there was confusion about this in practice. Many of the temporary staff were women and some branches excluded them from membership. There was strong resistance to having

[7] In fact its activities were confined to England and Wales.

messengers in the Guild. It was maintained that if they were allowed to join, the prestige of the Guild would be lowered in the eyes of the bank directors.[8] Even though the National Provincial Bank put messengers on a salary scale and Barclays Bank included them in a bonus system, the bank clerks maintained that they had nothing in common with them and excluded them from membership.[9]

Two full-time officials, a president and general secretary, were elected in October 1919.[10] The annual general meeting was designated the supreme policy-making body of the Guild. It consisted of elected delegates and any ordinary member of the Guild provided he paid his own expenses and gave notice of his attendance. Certain officials were allowed to attend *ex officio*. The executive committee attended but had no voting power. The administration of the Guild was put in the hands of the executive committee which had the power to interpret the rules and to call for the opinion of the branches or members on any issues, though it was not bound to accept that opinion.[11]

The number of branches increased from seventeen in August 1919 to 190 in 1922. The extra work which this expansion entailed caused the Guild to appoint two full-time organizing secretaries in 1921. The general fund of the Guild grew from £4000 in 1919 to almost £10,000 at the end of 1920. The Guild was clearly established by that time. It was national in scope and was well equipped to negotiate on behalf of bank clerks.

Employers' reactions

The bank employers responded quickly and firmly to the formation of the Bank Officers' Guild. They did nothing which was likely to intimidate or antagonize bank clerks to the extent of uniting them against their employers. The Guild was not proscribed, nor were its members victimized openly. The employers simply consistently refused to recognize the Guild and set up their own associations through which they could channel concessions after a semblance of consultation with staff representatives.

Various methods were used to establish these associations. In November 1918 the first intimation that consultation with the staff about working conditions was either necessary or desirable was given

---

[8] President of the Guild at the first annual meeting, April 1919.
[9] Messengers were not admitted to the Guild until 1941.
[10] Frank Clegg became president and J. R. Hannan became general secretary.
[11] *Bank Officers' Guild Rules*, 1922.

when Lloyds Bank established a Staff Representation Committee. The Committee was without a constitution until 1921. On 23 December 1918 the staff of the National Provincial and Union Bank met and elected a provisional committee to consider a proposal to form a guild. The committee presented a detailed and convincing case against an internal association and concluded that apart from sentimental reasons it could see no advantage in having a guild composed exclusively of members of its own bank. It recommended that the Bank Officers' Guild should be strongly supported. Nonetheless an internal association was formed in 1919.

During February 1919 both the London City and Midland Bank and the Westminster Bank took steps to form internal associations. The chairmen and general managers of the London City and Midland Bank invited thirty-six branch managers to London to consider questions relating to the staff. The branch managers recommended to the Board of Directors that a salary increase of 20 per cent should be given to all the staff, that holidays should be extended and that pensions should be improved. A circular letter was sent to all branch managers on 4 February 1919, informing them of these recommendations and that it had been 'decided to take immediate steps to form an Internal Staff Association'. Each branch manager was asked to send a list of the members of his staff (including himself), indicating by an asterisk those who were willing to become members of the Association. On 5 February the directors of the Westminster Bank called a meeting to hear an explanation of the principle of an internal association.[12] The general secretary of the Bank Officers' Guild was present but he had little influence. The meeting did as the directors advised.

With the establishment of internal associations in Barclays and Martins Banks in 1921 all the big joint stock banks had their own associations. In 1923 a central committee was formed to coordinate the activities of the internal associations.

The composition and methods of these associations showed slight variations. In Lloyds Bank, membership of the Staff Representation Committee was automatic for all members of the permanent and supplementary staff and they paid no subscriptions. Representatives were elected for a three-yearly period at a general election throughout the Bank and at each election managers and departmental principals were asked to give all possible assistance. The general secretary of the association was appointed by the directors and only they had power to remove him. In the London City and Midland Bank the membership consisted of 'as many members of the permanent and temporary

[12] *County Westminster and Parrs' Magazine*, March 1919.

clerical staff as may be willing to join . . .'.[13] Women were not eligible for membership and a nominal annual subscription was paid. Local committees 'selected from and appointed by the Staff of the Bank in the respective districts' were established in twenty-one towns.

The bank employers rarely said that the internal associations were established to weaken trade unionism. They justified their actions by stating that banking was an individualist and exceptional occupation. One of the reasons given for the formation of the Midland Bank internal association was that the branch managers did not 'consider it right that any persons other than our own officers should interfere in the affairs of this Bank'.[14] Soon after its formation in 1920 the British Bankers' Association on which all the big joint stock banks were represented stated that a method of direct communication between the directors of each bank and its staff by means of an internal association elected by the staff, was the best basis for solving the problems of banks. The Association added that brains and ability, not strength of limb, were the measure of efficiency and that promotion should be made on merit through the management of each branch, without external interference.[15]

The aims and methods of the Guild

There is an obvious correlation between the determination of employers to oppose trade unionism and the methods needed to obtain recognition from them. The stronger the employers' opposition the greater is the need for militant action. This correlation evaded the majority of the members of the Bank Officers' Guild so that at no time did the Guild adequately match its policy with that of the bank employers.

It was the broad aim of the Guild to improve the conditions and protect the interests of its members; to settle disputes between employers and members; to assist the unemployed; to give assistance to other guilds or trade unions and to amalgamate with other organizations of a kindred nature. It had a general aim to promote and guard the interests of the banking profession.

The first main task of the Guild was to obtain recognition as a negotiating body. Bank employers could either be persuaded or forced to accede recognition. Persuasion involved convincing the employers that the Guild was beneficial to banking and would not

[13] Circular letter, 4 February 1919.   [14] *Ibid.*
[15] Letter to Frank Clegg, president of the Guild, from R. Holland Martin, chairman of the British Bankers' Association, 16 June 1920.

harm the employers' interests. Force entailed the ability to withdraw labour from the banks on a scale sufficient to disrupt their operation. For both methods it was necessary for the Guild to organize a majority of all bank clerks.

The organizers of the Guild believed that bank clerks would not accept the collective standards of manual workers: that they would not be aggressive in their methods. From the beginning they therefore tried to establish a form of collective action which did not unduly violate their social values. The president of the Guild reflected their intention in 1919 when he said: 'We want to find not a basis of antagonism, but . . . a basis of cooperation.'[16] He added that if any of the Guild's 'proposals are proved to be unreasonable or unjust, it would certainly waive its claim to them. . . . The Guild is seeking a basis of co-operation. . . . Hostility to the Banking Directorates is not in the minds of the leaders of the Guild movement.'

The only effective standard of collective action which the Guild organizers knew about, however, was that of the manual workers' unions. In many industries unions had achieved recognition through the use of the strike weapon; through an aggressive, sometimes painful, defiance of the power of employers. The first year of the Guild's existence, 1919, was characterized by strikes and threats of strikes from the most powerful unions of the country. In this atmosphere bank clerks found it difficult to isolate their thoughts and proposals from known trade union methods. They inevitably became confused and contradictory in their statements and advice.

1. Strike action

A clause to give the Guild the authority to call a strike was included in the draft constitution and was accepted. It gave the executive committee the power to declare a strike, but only after a ballot had been held showing that five-eighths of the total membership were in favour of it.[17] The clause was the subject of much discussion at the initial conference. One delegate from Liverpool thought that the Guild was being based on 'Rules and regulations which are adaptable to coal-heavers, and not to intelligent men'.[18] Others opposed its inclusion on principle but the majority felt it was desirable to have their power to withhold labour stated explicitly because it might assist them in negotiations with the bank employers. The chairman, who was in favour of the clause, added that he would fight against it being

[16] Meeting of representatives from branches, April 1919.
[17] *Rules*, 1922, section 2.
[18] Minutes of the first General Meeting, April 1919.

used.[19] Opposition to the clause continued in subsequent years but it remained in the rule book. Its use was never contemplated.

The equivocal attitude of the Guild members to strike action came out more clearly in a discussion about another constitutional clause. One of the stated aims of the Guild was 'to protect the Banks and the Members hereof against any strikes or disputes between the Guild employers, and employees in any trade'. The clause, the Guild's solicitor stated, was a covering clause which might be useful. 'You might', he said, 'be able to squash any strike by striking yourselves.'[20] A delegate elaborated on this by saying 'if everybody else went on strike we might go on strike ourselves to bring them to their senses in combination with the Banks'. His intention was to make it impossible for strike benefit to be paid. The attitude that bank clerks ought to be able to compel settlements in other disputes persisted. It occurred to few bank clerks that their intentions were contrary to trade union ethics.[21] This clause was not used either.

This conception of collective action stemmed from the view which bank workers held of themselves as a social élite. They regarded manual workers in much the same way as nineteenth-century craftsmen looked at unskilled workers. When, for instance, the merits of a rule about assisting other guilds or unions was discussed in 1919 it was argued that it might be necessary for middle-class organizations to take collective action against the working class which frightened the community and threatened a breakdown in society.[22]

2. Collective bargaining

The Guild was in a difficult position. It had refused to use the strike weapon as a rallying force and recruiting medium. It therefore had to reason with unorganized bank clerks and show them that collective action produced material results. This entailed obtaining concessions from the bank employers. But this could only be done obviously and systematically through established negotiating procedures.

The Guild made a number of attempts to establish negotiating machinery. An official of the Ministry of Labour attended a meeting of London bank clerks in May 1919 to explain the Whitley system and its application to the banking industry. The meeting recommended that the Government should be approached to establish a

---

[19] Minutes of the first General Meeting, April 1919.

[20] *Ibid.*

[21] A few delegates at the Annual General Meeting in October 1919 did protest that they should not have the power to act against strikers or interfere in other disputes or dictate to trade unions.

[22] General Meeting, April 1919.

Whitley Council and the Minister of Labour and the chairman and secretaries of various banks were informed of the recommendation. The Minister of Labour gave his approval but the replies from the banks were mixed: some cordial, some noncommittal and some hostile. No replies were received from the Midland, Westminster and National Provincial and Union Banks.[23] From the chairmen of Lloyds and Barclays Banks came polite rebuttals. But the Guild, even on this matter, was prepared to be slow-moving. 'The idea of the application of the scheme to the profession', it stated, 'is so entirely novel, as also is the fact of bankmen combining into one association to realize their ideas, that the process will necessarily be slow.'[24]

The national executive of the Guild produced a national programme, after the annual general meeting in October 1919, which dealt with salaries, bonuses, employment of women, overtime, balance dates, holidays, pensions, windows and orphans and education. It suggested also that a Whitley Council for the banking industry should be established and a number of prominent people commented favourably about it.[25] The programme was intended as a basis for negotiations. The *Daily Express* gave it some prominence.

> We hope [it stated] that officials of the Guild will also take care that it reaches the hands of all bank directors. It is so moderate and has so little of the Bolshevist touch about it that it should bring considerable relief into boardrooms, from which the progress of the Guild has been watched with some trepidation. If there are points in the programme which, in the directors' view, need further consideration, the proposed formation of a Whitley Council provides an admirable field for discussion.[26]

The bank employers made no concessions to the Guild. Yet when the 1920 annual general meeting of the Guild discussed its inability to make any impression on the bank employers it rejected the suggestion that all the bank staffs should be balloted on whether or not they wanted a Whitley Council. The Minister of Labour was asked in December 1920 to proceed with the establishment of a Council, but he could do nothing without the approval of the bank directors. Finally the Guild dropped the suggestion from its policy, ostensibly because it wanted negotiating machinery with recourse to arbitration and felt that a Whitley Council would not help to achieve this end.

The Bank Officers' Guild was faced with the problem of handling

---

[23] *The Bank Officer*, September 1919.   [24] *Ibid*.
[25] Some of these were Cardinal Bourne, Lord Robert Cecil, Lord Cavendish Bentinck, T. P. O'Connor and Mr J. H. Whitley.
[26] 19 December 1919.

the internal associations. In 1919 it had rejected an offer from the provisional committee of the Westminster internal association to affiliate to the Guild whilst retaining control of its own members. Until 1923 it doubtfully pursued a policy of permeation. When Barclays Bank formed an internal association in 1921, twenty-seven out of twenty-eight members of its executive committee were members of the Bank Officers' Guild. Other internal associations were treated similarly. This course was aimed at directing the policy of the associations to coincide with that of the Guild. But it was bound to end in failure for the associations had no policy which they could claim as their own. They were instruments of the management and were used largely to express management wishes. The Guild faced another difficulty. Once its members sat on committees of the associations they saw the promotion possibilities which would be opened up to them if they left the Guild. They were continually confronted by a temptation which tended to neutralize their initial purpose.

The internal associations caused the Guild most worry during 1921, the first year in which they were all active. They rejected a proposal by the Guild to convene a joint conference; they refused to cooperate with the Guild over the introduction of an unemployment insurance scheme. A clause in the Unemployment Insurance Act 1920 permitted an industry to contract out of the national scheme provided a special one, drawn up by representatives of employers and workers, was approved by the Minister of Labour. The Bank Officers' Guild wanted a scheme to be introduced which was appropriate to the banking industry. The British Bankers' Association also refused to cooperate because it considered that cooperation would be tantamount to recognition.[27]

The membership of the Guild reached its peak in December 1922 when, with 30,173 members, it organized about 50 per cent of the clerical and managerial bank employees in England and Wales. But it was further away from recognition than at almost any time since its formation. It could do nothing, it seemed, to displace the internal

[27] The British Bankers' Association submitted a scheme which was not accepted by the Minister of Labour because by not being jointly drawn up by representatives of workers and employers it did not conform with the Act. Eventually, after a long-drawn out controversy, a scheme which had been submitted to a few internal associations was submitted to a ballot of bank employees. The Bank Officers' Guild advised its members to support the scheme to avoid further delay and it was endorsed by 53,267 votes to 1268. An unemployment insurance scheme for the banking industry was approved by the Ministry of Labour in June 1924. Representatives of the Bank Officers' Guild were elected to the banking Unemployment Insurance Board which was then set up.

associations. At the 1923 conference a resolution was passed calling upon all members of the Guild to sever their connections with internal associations. Thereafter a policy of non-cooperation was pursued. The issue, however, was not settled. In 1924 and 1925 attempts were made to persuade the Guild to readopt the policy of permeation. The attempts failed because so many Guild members had witnessed the futility of that policy. The Guild hardened its attitude and decided in 1924 that no voluntary member of an internal association could hold office in the Guild.

At every move it was disarmed by its own estimate of the conservatism of bank clerks. There was a request at the Guild's delegate conference in 1922 for a petition in favour of recognition to be organized and presented to the British Bankers' Association. The conference turned the request down mainly because it believed that bank clerks would not sign a petition. The dominant opinion at the conference was that there were many bank clerks, even members of the Guild, who were afraid of putting their names down on a piece of paper in case anybody should see it.[28] It was decided instead to approach the British Bankers' Association for recognition, and if refused, to ask for its reasons. In 1924 the Guild would not even ask the Association to conduct a secret ballot among bank staffs to determine whether the Guild should be given recognition.

3. Political action

The need for political action was raised seriously in 1923. The Guild did not have a political fund so it could not finance political activities, but some of its members felt that their interests should be represented in Parliament. In 1923 there were nineteen bank directors in the House of Commons and others in the House of Lords. The members of the Guild did not make it clear what they thought could be achieved by political representation. The matter seemed to have been raised more out of despair than as a serious attempt to tackle a problem.

A motion at the delegate conference of the Guild in 1922 that bank clerks should adopt a political policy in combination with other professional groups but without allying themselves with any one political party, did not even produce a seconder. Various bodies, including the National Federation of Professional Workers, had approached the Guild to join with them in seeking parliamentary representation but the Guild had not responded. Even its executive could not reach agreement over the matter.[29] Then in 1923 the delegate conference, by

[28] Minutes of the Annual General Meeting, 1922.
[29] Minutes of Annual General Meeting, 1923.

22,351 votes to 5707, agreed 'that parliamentary action should be taken by putting forward our own candidates in conjunction with other professional workers'. The delegates had obviously been encouraged by the House of Commons debate on 18 April 1923, when a motion calling for the recognition by employers of professional workers' organizations and for the establishment of collective bargaining machinery for them, had been passed on a free vote.[30] Bank clerks had been mentioned frequently in the debate and only bank directors had spoken against giving the Guild recognition. Another possible reason for the Guild's change of mind may have been the decision of the National Provincial Bank to reintroduce a clause forbidding bank clerks to participate in the activities of political parties.[31]

The feeling at the 1923 conference was that the Guild should avoid a party political affiliation but the leaders of the Guild realised that this was a difficult condition to meet. The Guild could not finance an independent candidate and in any case the chances of such a candidate being elected were remote. So the executive proposed in 1924 that an attempt should be made to get a candidate from each of the main political parties to represent the interests of the Guild in Parliament. This was agreed and a special committee was appointed to explore the ground. The matter was resolved in 1925 when three existing Members of Parliament, one from each main political party, agreed to act as representatives of the Bank Officers' Guild.[32] Political representation, however, made no impression on the banks. They ignored it as they had ignored the resolution of the House of Commons in 1923 which had favoured recognition for bank workers.

4. Federation

Occasionally after 1922 the Guild turned its attention to the possibility of federating with similar bodies. Its president advocated federation in 1923 and in 1924 the issue was debated. The executive of the Guild wanted to form a confederation with the Guild of Insurance Officials, the Scottish Bankers' Association and possibly the Stock Exchange Guild and the Shipping Guild. It recommended to the 1924 conference that this confederation should then join the National Federation of Professional Workers as a 'non-manual,

[30] See *Hansard*, vol. 162, col. 2162, 18th April 1923.

[31] The Guild protested and drew attention to the clause through the Press, but the bank did not withdraw it until November 1924.

[32] They were Sir C. Kinlock-Cooke (Conservative), L. Hore-Belisha (Liberal) and Arthur Greenwood (Labour).

middle-class organization'. A number of delegates expressed doubts. Would this mean that bank clerks would contribute financially to strikes? Some of the unions in the Federation had political funds and reputations for militancy. Should the Guild associate with such unions?

The constitution of the National Federation of Professional Workers was considered to be questionable. One clause stated that it was an object of the Federation 'to promote friendly relations between the federated organizations and the organizations representing the manual workers'. This involved too much for some clerks. Another clause aimed to assist professional workers to contribute to the democratic control of their respective industries and services. But the Bank Officers' Guild, it was maintained, was not antagonistic to employers; it believed in cooperation with the British Bankers' Association. Despite these doubts, the executive's recommendation was accepted by the conference but nothing came of it. In 1925 the Guild executive was divided about what it should do. By 1926 it had resolved its doubts. It and the delegate conference of the Guild unanimously agreed to have nothing to do with the National Federation of Professional Workers. At the same time the Guild, to show how different it was from most other unions, rejected a motion for affiliation to the Trades Union Congress by 23,431 votes to 161.

During the General Strike the Guild offered to supply mediators because its members considered that they stood apart from the dispute. In reality they did not stand apart. Bank employers, like other employers, gained strength from the collapse of the strike. The Bank Officers' Guild found itself in a weaker and more vulnerable position than ever before. And as in the case of trade unions in general, the General Strike ended a phase for the Bank Officers' Guild. By 1927 the Guild had considered all the known industrial and political methods for gaining recognition. Those it had tried failed in their purpose. The enthusiasm which had marked its early years had been dissipated. Its membership, which had declined slowly since 1922, fell sharply in 1926 and 1927. In the five years after 1922 it lost almost one-third of its membership and slipped into a long period of relative stagnation.

Conclusion

The Bank Officers' Guild indirectly obtained benefits for bank clerks. Its propaganda drew attention to the deficiences in the salaries and conditions of work in banks, and its presence impelled the bank employers to remedy some of them. But it failed to obtain direct benefits through negotiation because the bank employers steadfastly refused to recognize the Guild as a negotiating body. It failed, therefore, in a fundamental sense. The Guild could not operate fully as a trade union until it had established a working relationship with employers. Its failure was emphasized by the success of other non-manual groups. Organizations of civil servants, railway clerks, some clerks in the iron and steel industry, and of bank clerks in other countries successfully claimed recognition from employers shortly after the First World War.

The bank clerks' failure to gain recognition, compared with the efforts of other non-manual groups, cannot be explained by differences in market conditions. The members of all these groups sold their labour in markets over which, as individuals, they exercised very little influence; and they encountered few possibilities of moving out of that situation. Nor can it be explained simply by reference to differences in social and work situations.[33] The explanation lies in the manner in which the bank employers made use of factors in these situations to counter trade unionism.

The bank clerks regarded themselves as the social élite of non-manual workers. This phenomenon of status differentiation was not confined to them or to non-manual workers in general; nor did it have any special significance by itself for trade unionism. There is not a straightforward connection between social status and attitudes to collective action. Some groups with relatively high social standing, for instance bank clerks and insurance officials, did not accept the methods of trade unionism, while others such as stationmasters and teachers did. Craftsmen had differentiated themselves from unskilled workers and from each other. In the nineteenth century they had practised trade unionism but had regarded unskilled workers as unfitted for it.[34] But status differentiation indicated a social attitude which could influence collective responses. In the case of the bank clerks this attitude assisted the employers.

The work situation consisted of such factors as skill, grading, promotion, size of office unit, degree and kind of contact between workers in the same and other occupations, and the relationship with employers. No particular type of work situation was associated with

---

[33] The differences in the extent of trade unionism among non-manual workers were explained in terms of work situation by Lockwood, pp. 137 ff.

[34] See E. J. Hobsbawm, 'The labour aristocracy in 19th-century Britain', in *Democracy and the Labour Movement*, ed. John Saville, Lawrence & Wishart, 1954, pp. 201 ff.

the spread of trade unionism. There was no direct correlation between bureaucratic work situations and the use of collective action. Civil service employment was barely more regulated than that in the banks until after the civil service unions had gained general recognition in 1919.[35] Clerical employment in the sections of the iron and steel industry where the clerks' organizations were recognized was less regulated than bank employment; railway clerical and supervisory work, on the other hand, was subject to stringent regulation. There was no connection between the size of the office unit and the acceptance of trade unionism. The London civil service offices were large but the organized local government ones were frequently small and scattered; the workers in the large London bank offices were less organized than those in the dispersed and relatively small provincial branches.[36]

The behaviour of employers was, however, a relevant aspect of the work situation. The Government was the employer of civil servants and a temporary war and postwar employer of railway clerks. It had accepted the report of the Whitley Committee in 1917 which recommended that joint industrial councils consisting of workers' and employers' representatives should be established in industry, but had refused to implement the recommendations in the case of its own non-manual employees. This had placed the government in an anomalous position. It was subjected to criticism and protests from politicians and civil service unions for discriminating between manual and non-manual workers and for failing to do what it advocated private employers should do. It was amenable to sustained pressure. It granted recognition to civil service unions in June 1919. The Railway Clerks' Association had been granted a limited form of recognition by the Government controlled Railway Executive in May 1918—it was not given the right to negotiate for stationmasters, agents and supervisory clerks. The Association had refused to accept recognition on such terms and its members who belonged to the disputed grades were victimized. The railway companies, which operated under the control of the Railway Executive, sponsored the formation of sectional organizations, such as the National Federation of Stationmasters' Association. Then, in a determined attempt to gain recognition, the Railway Clerks' Association called a strike of

[35] Civil service employment was reorganized and given precise functional grades between 1919 and 1924.

[36] There is a common misunderstanding about the effect of factory and large office organization upon trade unionism. It does not create trade unionists, but makes union organization easier once workers have accepted the principle of collective action.

the disputed grades for 6 p.m. on 4 February 1919. The Cabinet at first supported the Railway Executive; then three hours before the strike was due to begin, disregarding the Railway Executive, it granted recognition to the Association.

The bank employers were in an anomalous position too because many of them were directors of industrial firms which had accorded recognition to trade unions. The anomaly did not worry them. Unlike the Government, they were not amenable to public pressure; and they were determined to frustrate the growth of trade unionism in the banks.

British employers in general had not tried to circumvent trade unions through the creation of 'company' unions or 'internal associations' as American employers had done. They had openly opposed trade unionism; trade unionists had been victimized and union officials refused entry on to works' premises. In the odd cases, such as on the railways, where 'company' unions had been fostered, direct opposition had also been used.

Different methods were used by the bank employers. They largely ignored the existence of the Bank Officers' Guild and did not openly victimize or intimidate bank clerks who were trade unionists. Instead they adopted what appeared to many bank clerks to be the reasonable course of creating internal associations. They acted quickly and uniformly before the Guild had had the time to establish itself. The smallness of the number of bank employers made possible some form of collusive opposition.

The bank employers made full use of the factors in the work and social situations which favoured the creation of internal associations. Indeed, without these factors their methods would most probably have been unsuccessful. They emphasized the distinctive qualities of banking and the individual characteristics of banks to justify the repudiation of a single organization to represent all bank workers and representation by officials who were not employed by the banks. Many factors in the postwar situation contradicted this emphasis but there was one important one which did not. Clerks in the main banks were not able to move from one bank to another if they were dissatisfied and they knew that they could only make individual advancement within the bank which already employed them. The bank employers also attributed the pay concessions they made to the activities of the internal associations and laid stress on the economic advantages of bank employment. There was little evidence to support this emphasis until the end of 1920; then unemployment increased while bank employment remained secure and bank salary levels relatively stable. In the depression bank clerks saw little need for collective action.

The relevant factors in the social situation operated in the following manner. The officials of the Bank Officers' Guild believed that a militant policy would lose them rank-and-file support. Militancy did not necessarily involve strike action but it did imply a willingness to strike. It had been used effectively by manual workers' unions to overcome opposition from employers and sometimes it had been supported by non-unionists. There was no evidence to show that either the trait of irrationality among non-unionists or the willingness to strike was confined to manual workers. After the First World War school teachers, stationmasters and civil servants either talked of striking or actually went on strike. So did bank clerks in Ireland, Scotland, South Africa, Australia and New Zealand. And in most cases militancy achieved its objective.

Perhaps, then, the Guild Officials had misinterpreted the ordinary bank clerks' attitude to strike action and had under-estimated the self-charging, explosive nature of emotion in collective action. In the main, however, militancy had occurred in response to a provocative or obviously unreasonable attitude by employers and bank employers had not behaved in this manner. If the bank employers had offended the sentiments of their employees during 1919 and 1920 when the Guild's membership was growing fast to an extent unknown to the employers and when the internal associations were not fully established, a strike might have occurred. An indication of their possible behaviour was provided by the activities of insurance officials in 1920. Insurance officials came from the same social stratum as bank clerks and worked under comparable conditions. And they too were struggling to form a trade union, the Guild of Insurance Officials. In 1920 an insurance company dismissed some of its employees because of their union activities and a strike was called on 8 November 1920, after a ballot of the Guild's membership throughout the country had shown a majority was in favour of it.[37]

The promptness with which the bank employers established internal associations; the apparent reasonableness of their action and the extent to which it accorded with significant elements in the work

[37] The strike occurred at the head office of the General Accident Assurance Corporation, located at Perth. The Guild of Insurance Officials had about 20,000 members; of these 13,000 participated in the ballot and more than 10,000 were in favour of strike action. The Corporation had 529 employees of whom 325 belonged to the Guild. 150 insurance officials went on strike and were dismissed. All the strikers were given employment by other insurance companies (see *The Insurance Guild Journal*, October, November and December 1920).

and social situations of bank clerks made strong counter-action by the Bank Officers' Guild a necessary means of obtaining recognition. They also made it more difficult to attain. Bank clerks had barely been introduced to trade unionism before they were presented with an alternative which the majority considered to be adequate and more appropriate.

PART III

PART III

10

Rewriting the history of the TUC

There is, perhaps, no clearer illustration of the significance of using different conceptual approaches than when an analysis using one approach is based on secondary sources and can be compared with an analysis involving the same sources but using a different approach. In such a case one has two analyses based on the same empirical data and the contrast in the ordering of the data, in the emphases given to it and in the conclusions drawn from it represent the distinction between the approaches. The reason why such a comparison is possible is that there is no such phenomenon as an objective social fact; that is, a fact which retains its meaning and significance to all users and in all circumstances. Data derives its meaning from the manner in which it is used and this, in turn, depends on the conceptual orientation of the user.

This point was emphasized in Chapter 3 in connection with the work on trade unionism by Sidney and Beatrice Webb. In so far as there is a history of the British Trades Union Congress in the work of the Webbs it is a Webbs' interpretation, reflecting their values and within the framework of a particular, readily identifiable conceptual approach. The same can be said about the works of all other analysts of industrial relations. This does not mean to say that there are as many approaches as there are analysts. Each person may bring to bear on his work the peculiar characteristics associated with his own immediate environment, but his broad analytical approach must be one or the other of the two described earlier in this book. Various nuances differentiate the Webbs and most of their British successors, but in the main there is no qualitative difference between them. Indeed many analysts of industrial relations have not only used the data which rests in the large volumes by the Webbs, but have taken over their precise interpretations as well. In other words they have all operated the same conceptual approach.

When only the facts are taken from, say, an existing history and used in a completely different conceptual manner, then it is a case of

EIR

a rewritten history. The new version will show the analysed situations in a completely fresh light. Three of the four chapters about the Trades Union Congress in this Part are examples of rewritten history. They are based entirely on secondary sources and, therefore, contain little material which could help to throw fresh light on situations. The factual content of these chapters has been drawn from various sources; the main ones are A. E. Musson, *The Congress of 1868: The Origins and Establishment of the Trades Union Congress* (TUC, 1955), W. J. Davis, *The British Trades Union Congress—History and Recollections* (TUC, 1910), Sidney and Beatrice Webb, *The History of Trade Unionism* and B. C. Roberts, *The Trades Union Congress 1868–1921*.

The main work with which these chapters can be compared is *The Trades Union Congress 1868–1921* by B. C. Roberts. With the exception of parts of Chapters 13 and 14 they cover the same historical period and much of the material is drawn from or is the same as that in Roberts's book. The source material differs in one respect, however, and this should be mentioned. At various times criticisms were made of George Howell, secretary of the Parliamentary Committee from 1871 to 1875, and members of the Parliamentary Committee for their reluctance to oppose the Liberal Government on any important question. These criticisms were known to B. C. Roberts and he referred briefly to some of them.[1] In a footnote he referred to the accusation by Karl Marx that the union leaders concerned were in the pay of 'Disraeli or Gladstone' but made no further reference to it. Professor Roberts did not have the benefit of seeing any of the work on Howell's association with the Liberal Party leaders by Royden Harrison and which on unquestionable evidence shows that Howell was in the pay of the people whom he was purportedly opposing in his capacity as a trade union leader.[2]

Dr Harrison was not the first historian to describe Howell's two-sided political activities. This task had been done much earlier though in less detail by S. Maccoby in *English Radicalism, 1853–1886* (Allen & Unwin, 1938), and, as Royden Harrison points out in his review of Roberts's book, evidence against Howell and others had appeared in the pages of the *Beehive*.[3] The omission of this evidence

[1] *The Trades Union Congress 1868–1901*, p. 83.

[2] See 'The British working class and the General Election of 1868', *The International Review of Social History*, v, pt 3, pp. 424–55; and vi, pt 1, pp. 74–109, See also Royden Harrison, *Before the Socialists, Studies in Labour and Politics 1861–1881*, London, Routledge, 1964.

[3] Royden Harrison 'Practical, capable men', *The New Reasoner*, Autumn 1958, pp. 115–16.

must thus be attributed to Roberts's own values and conceptual approach. If Professor Roberts had acknowledged that some of the most prominent union leaders of the last quarter of the nineteenth century were receiving money for secretly supporting the Liberal Party his image of these men as 'practical capable men' could not have been maintained; this, in turn, would have damaged his support for the social engineering which these men engaged in. A belief that relative progress stems from social engineering, by which is meant *ad hoc* opportunist moves, follows from the more general belief that society has an organic unity, for it is only on the basis of this general belief that it is possible to conceive of improvement through isolated acts at various points.

On the other hand, the admission of the evidence of political opportunism, accompanied by the rejection of a belief in compromises and concessions as a means of achieving relative improvements, leads by the same logic to the belief that trade unionists can obtain no real changes without structural alterations. In other words, so long as the social relations to the means of production remain unaltered, other things will remain basically unaltered for employees and employers. The chapters in this Part largely reflect this conceptual approach and show, in consequence, a constancy of issues before the Trades Union Congress and an inability to do anything substantial about them.

In general the question of the interpretation of data which these chapters raise points to the need for social analysts to have greater access to primary source material on which books and reports are based. It would be too demanding, of course, to expect individual authors to make their basic data available; in any case the facts are usually available to others if they are prepared to put in sufficient work. But it is not too demanding to expect Government departments and agencies to make available the data on which they base their reports and surveys. Social survey information is a case in point. Royal Commissions meet this need by publishing minutes of evidence. It is not necessary that the evidence should be published, only that it should be freely available for consultation. It might then be easier to rewrite history in a more acceptably authentic manner.

11

The establishment of the Trades Union Congress, 1868–1875

Sufficient conditions for unity

Developments in the trade union movement were always, inevitably, responses to changes in the environment of unions. When markets for commodities, including labour, were small and localized, so were trade unions. As industrial units grew and became more complex in their organization, so the tasks of unions became more complicated and onerous and demanded organizational adjustments. The changes in the democratic structure of unions, involving the rejection of a rotating head office, the locally based executive committee, the rotation of officials and the decentralization of funds, were all responses to alterations in market structures which enabled firms to expand. The movement from complete lay administration to the employment of full-time officials was made necessary by the inability of lay officials to remain lay, that is to work in industry, in the face of determined opposition to unions from employers.

The first organizational movement involving trade unions was a vertical one through trades because the factors showing the need for unity were apparent first in single trades. A vertical centralization of activities began to occur through the process of unions absorbing each other or amalgamating. This process was dependent upon the ability of workers in the same trade to get to know each other. Many, such as bookbinders, were able to do this through the Tramping System whereby unemployed workers tramped from town to town until they secured work. At each town they were looked after by union members in the same trade. An effective organizational link between towns depended on the towns being linked by an efficient system of communications. Trade unionists had to be able to meet quickly in order to make common decisions; they had to be able to send communications to each other; they also had to have access to common information on which to base their decisions. Vertical unity waited on developments in these respects. Horizontal unity also had to wait on them. It was not possible to conceive of a regular horizontal unity without these conditions being satisfied.

By 1868 there was an extensive railway system: 12,319 miles of track had been laid by the beginning of the year. This was an increase of 7337 miles since 1848, the year of the great Chartist demonstration. In the year of the Grand National Consolidated Trade Union, 1834, there were only 298 miles of railway track and the union's organizers had to travel slowly and expensively by horse-drawn coaches or on foot. The track mileage in 1868 was more than half the total reached at the peak of railway activities and covered the main lines of subsequent developments. It was possible in 1868 for any of the main industrial centres, such as London, Manchester or Birmingham, to be used as centres for national union activities.

The same changes in transport communications, by widening market structures, encouraged the growth of firms and an economic network of interdependence. The Limited Liability Act of 1855 facilitated the expansion of firms within the wider markets. Thus there was a tendency for the industrial context within which unions operated to become national in character. In practical terms this meant that the power of employers became more concentrated; and that the insularity of small local unions was penetrated by widening common industrial links between workers in the same and different trades. The changes in size and scope between the years 1850 and 1870 were accompanied by significant technological advances which altered the exclusiveness of many and varied work operations by diluting them and giving them common features.

Unions were forced to change under such conditions simply in order to survive. Amalgamations then, as always, arose out of necessity. As unions grew in size so their assets accumulated, their involvement in the capitalist system became more entrenched, their identity with the ideological basis of the system grew closer. The period 1850 to 1867, though marked by acute troughs of depression, was in general one of rising prosperity and was a favourable one with which to become identified. It was estimated that real wages, allowing for unemployment, were 20 per cent higher in 1865 than they had been in 1850.[1]

The year 1868 belonged to, though it was at the margin of, the phase of Mid-Victorian optimism. Union leaders, in their positions of new assumed responsibilities, had contacts with politicians and sympathetic middle-class intellectuals. They condemned strike

[1] B. Mitchell and P. Deane *Abstract of British Historical Statistics*, p. 343.

action and publicly advocated conciliation and arbitration. This switch was not simply a reaction to the appointment of a Royal Commission, but a result of profound environmental pressures.

Early attempts at horizontal unity had been hampered, not only by the physical insularity of local unions, but also by the inadequacy of the means for making written communications. The introduction of the penny postage and the development of the telegraph system made it easier for workingmen to communicate with each other quickly and cheaply. The spread of ideas and of information about current political and economic events was facilitated by the removal of the newspaper tax in 1855. The cheapening of newspapers improved their geographical distribution and circulation. Even by 1861 the number of newspapers in the United Kingdom had increased by 400 and 123 towns had newspapers which did not have them in 1855.[2] Thus it became possible to have simultaneous reactions to events of common interest to trade unionists. There was much evidence that this was so in the 1860s, as was indicated in the previous chapter. But the most prominent and impressive illustration was over the demand for universal suffrage. This campaign moreover had a profound influence over the Government attitude to unions after 1868.

The Manhood Suffrage and Vote by Ballot Association, which had been formed in London in 1862 by the London-based union leaders, was merged into an all-embracing Reform League in 1865. There was little change in policy and Robert Applegarth and his coterie continued to play a prominent role in the activities of the new body. George Howell was the secretary of the League. Howell was a delegate of the Operative Bricklayers' Society to the newly formed London Trades Council in 1861, of which he became the secretary in 1861–62. Later, in 1871, he became the secretary of the Trades Union Congress but before then, in the critical period of labour law reform, he developed a close and unhealthy relationship with the leaders of the Liberal Party.[3]

The Reform League had a solid working-class basis. 'The activities of this league', Gillespie wrote, 'present the most complete picture of general working class politics between the date of its formation and its dissolution in 1869 that can be found.'[4] It had

[2] F. E. Gillespie, *Labour and Politics in England 1850–1867*, Duke University Press, 1927, pp. 200–1.

[3] For a detailed description see Royden Harrison, 'The British working class and the General Election of 1868', *The International Review of Social History [Irish]*, v, pt 3 (1960), 424–55; and vi, pt 1 (1961), 74–109.

[4] Gillespie, p. 250.

middle-class supporters, however, among whom were some wealthy Liberal manufacturers who gave the League financial assistance. Many demonstrations were organized by the League in 1866. At first they were for an electoral reform measure; then, after March, they were in favour of Gladstone's Bill of limited enfranchisement; when Gladstone's Bill was threatened by Conservatives and defecting Liberals, the demonstrations were again for reform but more vòciferously and aggressively. The whole tenor of the struggle for reform changed after Easter of 1866. The general strike and civil disobedience were discussed as ways of forcing a reluctant Parliament to take action. The demonstrations were popular ones, described, in familiar terms, as being 'composed of Chartists, extremists, artisans, Dissenters or rabble'.[5] They had little middle-class support.

The Bill brought down the Liberal Government led by Lord John Russell, and the Conservative Party was returned to power. But the agitation produced by working-class unity convinced Disraeli of the seriousness of the questions of electoral reform and persuaded the Conservative Government that, for it, reform was the lesser of two evils. During the early summer of 1866 a trade recession had set in. There was a bad domestic harvest. Real wages fell almost to the 1850 level and remained there until 1869. Economic distress, a rejection by Parliament of political democracy and an attack upon trade unionism by employers and the judiciary combined to give the protests the ingredients of a class war. The participation in the protests of organized labour gave them a discipline and form which left the Conservatives, led by Lord Derby, with no practical alternative to submission. In August 1867 a Reform Bill became law which added 938,000 voters to an electorate of 1,156,000 in England and Wales. The majority of the male industrial workers, excluding those in mining and agriculture, were given the vote.[6] The total population over the age of twenty in England and Wales at the 1871 census was 12,330,000. Of these 5,864,000 were males so that more than half of the males and all females were still excluded from the franchise.

Trade unions now had a new political significance. In so far as it was assumed that they could influence the voting behaviour of their members they had to be taken into reckoning by the two major political parties. A fickle courtship tentatively began with the general election in November 1868. The first Trades Union Congress met in that interregnum period between achieving an extended franchise

[5] Gillespie, p. 262.

[6] See Gillespie, chapter 9, and Maccoby, *English Radicalism, 1853–1886*, chapter 7, for a description of the Reform League's activities.

and applying it in an election. Trade unionists in June 1868 were not to know how the political parties were going to behave. But they did know how to achieve political success.

The first meeting of the Trades Union Congress

The intention of the Manchester and Salford Trades Council when it issued its circular in February 1868 was to initiate annual meetings of trade unionists which would 'assume the character of the annual meetings of the British Association for the Advancement of Science and the Social Science Association, in the transactions of which Societies the artizan class are almost entirely excluded'.[7]

Although the Congress was held in a crisis situation it was not an emergency meeting with the task of making vital decisions. It was intended 'that papers, previously carefully prepared, shall be laid before the Congress on the various subjects which at the present time affect Trades Societies, each paper to be followed by discussion upon the points advanced, with a view of the merits and demerits of each question being thoroughly ventilated through the medium of the public press'. No substantial elements for dissension were here. As it was conceived in no sense could it impinge on the autonomy of individual unions. Indeed at first it was intended to invite only trades councils and other federations. Owing presumably to lack of support a second circular was issued extending the invitation to individual unions.[8]

The Congress was held for four days from 2 to 6 June 1868 in the Mechanics' Institute, David Street, Manchester. It was attended by thirty-four delegates representing, it was claimed, 118,367 members. It was ignored by the Conference of Amalgamated Trades, both the London and Glasgow Trade Councils, and many prominent trade unions. The only two London representatives were George Potter, coming from the London Working Men's Association, and a delegate from the small London Pressmen's Society. Apart from Potter, the only well-known union leaders who attended were William Dronfield from Sheffield and John Kane from the Amalgamated Ironworkers. Most of the other delegates were from Lancashire towns and may not even have been sent by the executives of their unions.[9] The Congress elected W. H. Wood, the secretary of the Manchester and Salford Trades Council, as its president, and Peter Shorrocks of the Amalgamated Tailors as secretary.

---

[7] The original circular is reproduced as an appendix to this chapter (pp. 138–9).
[8] Musson, p. 33.   [9] Musson, pp. 35–36.

The Congress listened to papers on the range of topics which had been listed in the circular which summoned it, but it also passed resolutions on issues of moment for trade unionists, including one which criticized the composition and proceedings of the Royal Commission, and another, moved by John Kane, which pledged itself

in the names of the respective societies represented to aid and assist the London Committee of Amalgamated Trades in their laudable efforts to secure the legislation and protection of trade union funds, and hereby declares its determination to continue the agitation, and to make the support of this measure a condition for candidates for parliamentary honours before giving any pledge or vote at the ensuing election.

The activities of the Conference of Amalgamated Trades were also supported in a resolution concerning its attempts to alter the third section of the 1825 Combination Act relating to the law of 'conspiracy, intimidation, picketing, coercion, etc., which is . . . capable of such misconstructions that it is utterly impossible that justice can be done'.[10] Thus it was made quite clear that the Congress had no intention of usurping the leadership function which the London Conference of Amalgamated Trades had taken for itself in connection with the Royal Commission. But where the London leaders were not considered to have a prerogative, the Congress decided to take action. It was resolved: 'That it is highly desirable that the trades of the United Kingdom should hold an annual congress, for the purpose of bringing the trades into closer alliance, and to take action in all Parliamentary matters pertaining to the general interests of the working classes.' No special organizational machinery was recommended for this task. The delegates simply agreed to meet for the second time at Birmingham and to leave the details and organization of the Congress to the Birmingham Trades Council.

The seeds of Lib-Labism

The Congress passed virtually unnoticed. Trade union interest was still focused on the Royal Commission and the possibility of wholly repressive legislation being introduced. Attention, therefore, was on Parliament and its political composition; on the possibility of a general election and the consequences of the new Reform Act. A general election was held in November 1868. The trade union attitude towards it had been stated the year before when the General Council

---

[10] Musson, p. 37. For details of the first Congress see also B. C. Roberts, *The Trades Union Congress*, pp. 44ff.

of the Reform League had called for joint action with unions to secure the return of Labour representatives to the next Parliament in numbers 'proportionate to the other interests and classes at present represented in Parliament'. The London Working Men's Association also wanted working men in Parliament and recommended the creation of a Working Men's Parliamentary Election Fund to help achieve this end.[11] It also issued a manifesto on the 'Direct representation of Labour in Parliament'.

Neither the Reform League nor the London Working Men's Association set up a fund or established the machinery with which to fight an election. Indeed, after the passage of the Reform Act the League had so little finance that it found it difficult even to maintain its own existence. Various Liberal manufacturers gave odd donations in order to preserve its organization to provide mass support for the disestablishment of the Irish Church,[12] but no one with financial means wanted it to achieve its stated political objectives. George Howell, having lost his wealthy supporters, went to the Liberal Party itself for assistance and, during the middle of 1868, concluded a secret agreement with it whereby in return for financial support the Reform League would be converted into an electoral machine for the Liberals.[13] Howell, assisted by W. R. Cremer, a founder member of the Amalgamated Society of Carpenters and Joiners, provided reports for about eight-five constituencies showing the estimated effects of the Reform Act and the political role of unions. But, more important than this, Howell and Cremer successfully prevented working-class candidates nominated by League branches from either obtaining nominations or getting nomination in suitable constituencies. Alexander Macdonald, the miners' leader, J. J. Merriman, a member of the International Working Men's Association and the Reform League, Charles Bradlaugh, Ernest Jones, Edmund Beales and many others suffered through the intervention of Howell. Howell and Cremer were allowed to contest seats at Aylesbury and Warwick respectively, thus permitting 'the advanced Liberals of the House of Commons to have the League . . . decently interred during March 1869 without needing to fear the charge that they had betrayed their working-class allies'.[14] Both Howell and Cremer were unsuccessful, as were all other working-class candidates. Not even the usually vociferous, and, where Howell and Cremer were concerned, acri-

---

[11] Roberts, p. 41.   [12] Maccoby, p. 102.

[13] Details of this sordid story are given by Royden Harrison, op. cit., see also Maccoby, pp. 102–3.

[14] Maccoby, p. 103.

monious, George Potter attacked the Lib-Lab alliance, for he had concluded a quite separate agreement with wealthy Liberal employers from which he received finance to boost the circulation of the *Beehive* in return for support from the paper for the Liberal Party.[15] The parliamentary aims of organized labour were frustrated from their inception by the prostitution of union leaders by the Establishment.

The Royal Commission reports and legal recognition

The Royal Commission published two Reports in March 1869: a majority report, signed by the Commission Chairman Sir William Erle and others, and a minority one, signed by the Earl of Lichfield, Thomas Hughes and Frederic Harrison. The majority report, though less vindictive than had been anticipated, recommended that restrictions should be imposed on unions through a system of registration. It suggested that unions should not be allowed to register whose objects limited apprentices, prevented the introduction of new machinery, objected to piecework, enforced compulsory trade unionism. The report saw little value in trade unionism in general. The minority report objected to these restrictions and recommended that all legal discrimination against unions should be removed. Unions reacted against the majority report and agitated for the proposals in the minority one, which were embodied in a Bill drafted by Frederic Harrison and presented to the House of Commons by Thomas Hughes and A. J. Mundella. The attitude of unions was reflected by that of the leaders of the Boiler Makers' Society who wrote in their *Monthly Report* of April 1869:

> Trade Unions have been on their trial, and the verdict of some of their judges has been returned—to crush them in Parliament by acts of repression and oppression. . . . Shall those Commissioners who reported, and who wish to oppress Trade Unionists, be allowed to go forward in their career of class legislation, to the injury of labour and the ruin of every Trade Unionist who stands determined to protect his home, his family, and himself by an honest remuneration for his labours? Shall it be so? is the question of the day, not only of the Boiler Makers and Iron Ship Builders, but of every man, woman and child whose dependence is upon labour. . . . Upon your exertions depends your future freedom or slavery. . . . Take immediate action in petitioning, or the majority of the Trades Union Commission, with Lord Overstone and others, will take you back to the combination laws, which made the workman a subject slave to his employer.

[15] Harrison, *IRSH*, vol. vi, pt 1, 94–5.

> The case is in your hands,
> Be not slaves, but break the bands;
> He who would a free man be,
> Must strike the blow that will make him free.

The breach between George Potter and the leaders of the London-based amalgamated unions started to close when a meeting called by the Conference of Amalgamated Trades to organize support for the Bill of Hughes and Mundella on 28 April was attended by Potter and provincial leaders. At this meeting a committee was elected from both sides to press for the Bill to become law. This was a substantial step towards unity in the trade union movement.[16] Also in April, the Birmingham Trades Council issued a circular summoning the second Trades Union Congress. After a postponement the Congress met in the Odd Fellows Hall in Birmingham on 23–28 August 1869. This time the London Trades Council was represented but not the Conference of Amalgamated Trades whose leaders, it seemed, would undertake united action only if they initiated it. Both George Howell and W. R. Cremer were present, representing the Paddington lodge of the Operative Bricklayers' Society and the Marylebone and Chelsea Working Men's Association respectively. Howell was not at that time a practising bricklayer or an official of the union. Both had appealed successfully earlier in the year for financial support from G. G. Glyn, the Liberal Party Chief Whip, and at the time of the Congress, Howell was running a private Registration and Election Agency financed by Glyn, so that the 'good work' for the Liberal Party could be carried on.[17]

Apart from the presence of these few national figures, the Congress was again largely a provincial one. The main topics for discussion were the Royal Commission reports and labour legislation. As at the first Congress many issues were discussed, including that of the role of the International Working Men's Association. W. R. Cremer, a member of the General Council of the International, successfully moved a resolution calling on all workers and workers' organizations to affiliate to the International. Two not entirely consistent resolutions were passed on the subject of legislation,[18] and a committee was

---

[16] Harrison, *IRSH*, vi, pt 1, p. 95, wrote that the rapprochement between 'Potter and the Conference of Amalgamated Trades was achieved because "it was difficult to continue a quarrel in which both parties were receiving blessings from the same source".' At the end of 1869 the London-based leaders acquired control of the *Beehive*, and thus removed from Potter his most important weapon.

[17] *Ibid.*, p. 102. G. G. Glyn was one of the partners in the banking house of Glyn, Mills and Co.

[18] Cf. Roberts, pp. 57–8.

established 'to prepare a statement, in accordance with this and other resolutions, to go out to the world, to the trades' unions and legislators, as to the reasons why we hold the opinions therein contained'. A second committee, comprising six London members, including Odger, Potter, Cremer and Howell, was appointed to cooperate with the London Trades Council in making arrangements for the third Congress in London. It was decided to coincide the date of the third Congress with the introduction into Parliament of a Government Trade Union Bill. The first of these committees did not, it seems, meet after the Birmingham Congress. The second of the committees issued two circulars, one announcing that the third Congress would be held in October 1870, while the second one announced the postponement of the October Congress until the first Monday after the introduction of the Trade Union Bill before Parliament. The third Trades Union Congress eventually met on 6 March 1871, coinciding with the second reading of the Bill.

The Trade Union Bill, which had been drafted by Frederic Harrison and introduced into the House of Commons by Hughes and Mundella, made no parliamentary progress. The Government obstructed and opposed it. In June 1869, therefore, a mass demonstration, presided over by Samuel Morley, MP, who had provided most of the money with which to buy over the Reform League in the 1868 election, was held in London and 150 union leaders were deputed to protest to the Home Secretary about the matter. In the face of union agitation and on the understanding that Hughes and Mundella would drop their Bill, the Government agreed to introduce a temporary measure in order to provide legal protection for union funds. It promised to introduce a Bill in the next session. Unions were confined to waiting and agitating. The Conference of Amalgamated Trades called a meeting in February 1870, which included representatives of a wide range of London trades and brought together again William Allan, Robert Applegarth and George Potter. The factions which had previously divided unions were united in politics.

Following the dissolution of the National Reform League in March 1869 on the grounds, as Howell explained, that it 'had accomplished its main purpose; that he had every confidence in Mr Gladstone and that continual political agitation was bad for the country',[19] a new body was formed called the Labour Representation League. The policy of this new body was, given the circumstances of the 1868 election, both hypocritical and paradoxical: it aimed to secure the

[19] Harrison, *IRSH*, vi, pt 1, 100.

return of workingmen to Parliament, to promote the registration of working-class voters throughout the country 'without reference to their opinions or party bias' and 'where deemed necessary, (to) recommend to the support of working-class electors candidates whose attitude on labour questions commended them to the movement'.[20] The Chairman of the League was William Allan, its secretary was Lloyd Jones, an old Owenite, while ten other members of its executive were past, present or future members of the General Council of the International Working Men's Association along with Karl Marx. The Labour Representation League did not include the leaders of the northern unions and its activities were confined to by-elections in the south of England. Its true affiliation was with the Liberal Party, for it was in every sense an offspring of the Reform League, but the attitude of Gladstone's Liberal Government towards labour legislation prevented the alliance from being made explicit.

The waiting ended for unions in February 1871, when the Government introduced its Trade Union Bill, but the agitation only then really began. The Bill aroused widespread union opposition for whilst it granted legal recognition and enabled unions to protect their funds by registering under the Friendly Societies Act, it denied unions the right to strike by a third clause which left unionists liable to criminal prosecution for the obscure acts of intimidation, obstruction and the like. Under this third clause the position of unions was worse than it had been after the 1825 Act for it put into legislative form the judicial decisions which had attacked trade unionism in the interim.

The third Trades Union Congress, which met in London on 6 March 1871, was almost wholly concerned with the criminal aspects of the Bill, for it was at the core of a crisis situation for unions. The success after the dramatic struggle for the franchise had soured as the Liberal Party, portrayed by so many union leaders as the friend of Labour, had showed its true class allegiance. Unless the unions could use their newly acquired political strength to change the Bill the Reform Act would seem to be an empty achievement indeed. It was a testing time. Fifty-seven delegates from forty-nine unions, representing 289,430 members, were present. The London as well as provincial leaders were present for the first time. This was the first truly representative Congress. A deputation was sent to protest to the Home

[20] See G. D. H. Cole, *A Short History of the British Workingclass Movement, 1789–1947*, p. 211.

Secretary about the Bill's third clause, but it met with no success. Then a resolution was passed, stating:

> That this Congress, having considered the Trades Union Bill in connection with the explanations and representations of the Home Secretary, hereby resolve that, whilst they are anxious to obtain from Parliament any legislation that may enable them to carry forward their efforts on behalf of the legitimate interests of their fellow workmen, refuse in any way to sanction any Bill that, in its provisions, pre-supposes criminal intentions or tendencies on the part of English workmen, as a class.

In this same mood, the delegates appointed a parliamentary committee to work with the committee of the Amalgamated Trades in agitating against the Bill. George Potter was elected chairman while George Howell became its secretary. With them were Alexander Macdonald of the Miners' National Association, Joseph Leicester of the Flint Glass Makers' Society and Lloyd Jones, representing the Manchester Fustian Cutters. The Parliamentary Committee dispatched a letter, embodying the resolution, to each Member of Parliament. The only result of these pressures, however, was that the Bill was split into two, the 'Trades Union Bill' and the 'Criminal Law Amendment Bill'. The latter had an amendment added to it in the House of Lords which made virtually all picketing impossible.[21]

When the Bills became law the Conference of Amalgamated Trades dissolved itself because it considered that it had fulfilled its purpose. Its leaders, William Allan and Robert Applegarth, had always emphasized the achievement of legal status as the most important factor, and had played down strike activities. The Criminal Law Amendment Act was not all that important from their point of view. In any event Applegarth resigned from his union post shortly after the Congress and was lost to the trade union movement. Allan without Applegarth was publicly inarticulate; he slowly became indisposed and withdrew from active politics.[22] In addition the structure of the trade union movement changed. The amalgamated unions were overtaken by unions of miners, cotton operatives, shipbuilders, and iron workers, which had their head offices in the provinces. The London Trades Council began to play a subordinate role. In this situation the Trades Union Congress had little difficulty in assuming the role of the sole national representative body. When, therefore, the fourth Congress met in January 1872, shortly after the two new Acts

[21] Roberts, p. 66.
[22] Applegarth became private secretary to one of the Education League politicians and ran errands for Glyn, the Liberal Party Whip. Allan suffered from Bright's disease.

took effect, it had no contenders. The Congress, held in Nottingham, elected its Parliamentary Committee and defined its functions. It resolved:

> That a Committee be appointed by this Congress to be called the Parliamentary Committee, for the purpose of taking any action that may be necessary to secure the repeal of the penal clauses of the Criminal Law Amendment Act, the Truck Act, the getting of a proper Compensation Act and to watch over the interests of labour generally in the proceedings of Parliament, the Committee to continue in existence till the next meeting of Congress. That the Committee shall consist of nine members. Further that it be remitted to the constituencies to see if they will make a levy per member, or pay voluntarily such a sum as will maintain the action of the Committee . . .[23]

A. J. Mundella addressed the Congress on the passage of the trade union legislation through Parliament, the delegates discussed the address and went on to recommend that every legal means should be used to secure the repeal of the Criminal Law Amendment Act and

> That united action shall be taken by Trades Societies and working men generally to resist the return to Parliament of any candidate who may refuse to pledge himself to vote for the repeal of the enacting clauses of the Criminal Law Amendment Act, and in the meantime this Congress recommends the working class electors of the United Kingdom to use their influence with their present members of Parliament to vote for the repeal of the enacting clauses of the Criminal Law Amendment Act.

This last motion was supported by George Howell, but its application tested the allegiance of Howell to the Trades Union Congress. Professor E. S. Beesly had attributed the passage of the Criminal Law Amendment Act to 'the fact that workmen had been sold at the election of 1868. He said that some trade union officers had got money or "money's worth" by working for wealthy politicians instead of for their members.'[24] Now some of these officials were being deputed to organize a withdrawal of support from the wealthy politicians if they could not guarantee support for trade union aims. Howell could not associate himself fully with the agitation against the Government. His industrial and political policies came into conflict with each other. 'Congress', Harrison wrote, 'would have better understood the strange reticence of its secretary had it known that he had made an impressive contribution to the Government's majority and that he had been set up in business by the Whips on the understanding that he would continue to work for the Party'.[25] While he was secretary

[23] Roberts, p. 71.   [24] Harrison, *IRSH*, iv, pt 1, 93.   [25] *Ibid.*, p. 106.

of the Parliamentary Committee in 1871, Howell had written for favours from the Government. He wrote:

Mr Glyn should remember not merely good offices rendered, but the abstention from adverse criticism upon many points of the Government promise and performance. I, of course, could not do anything which would run the risk of a Liberal defeat, but upon some questions they have really invited it, and if we had been hasty in taking up the cudgels I think considerable dissatisfaction would have been the result. I wonder if Mr Stansfield ever remembers how some of us worked for him, now that he is reconstructing his office. Surely there would be a chance of some good appointment where my qualifications would be a fair test.[26]

Fortunately Howell could not curb the dissatisfaction of trade unionists with the Government. Nor could he stop the involvement of the Trades Union Congress in the agitation. He did endeavour to evade the instructions of the 1872 Congress by trying to negotiate minor amendments to the Criminal Law Amendment Act privately with 'well-disposed' Liberals, but his antics were revealed through articles in the *Beehive*. Protests demanding an uncompromising stand poured in to Howell.

The mass campaign which was built up by 1873 to secure the repeal of the Act was encouraged by a number of judicial decisions concerning strikers. The 1871 legislation had made strikes legal, but had pronounced the means whereby strikes were enforced as illegal. In South Wales seven women were imprisoned for saying 'Bah' to a blackleg in 1871. The next year five leaders of a gas workers' strike in London were sentenced to a year's imprisonment for conspiracy. There were numerous other cases of arrests, even for using bad language during strikes.

The intolerable injustice of this state of things [the Webbs stated] was made more glaring by the freedom allowed to the employers to make all possible use of 'blacklists' and 'character notes', by which obnoxious men were prevented from getting work. No prosecution ever took place for this form of molestation or obstruction. No employer was ever placed in the dock under the law which professedly applied to both parties. In short, boycotting by the employers was freely permitted; boycotting by the men was put down by the police.[27]

Massive demonstrations were held in 1873 in many large industrial centres. In June an estimated crowd of 100,000 people demonstrated

---

[26] Letter to Edmond Beales, quoted by Harrison, ibid., pp. 102–3. The Mr Stansfield was James Stansfield, brewer and Liberal politician.
[27] S. and B. Webb, *History*, p. 284.

in Hyde Park. In Glasgow 20,000 trade unionists demonstrated with banners saying 'Down with all Class Legislation'. Unorganized workers became organized in the process. Even the Trades Union Congress at the beginning of 1873 reported an aggregate membership of 750,000 compared with that of 255,710 in 1872. In January 1874 the affiliated membership of the Congress was 1,191,000. The Parliamentary Committee consulted with its middle-class friends against the background of the agitation. Thomas Hughes was against a total repeal of the Act but E. S. Beesly and Henry Crompton were in favour of it. Howell's special friends were Vernon Harcourt, described by Mundella as 'a Tory who plays the game of radical brag',[28] another Liberal lawyer, Henry James, and A. J. Mundella himself, condescending to trade unionists and considered by Sir Charles Dilke as a windbag.[29] Howell's friends had tried to bring in an amending Bill during 1872, but it was acceptable to neither side. The memorials, deputations and petitions of the Parliamentary Committee had no impact on the Government. The Prime Minister, W. E. Gladstone, refused in 1872 to take up the matter of legislation at all and in 'that session the Parliamentary Committee were unable to find any member willing to introduce a Bill for the repeal of the Criminal Law Amendment Act'.[30]

A week after the end of the 1874 Trades Union Congress, Parliament was dissolved and a general election was called. The Labour Representation League, directly and indirectly, sponsored about a dozen candidates, but only two, Alexander Macdonald and Thomas Burt, were successful. These two miners' leaders were returned for Stafford and Morpeth respectively, without Liberal Party opposition. The election was noted, however, not for the minor marginal encroachment of workingmen into power politics, but for the rejection of the Liberal Party by the new working-class voters. Vote catching through the use of policies rather than manipulation resulting in pendulum swings of allegiance began to characterize elections. The Liberal Government had offended many interests but not the least was that of trade unionism. The election resulted in the return of a Tory majority of forty-eight in place of a Liberal one of about 120. The Parliamentary Committee of the Trades Union Congress had to face a Conservative Government led by Disraeli.

The new Prime Minister showed his gratitude by establishing a Royal Commission to examine the Master and Servants Acts and

[28] W. H. G. Armytage, *A. J. Mundella*, Benn, 1951, p. 118.
[29] Roy Jenkins, *Sir Charles Dilke*, Collins, 1965, p. 148.
[30] S. and B. Webb, p. 286.

the Conspiracy Acts. The Parliamentary Committee was not pleased and stated that it considered

> the action of the Government in appointing a Royal Commission to be a mere excuse for delay, and we adhere to the resolution already passed deprecating the appointment of the Commission, and we pledge ourselves to continue to protest against the whole scheme as being a surprise, an intrigue, and a fraud; and we further recommend the whole Trade Unions of the country to refuse to have anything to do with the Commission . . . in any way.[31]

In spite of this opposition Alexander Macdonald, the chairman of the Parliamentary Committee, had agreed, with Thomas Hughes, to serve on the Commission. He resigned from the chairmanship of the Committee as a consequence. The Commission's report was inconsequential. It recommended the abolition of the penal clauses of the Master and Servants Acts, but thought that only a slight amendment in the Criminal Law Amendment Act was necessary. The report was evidence in support of the apprehension of the Parliamentary Committee. Then in June 1875 the Home Secretary, R. A. Cross, ignoring the Royal Commission report, introduced two Bills into Parliament for altering the civil and criminal law concerning labour. The two Bills, amended in committee by the friends of unions, became the Employers and Workmen Act which replaced the Master and Servant Act of 1867, and the Conspiracy and Protection of Property Act which repealed the Criminal Law Amendment Act and expressly legalized peaceful picketing. The terms coercion and molestation did not appear in the new Act. Simple criminal conspiracy was no longer involved in trade disputes. The British workers had achieved, it seemed then, the right both to organize and to take effective industrial action.[32]

The Parliamentary Committee was duly pleased. It moved that a vote of thanks be sent to the Home Secretary. George Odger, a member of the Committee, 'paid testimony to the "immense singleness of purpose" with which the Home Secretary "had attended to every proposition that had been placed before him" and accorded them "the greatest boon ever given to the sons of toil".'[33] The Trades Union Congress which met in October 1875 was fulsome in its praise of Cross. An amendment critical of such praise being accorded to the Conservative Party only received four votes. The delegates met

---

[31] Roberts, p. 82.
[32] Wedderburn, *The Worker and the Law*, pp. 222–3.
[33] S. and B. Webb, p. 291n.

in a mood of complacency. The secretary of the Parliamentary Committee, George Howell, resigned because he felt that the major work of the Trades Union Congress had been completed. In so far as there was an achievement, however, it did not belong to the shady Howell or the Parliamentary Committee. It rested with the rank and file trade unionists who had agitated in the streets, through the Trades Union Congress and the ballot boxes. As Disraeli explained to Queen Victoria, the new Labour laws would 'help to soften the feelings of the working multitude',[34] for it was these feelings which were disturbing the ruling class.

Appendix

PROPOSED CONGRESS OF TRADES COUNCILS
and other
Federations of Trades Societies

Fellow-Unionists,   Manchester, February 21st, 1868.

The Manchester and Salford Trades Council having recently taken into their serious consideration the present aspect of Trades Unions, and the profound ignorance which prevails in the public mind with reference to their operations and principles, together with the probability of an attempt being made by the Legislature, during the present session of Parliament, to introduce a measure detrimental to the interests of such Societies, beg most respectfully to suggest the propriety of holding in Manchester, as the main centre of industry in the provinces, a Congress of the Representative of Trades Councils and other similar Federations of Trades Societies. By confining the Congress to such bodies it is conceived that a deal of expense will be saved, as Trades will thus be represented collectively; whilst there will be a better opportunity afforded of selecting the most intelligent and efficient exponents of our principles.

It is proposed that the Congress shall assume the character of the annual meetings of the British Association for the Advancement of Science and the Social Science Association, in the transactions of which Societies the artizan class are almost entirely excluded; and that papers, previously carefully prepared, shall be laid before the Congress on the various subjects which at the present time affect Trades Societies, each paper to be followed by discussion upon the points advanced, with a view of the merits and demerits of each question being thoroughly ventilated through the medium of the public press. It is further suggested that the subjects treated upon shall include the following:

1. Trades Unions an absolute necessity.
2. Trades Unions and Political Economy.

[34] R. Harrison, 'Practical, capable men', *The New Reasoner*, Autumn 1958, p. 115.

3. The Effect of Trades Unions on Foreign Competition.
4. Regulation of the Hours of Labour.
5. Limitation of Apprentices.
6. Technical Education.
7. Arbitration and Courts of Conciliation.
8. Co-operation.
9. The Present Inequality of the Law in regard to Conspiracy, Intimidation, Picketing, Coercion, &c.
10. Factory Acts Extension Bill, 1867: the necessity of Compulsory Inspection, and its application to all places where Women and Children are employed.
11. The present Royal Commission on Trades Unions: how far worthy of the confidence of the Trades Union interest.
12. The necessity of an Annual Congress of Trade Representatives from the various centres of industry.

All Trades Councils and other Federations of Trades are respectfully solicited to intimate their adhesion to this project on or before the 6th of April next, together with a notification of the subject of the paper that each body will undertake to prepare; after which date all information as to place of meeting, &c., will be supplied.

It is also proposed that the Congress be held on the 4th of May next, and that all liabilities in connection therewith shall not extend beyond its sittings.

Communications to be addressed to MR. W. H. WOOD, Typographical Institute, 29, Water Street, Manchester.

By order of the Manchester and Salford Trades Council,

S. C. NICHOLSON, *President*.

W. H. WOOD, *Secretary*.

12

The Trades Union Congress before Socialism, 1875–1886

The conditions following the first meeting of the Trades Union Congress were propitious for the spread of trade unionism. Trade improved; the level of employment rose and so did real wages. Unemployment among the members of unions which made employment returns fell from 7·9 per cent in 1868 to 0·9 per cent in 1872 and rose only slightly afterwards to 2·4 per cent in 1875. Average real wages, not allowing for unemployment, after being relatively stable for many years, rose by almost 25 per cent between 1868 and 1875. Everywhere, even in agriculture, the economy was buoyant. Trade unionism spread in the wake of these conditions to an unprecedented level of activity. It reached new trades and was intensified in old ones. In some activities, as in coal mining, employers strongly resisted the spread, but in the main trading prospects discouraged anti-union pressures.

These conditions placed the Trades Union Congress in an historically unique position. Hitherto attempts to achieve a horizontal unity either had coincided with falling trade and employment which had strengthened the opposition of employers, or had occurred in a situation in which powerful opposition from employers was possible anyway. But not only was it inappropriate for the employers to attack the Trades Union Congress. It was also unwise for the Government to do so because of the extension of the franchise in 1868. On previous occasions the employers were always able to depend upon Government support to restrain unions whatever the reason. Nothing in the period 1868 to 1875 had altered the basic identity of interests between Conservative and Liberal Governments on the one hand and employers on the other but the Reform Act had modified the relationship between their respective responses to union behaviour. No longer, it seemed, could a government oppress trade unions with impunity for, as the events showed, the working-class vote could influence the duration of a government's life. The political parties competed for electoral favours from trade unionists by courting their unions.

The situation of the TUC changed in important respects in 1875. A number of union leaders, in addition to George Howell, considered that with the repeal of the Criminal Law Amendment Act, the purpose of the TUC had been fulfilled. It was advocated that the organization should be wound up and if it had not been for the pressure of provincial union leaders who wanted to keep the TUC intact this might have happened.[1] The provincial leaders did not want to leave affairs in the metropolitan centre solely in the hands of the London Trades Council. This view was reflected in the choice of a successor to Howell. George Shipton, the secretary of the London Trades Council, was defeated in competition for the post with Henry Broadhurst by twenty-seven votes to seventy-four. Shipton represented domination by the London leaders and complacency in the eyes of provincial leaders. In his Trades Council annual report for 1875 he had written that all that was necessary was for workers to 'be faithful to their own cause and the principles of justice and they have every means within their power by which they may obtain all they may rightly claim, and greatly advance the cause of human happiness and progress together'.[2] Henry Broadhurst, on the other hand, had different associations. He came from Oxford, had belonged to Potter's Working Men's Association and was a member of the Operative Stonemasons' Society, which was not identified with the London-based amalgamated unions. Broadhurst became a delegate to the TUC in 1872 and was immediately elected to the Parliamentary Committee. He became secretary to the Labour Representation League in 1873 and continued in this post after he was elected as the Parliamentary Secretary of the TUC.[3] But it was one thing to maintain the formal existence of the TUC and quite another thing to involve it in working-class struggles in a leadership position. None of the union leaders who wanted to maintain the TUC in existence had clear ideas about its purpose. They had no industrial or political programme for it. At the most it was envisaged as having a limited watchdog function; keeping an eye on legislation, seeking improvements in such matters as factory legislation. In effect the TUC had to rejustify its existence from 1875.

---

[1] See Davis, *The British Trades Union Congress*, p. 52.
[2] *London Trades Council, 1860–1950*, p. 46.
[3] See Henry Broadhurst, MP, *Story of His Life from a Stonemason's Bench to the Treasury Bench*, told by Himself, Hutchinson, 1901.

Already by 1875 the employment situation was changing. Unemployment increased each year until in 1879 it reached the level of 11·4 per cent.[4] In the engineering, metal and shipbuilding industries approximately 15·3 per cent of the union memberships were unemployed in that year. The employers' ideological opposition to unions, fortified by the power they derived from unemployment, became an outright attack. Many unions disappeared under the impact. Their strength was undermined by more insidious forces. The period between 1868 and 1875 was characterized by the emergence of voluntary methods of conciliation and arbitration to settle industrial disputes. Starting with A. J. Mundella's experiment in the Nottingham hosiery trade a number of joint boards were established, in the hosiery trade in Leicester, the Staffordshire pottery trade, the glass bottle industry, the building industry in various provincial towns, the North of England iron trade and other trades.[5] The idea of using independent arbitrators became popular. There was in 1875 an 'arbitration craze'. A National Conciliation League was formed in December 1875, to encourage the craze. The Christian Socialists and the Positivists along with a few lawyers not connected with these groups encouraged the settlement of disputes by 'reason' and some of them participated as arbitrators. The consequence of the advocacy of arbitration was near disastrous for some unions, as its logical result was the acceptance of sliding-scale agreements which related wages to changes in selling prices. With such a clearcut automatic means of regulating wages trade unions appeared to many workers to be unnecessary. After the introduction of sliding-scale agreements trade unionism in some mining and iron industry areas virtually died. The membership, for example, of the Association of Ironworkers fell from 35,000 in 1873 to 1400 in 1879.

The affiliated membership of the TUC fell from 1,191,922 in 1874 to 541,892 in 1879. In the same period the number of affiliated unions fell from 153 to 92. The membership continued to fall until 1881 when it reached the trough figure of 463,899. Understandably the unions were too concerned with their own question of survival to bother much about interunion unity. Indeed the impact of the depression pitted unions against each other. One of the paradoxes of trade unionism is that when their need for unity is greatest, in that only united action can achieve their ends, their ability to fight is weakest. The period after 1875 showed the paradox in a vivid form.

Neither the unions nor the delegates they sent to the TUC each

---

[4] Cf. Mitchell and Deane, *Abstract of British Historical Statistics*, p. 64.
[5] On the spread of industrial conciliation and arbitration see Chapter 6.

year recognized the paradox. The value of interunion unity had been empirically illustrated, but as yet it did not have any continuing political significance. There was no coherent ideological basis for unity: no reasoned case for heightening workingmen's consciousness in their class solidarity. Socialism had no organized basis except in the sect of Christian Socialism, headed by F. D. Maurice and J. M. Ludlow. It was identified through the acts of isolated individuals, mainly Owenites. With the Criminal Law Amendment Act out of the way the union leaders were able to consolidate their relationship with the Liberal Party.[6] The real phase of Lib-Labism began.

In the absence of a coherent Socialist ideology the only alternative political philosophy which could attract working-class support was Positivism. The Positivists, E. S. Beesly, Frederic Harrison, Henry Crompton and others, were followers of Auguste Comte, the French advocate of secular, or rational religion.

> They sought to exchange the consolations of theology [Royden Harrison wrote] for those of history. By the Religion of Humanity they expected to resolve the conflicts of capital and labour; order and progress; religion and society. . . . It is largely through secular religion that the intimate alliance of philosopher and proletarian is sealed and the intellectual becomes progressively identified with the Labour Movement.[7]

The Positivists made little impact upon trade unions but, as the intellectual advisers of Applegarth, Allan and others, during the period when unions were struggling for legal recognition, they undoubtedly made an impact upon the political course of trade unionism. Through their advocacy of arbitration and conciliation in the industrial sphere they also made an impact which in essence was no less significant.

The Positivists did not sever their connections with the trade union movement after the 1875 political achievements. They remained closely connected to the Parliamentary Committee of the TUC and largely provided it with whatever programme of action it possessed. Henry Crompton served as the legal adviser to the TUC and directed its attention to both the codification and the administration of the criminal law in general. The TUC became, as it was initially intended to be, a debating society. It debated each year a variety of legal reforms, some of which, such as employers' liability for accidents, were directly relevant to the work situation, while others, such as imprisonment for debt and the reform of magistrates courts, had a

---

[6] See Harrison, *Before the Socialists*, Routledge, 1965, pp. 2–6.
[7] *Ibid.*, pp. 252 and 253.

general significance. In tackling piecemeal reform while neglecting the cause of legal discrimination against the working class which was the concentration of power in the hands of the relatively small number of owners of the means of production and the use of that power to provide legal protection for their property, the Parliamentary Committee reflected the attitude of the Positivists. The reform of the criminal law was not, Henry Crompton insisted, a class question.[8]

Occasionally the debates produced action. In 1876 the Parliamentary Committee launched a campaign to get a reform of the jury laws and organized a large deputation of delegates in support of the Merchants' Shipping Bill introduced by Samuel Plimsoll. In 1880 it protested at an attempt by the House of Lords to wreck an Employers' Liability Bill. Henry Broadhurst, the new secretary of the Parliamentary Committee, drafted his own Bill for the abolition of the property qualifications attached to membership of local authorities. The Bill became law in 1878. The Parliamentary Committee framed amendments for the Consolidating Act dealing with factory and workshop laws in 1877 and 1878. In the main, the activities of the Parliamentary Committee were consistent with the aims of many members of the Liberal Party and drew support from people who had little sympathy for trade unions. The Parliamentary Committee, Broadhurst wrote:

> fulfilled the functions of the Radical wing of the Liberal Party. Reform of the Jury Laws, amendment of the Summary Jurisdiction Act, reduction and restriction of legal costs and payments to Clerks of the Peace, modification of the Shipping and Patent Laws were all planks in our platform, which, affecting the working man chiefly, undoubtedly touched much wider interests. This phase of our work procured for us the cooperation of many men entirely unassociated with the Labour cause, who manifested a keen interest in the wider aspects of our work. Some even went so far in their appreciation as to offer liberal contributions to our funds.[9]

Neither the TUC nor its Parliamentary Committee displayed any interest in foreign policy issues in the 1870s. Broadhurst became associated with the Eastern Question Association, which pursued Gladstone's policy over the atrocities of the 'Unspeakable Turk in Bulgaria'. He organized a Workmen's Committee to the Association but the Parliamentary Committee as such was not involved. Throughout Disraeli's Tory administration the TUC failed to debate any of

[8] *Ibid.*, p. 308.
[9] *Henry Broadhurst, M.P. The Story of his Life from a Stonemason's Bench to the Treasury Bench*, 1901, p. 77.

the Government's imperialist interventions. Its attitude produced disillusionment even amongst the Positivists who had supported trade unions for about twenty years. Henry Crompton eventually concluded that trade unions had 'hindered rather than promoted political progress'.[10] He added that they were

> altogether indifferent in respect of the crimes committed by England against other nations. It is impossible to interest even their leaders upon such questions as England's wrong upon the Chinese. . . . They are easily deceived and led by a few rhetorical speeches: forgetting how they have been cheated and thrown on one side when used, they are ready to believe any specious vague platitudes about 'Liberals' and 'Liberal principles'. We shall see them trust again and again to the promises of the party politicians who have deceived them so often.[11]

The Parliamentary Committee gave more than tacit support to British imperialism in Africa when it invited J. Bradshaw, a Manchester merchant, to read a long paper on 'Africa, the Remedy for the Trade Depression of England', before the 1879 TUC. Bradshaw wanted trade unionists to invest in an African trading corporation which had the backing of the Duke of Manchester and Lord Shaftesbury. 'How', Bradshaw asked, 'could Africa best be utilized for the benefit of British industries?'[12] The answer he gave was mildly approved by the Congress. After the 1880 general election when Broadhurst, in addition to Alexander Macdonald and Thomas Burt the miners' leaders, was elected to Parliament, the Parliamentary Committee became even more closely identified with the Liberal Party and supported Gladstone's policy of coercion in Ireland. At this point the connection between the Positivists and the TUC was severed. The TUC was not left, however, safely in the hands of the Liberal politicians for very long. A disillusionment with mid-Victorian capitalism was setting in. Progress for the working class was being seen for what it was, an illusion. As the Positivists bowed out, working-class socialists moved in.

The Lib–Lab Alliance was an alliance of persons, not social forces. It was expressed through the activities of parliamentarians, not rank and file movements. So far as the Liberal side was concerned the Alliance made few demands. All that was necessary was for Gladstone's Government to receive Parliamentary Committee deputations cordially, to take some notice of their wishes and to make small legislative concessions accordingly, and to allow openings so that

---

[10] Harrison, *Before the Socialists*, p. 311.
[11] Quoted in *ibid.*, p. 311.   [12] *Ibid.*, p. 312.

some union leaders could satisfy the social and occupational aspirations which affinity with power-holders was creating. The Alliance did not require the Liberal Government to make substantial and consistent concessions to labour for had it done so it would never have existed. The Lib–Lab Alliance was based on the allegiance of Broadhurst and his like to the Liberal cause not on the allegiance of Gladstone to the interests of labour or on an identity between the interests. The Alliance, therefore, was never in real terms an alliance, and this became obvious quite early on as even the marginal reforms achieved by Parliamentary Committee pressure were seen to lack substance. One of Broadhurst's first moves after becoming a Member of Parliament was to press for the passage of the Employers' Limited Liability Bill. This Bill became law in January 1881 and was hailed by Broadhurst as 'a great triumph for the trades unions, which for fourteen years had persistently agitated for the recognition of the principle'. Very soon afterwards, however, the TUC was complaining bitterly about the Act's permissive character, and about the fact that 'hundreds of thousands of workers were forced to contract themselves out of the benefits of the Act by railway and other Companies'.[13] Workmen's compensation was not to be restored to the TUC agenda until 1896. A realization that reform of land laws was inadequate was expressed at the TUC in 1882 when a motion was passed stating 'that no reform will be complete short of nationalization of the land'. Though this decision was reversed the following year when the Parliamentary Committee reasserted its authority it was a sign of what was to follow.

The Parliamentary Committee, while it could, gave full value to Gladstone's Government. It defeated a move in 1883 to commit the TUC to manhood suffrage instead of franchise extension and in the following year restrained the TUC from embarrassing the Government in its attempts to get a Franchise Bill through the House of Lords. It was thought that views from the TUC which were highly critical of the House of Lords would increase the Lords' determination to resist the Bill. Broadhurst even stage-managed a deputation of 240 trade unionists to Gladstone in January 1884 to petition for 'an extension of the rights of citizenship' in order to create a positive political effect for Gladstone. 'Everything', Broadhurst wrote, 'went like clockwork. The speeches were short, sharp and to the point. . . . It was a memorable day's work and its influence reached all political circles.'[14] When the question of achieving labour representation in

---

[13] Davis, *The British Trades Union Congress*, p. 95.
[14] Broadhurst, p. 125.

Parliament was raised, as it was each year, it was always tackled by the Parliamentary Committee so as to benefit the Liberal Party. There was never any doubt that increased Labour representation had to be achieved within the organization of the Liberal Party. Broadhurst, following closely in George Howell's steps, did everything possible to enhance the electoral prospects of the Liberal Party. He was secretary of the Labour Representation League, but allowed it to lapse. Only five candidates stood in the 1880 general election as representatives of labour and only one of these opposed the Liberal Party as well as the Tories. The Labour Representation League ceased to exist altogether the next year. When labour representation in Parliament was raised at the 1882 TUC a resolution stating that 'the time has arrived when this question should pass from the region of abstract discussion to the domain of practical Labour politics', was passed but still the practical men on the Parliamentary Committee did nothing. A TUC resolution in 1885 to support the formation of local Labour Associations was also ignored. The main contribution of the Parliamentary Committee in the 1885 general election was an arid election manifesto of eleven points:

1. A Bill to amend the Employers' Liability Act of 1880.
2. An increase in the number of factory inspectors.
3. An increase in the number of mine inspectors.
4. A Bill to prevent further loss of life at sea.
5. An extension of the Employers' Liability Act to shipping.
6. A Bill for the better regulation of safety on the railways.
7. A Bill to make a certificate of competency compulsory for all those who have charge of an engine.
8. The removal of unnecessary obstacles to the appointment of workmen to the civil and magisterial service.
9. The abolition of the property qualification in local government.
10. Such reforms of the land laws as was best calculated to set free the springs of natural industry and to promote home consumption of manufactured goods.
11. The restitution of educational and other endowments to the service of those for whom they were originally intended.[15]

The manifesto demanded nothing in concrete terms which the Liberal Party was incapable of conceding. It was just a further jot of evidence of the limited political horizons of the union leaders. Nothing was said about the Irish question which dominated the political scene. On that and foreign policy issues the Parliamentary Committee

[15] Cf. Roberts, *The Trades Union Congress*, p. 106.

put its trust in Gladstone. More than this, for when the general election came at the end of 1885 the Committee put its trust in the election managers of the Liberal Party. It had no election machine of its own and depended on the generosity of party officials for constituency openings for Lib-Lab candidates. Eleven such candidates were elected but the increase was due, not to intensified trade union efforts, but to the extended franchise and redistribution of parliamentary seats. Gladstone's third Government lasted for less than six months, as a result of the defection and disruption of the Liberal Party's radical wing under the leadership of Joseph Chamberlain over the Irish question. At the next election in July 1886 the Lib-Lab candidates lost three seats and gained one. The parliamentary score for Lib-Labs was nine from 1886 until the next election in 1892, when it increased by one. This dismal record was poor compensation for the unqualified commitment of the TUC to the Liberal cause. There were other items, but they simply made matters look worse for they were like crumbs from the capitalists' table.

The Parliamentary Committee, including the secretary, had eleven members. Its membership changed slightly most years, mainly as the leadership of unions altered and as the fortunes of unions varied in sharply changing economic conditions. The relatively stable core of members came from the dominant unions of the time, those representing the engineers, carpenters, boilermakers, cotton textile workers and sections of the miners. This core comprised the statesmen of labour who ensured the continuing allegiance of the TUC to the Liberals and to whom the crumbs occasionally fell.

After the passing of the Factory and Workshop Act 1878, the TUC pressed the Government to appoint 'practical' working men as sub-inspectors of factories. A deputation of forty-six delegates presented a memorial on the question to the Home Secretary, Sir William Harcourt, in January 1881, and in response shortly afterwards, as an experiment, he offered Henry Broadhurst the job of assistant inspector of factories. Broadhurst refused and suggested the name of J. D. Prior, successor to Robert Applegarth as the general secretary of the Amalgamated Society of Carpenters and Joiners, and a member of the Parliamentary Committee.[16] Prior accepted the offer and commented in his union monthly report: 'After mature consideration, I determined to accept the responsibility thus entrusted to me, feeling that the offer was a compliment not only to myself but to the Society.' Contrary to Broadhurst's contention, Prior believed that he had been recommended for the post by '. . . some gentlemen who, although not

[16] Broadhurst, p. 137.

trade unionists, have rendered invaluable services to the cause of labour'; members of the Carpenters' Union were so delighted that they suggested a fund be set up for Prior 'to give expression to our unfeigned pleasure at the great honour done to our esteemed chief officer'.[17] Two years later, W. J. Davis, the vice-chairman of the Parliamentary Committee and general secretary of the National Society of Brassworkers and Metal Mechanics, was also made a factory inspector. Davis was followed by G. Sedgwick, and W. Paterson, both fellow-members of the Parliamentary Committee. Four trade unionists were appointed as magistrates in 1885, for the first time. They all came from Lancashire and two, H. Slatter and T. Birtwistle, were core members of the Parliamentary Committee. The biggest crumb of all, however, fell to Broadhurst himself.

Eight of the eleven Lib-Lab candidates returned to the House of Commons in 1885 either were, had been, or were shortly to be, members of the Parliamentary Committee. George Howell, the former secretary, was among the eight and was at last rewarded for his devotion to Gladstone, Morley and Glyn. Broadhurst was returned for his second Parliament and was offered the post of Under-Secretary of State for Home Affairs in Gladstone's Government. The offer, Broadhurst recalled, was in part a reward for his 'services to the Eastern Question Association'.[18] He accepted 'this flattering proposal', and the Parliamentary Committee sent a resolution to the Prime Minister thanking him 'for his recognition of the organized trades'.[19] Broadhurst resigned from the secretaryship of the Parliamentary Committee, and George Shipton, secretary of the London Trades Council, was elected in his place. When Gladstone's Government was defeated over the Home Rule for Ireland Bill a few months later Broadhurst lost office. He reappeared at the 1886 TUC as a delegate for the Operative Stonemasons' Society and was re-elected to the secretaryship of the Parliamentary Committee. Thus Broadhurst was by now no ordinary delegate and bore no resemblance to the man the provincial union leaders thought they were electing to office in 1875 as a reaction to the shady Howell. He was a friend and admirer of the Liberal manufacturers, in particular John Brunner the head of the armaments producing firm, Brunner, Mond and Co. He was flattered by attention from royalty and related with obsequious delight the attention he received on his visit to Sandringham. 'I left Sandringham', he wrote, 'with a feeling of one who had spent a weekend with an old chum of his own rank in society rather than one

[17] V. L. Allen, *Trade Union Leadership*, Longmans, 1957, p. 20n.
[18] Broadhurst, p. 188.   [19] Davis, p. 116.

who had been entertained by the Heir-Apparent and his Princess.' In 1887 Broadhurst supported John Brunner in his by-election campaign and drew upon himself charges of receiving shares in Brunner-Mond as payment for the support.

During the brief tenure of Gladstone's third Government, A. J. Mundella, the President of the Board of Trade, started a Labour Bureau for 'the full and accurate collection and publishing of Labour statistics'. John Burnett, general secretary of the Amalgamated Society of Engineers, who had made his name as the militant leader of the rank and file movement for a nine-hour day in 1871 and a member of the Parliamentary Committee since 1876, was given the job as sole Labour Correspondent to the Bureau. It was probably inevitable that the Government should look to the Parliamentary Committee as its source for union leaders as it mildly and marginally democratized Government institutions. But on the other hand the virtual monopoly which Parliamentary Committee members had over the relatively lucrative jobs the Government offered appeared to justify the charges which began increasingly to be made against them after 1885 that they were 'a gang of place-hunters scheming to obtain Factory Inspectorships and other appointments under Government'.[20]

The Congress met in September 1886 against the background of defeat and disillusionment in the Liberal Party and was more inclined than in many previous years to be practical about Labour representation in Parliament. George Shipton raised, as he had done on a number of previous occasions, the issue of providing funds to support working-class parliamentary candidates so that they were not driven to depend upon the machinery and backing of the established parties. During the debate, R. T. Threlfall, the secretary of Southport Trades Council, successfully proposed that a Labour Electoral Association should be established. The objects of the Association were not to create an independent Party to promote working-class issues but to secure: '1. More Labour representatives in Parliament. 2. Increased representation on local governing bodies. 3. Annual conferences, delegates to which to be appointed only by *bona-fide* workmen's associations, and the expenses of the delegates to be borne by the societies appointing them.'[21]

The Association was to be financed separately from the TUC and governed by a Labour Electoral Committee, which was to work in conjunction with the Parliamentary Committee. In effect the Association was run entirely independently of the Parliamentary

Committee. It formed branches in many centres and in 1888 claimed an affiliated membership of 600,000.[22] But its identity was separate from that of the TUC in organizational terms alone, for it pursued a policy of collaborating with the Liberal Party which would have done justice to Broadhurst himself. It encouraged the adoption of its candidates by local Liberal and Radical Associations so that they stood as Liberals and to this end it opposed three-corner electoral contests. The Labour Electoral Association was a continuation of the National Reform League and was therefore incapable of satisfying the rising mood of dissatisfaction among trade unionists with capitalism and its governing institutions. Its allegiance to the Liberal Party compelled it to resist that mood, and it spent much of its short life struggling against efforts to obtain independent labour representation.

There was little sign during these years that the TUC and its executive belonged to a wider movement which was rising out of the tortuous contradictions of capitalism. Occasionally delegates at the annual Congresses referred to 'the dearth of trade' or unemployment, but regarded them as inevitable features of their lives to be accepted, like their 'stations in life', without question. Much less occasionally, this fatalistic view was penetrated by observations about causality as when James Mawdsley, the conservative leader of the cotton spinners, moved at the 1885 Congress "That this Congress, believing the present stagnation in trade is greatly due to over-production—a remedy for which is not to be found in a curtailment of the earnings of the workers.'[23]

Mawdsley's intention was to express sympathy with the cotton workers in Oldham who were striking against wage reductions. The failure of the Parliamentary Committee to take account of social pressures in their policy formulation was not due, however, to a lack of understanding of them by its individual members. Some members showed an acute awareness of what was happening at the base of the Labour Movement. Outside of the TUC, for instance, James Mawdsley displayed a greater perception. In 1886 he attended the International Trades Union Congress in Paris, in his capacity as chairman of the Parliamentary Committee, and described the situation in Britain.

Wages had fallen, and there was a great number of unemployed. . . . Flax mills were being closed every day. . . . All the building trades were

[22] G. D. H. Cole, *A Short History of the British Working-Class Movement, 1789–1947*, p. 231; also Roberts, pp. 109–10.
[23] Davis, p. 111.

in a bad position; . . . ironfoundries were in difficulties, and one-third of the shipwrights were without work. . . . Steam-engine makers were also slack. . . . With a few rare exceptions, the depression affecting the great leading trades was felt in a thousand-and-one occupations. Seeing that there was a much larger number of unemployed, the question naturally presented itself as to whether there was any chance of improvement. He considered there was no chance of improvement so long as the present state of society continued to exist. . . . He did not understand their Socialism; he had not studied it as perhaps he ought to have done. The workmen of England were not so advanced as the workmen of the continent. Nevertheless they, at least, possessed one clear conception: they realized that the actual producers did not obtain their share of the wealth they created.[24]

On the Parliamentary Committee with Mawdsley for many years sat Robert Knight, the general secretary of the Boiler Makers' Society. In 1886 piecework prices and time rates in the shipbuilding industry were lower than they had been for twenty years and as low as any point reached during the forty years' life of the union.[25] In his annual report for that year Knight described the starvation and sickness and privation of the unemployed boilermakers and their families, and compared this position with 'the lavish display of wealth in which he has no part'. He concluded that the workman 'cannot fail to reason that there must be something wrong in a system which effects such unequal distribution of the wealth created by labour'.[26] James S. Murchie, who followed J. D. Prior as leader of the Carpenters' Union in 1861 and as a member of the Parliamentary Committee, also showed an awareness of social issues in his dealings with his members. After the extension of the franchise in 1884 he wrote in his annual address that 'the old lines of party politics, which have hitherto divided us, are not likely to continue. There must be no more crushing of necessary social reforms by the mere weight of vested interests.'[27]

Not all the members of the Parliamentary Committee went through the experiences of Mawdsley and Knight and those who did not remained conservative and solidly committed to the existing way of things at all levels of their activity. The Typographical Association experienced between 1881 and 1891 the most prosperous decade of its existence prior to 1914. Its general fund rose from less than £1500

---

[24] S. and B. Webb, *The History of Trade Unionism*, p. 379.

[25] D. C. Cummings, *A Historical Survey of the Boiler Makers' Society*, Newcastle upon Tyne, Robinson, 1905, p. 117.

[26] S. and B. Webb, *op. cit.*, pp. 378–9.

[27] S. Higenbottam, comp., *Our Society's History*, Manchester, Amalgamated Society of Woodworkers, 1939. p. 301.

in 1879–80 to over £25,000 in 1892.[28] Its general secretary, H. Slatter, sat on the Parliamentary Committee from 1877 to 1889, adopting what he would have described as a non-political attitude, wanting 'to see trade unions carried on in the same sober and steady lines as in the past'.[29] The Manchester Society of the Typographical Association, over which Slatter had a particularly powerful influence, voted as late as 1892 not to join even the Labour Electoral Association.

It is clear that the way in which trade union leaders thought depended to a large extent upon the nearness of their positions to the impulses of rank and file pressure. As general secretaries of unions they could ill-afford to ignore those impulses, but as members of the Parliamentary Committee they experienced virtually no pressures from below, except, perhaps, an annual haranguing from a small minority of Congress delegates and this was often external to their own union interests.

Their role as they saw it was a purely political one, so all industrial movements were excluded from their reckoning. In any event, industrial movements were the concern of individual unions over which the TUC had no jurisdiction. They did not consider that for their purposes the TUC needed to be a stronger, more centrally organized body. The TUC debated the possibility of forming itself into a federation in 1874, and in 1879 actually voted to do this but only by a majority of two. The Parliamentary Committee ignored the decision and carried on with its politics. The environment of the TUC leaders, from which decision-making pressures directly emanated, was dominated by Parliament and the institutions it comprised. That was where power seemed to lie, where political decisions were made, from where patronage was doled out. All that seemed necessary was to move into formal positions in the Government and the civil service and exercise the power which those positions appeared to possess. Hence the concentration of the union leaders on the mechanics of assimilation. They tried to identify themselves as nearly as possible with the Liberal leaders. They accepted their conventions and, with undying gratitude, their patronage, and they sought and accepted responsible, respectable, advice. The willingness to accept advice was a willingness to conform. When, in 1883, the Parliamentary Committee received 'an important communication . . . from Paris, in reference to an effort to bring about a better understanding between trade organizations of Great Britain and the continent', Broadhurst

[28] A. E. Musson, *The Typographical Association origins and history up to 1949*, Oxford University Press, 1954, p. 123.
[29] *Ibid.*, p. 349.

sought the advice of A. J. Mundella. Broadhurst stated that 'as Mr Mundella had not been unfavourably impressed by the letter, he would not ask Congress to reject the invitation to send representatives to attend an international congress to be held in Paris'.[30] But he advised caution. They welcomed, of course, only advice which assisted assimilation. Though for many years the advice of the Positivists had been acceptable, when this sprung from disillusionment with the established political system it was rejected. It marked the end of a relationship when, in 1881, Henry Crompton stated that 'The working classes must come sooner or later to see their position is not that of ragtag or bobtail to a party; to be silenced and satisfied by judicious legislative sops thrown to the Congress from time to time; or even by half a dozen workingmen Members of Parliament being cautiously and generously treated and listened to.'[31] The advice of the Positivists was no longer required.

The desire to be 'practical' was a part of the process of conforming. The case of the Parliamentary Committee for the introduction of workingmen into factory and mines inspection was based on the need to have 'practical' men in those positions. 'Practical' in this sense meant an acquaintance with the job through doing it. It also meant bringing to bear on issues a knowledge which would enable the machinery of operation to work more smoothly and in this sense it had a wide political significance. The TUC deputation of three which went to the 1883 International Trades Union Congress in Paris reported back to the Parliamentary Committee in such terms that the Committee felt 'there was too much talk on revolutionary principles, and too little on practical questions, for the Congress to be of service to the workers'.[32] Revolution, meaning a qualitative change in the system, was not seen at the Parliamentary Committee level as having any relevance for the solution of 'practical' questions of improving wages, working conditions and living standards in general.

The Congress and its Parliamentary Committee could remain insulated from the worsening condition of workers only so long as they were regarded as being of no consequence as means of improving that condition, and that, in turn, depended mainly upon three factors. First there was the extent to which the TUC was representative of the workers. It has been estimated that about 5 per cent of the occupied population was organized in 1888 and that this amounted to about 10 per cent of the adult male manual workers.[33] The majority

[30] Roberts, p. 113.   [31] Harrison, p. 335.   [32] Davis, p. 104.
[33] H. A. Clegg, Alan Fox and A. F. Thompson, *A History of British Trade Unions since 1889*, Oxford University Press, 1964, vol. i, *1889–1910*, 1–3.

of trade unionists were in the metals, engineering, shipbuilding, mining, cotton textiles, building and printing industries, and apart from those in the mining and iron industries, the bulk of them were craftsmen. Although a number of unions had been formed among semi-skilled and unskilled workers from the 1860s, few of them had survived the depression following 1874. Many workers in the 1880s were virtually untouched by trade unionism. It seems likely that most of those who were organized were in unions affiliated to Congress. The TUC, then, in 1886, with its 635,580 members, was a minority, craft-dominated body. It represented the 'aristocracy' of labour which was variably affected by the conditions of depression.

Secondly, the extent to which even the craft unions regarded the Congress as being useful depended on the existence of an acute common need. The persistence and pervasiveness of the depression was beginning to create the conditions for united action which earlier the Criminal Law Amendment Act and electoral reform had created. Few groups could insulate themselves from the economic crises. Frederick Engels described the developing situation in a letter to August Bebel, a prominent member of the German Labour movement, in January 1886:

> Six weeks ago symptoms of an improvement in trade were said here to be showing themselves. Now this has all faded away again, the distress is greater than ever and the lack of prospects, too, added to an unusually severe winter. This is now the eighth year of the pressure of overproduction on the markets and instead of getting better it is steadily getting worse. There is no longer any doubt that the situation has essentially changed from what it was formerly; ever since England has had important rivals on the world market the period of crises, in the sense known hitherto, has been closed. If the crises become chronic instead of acute and at the same time lose nothing in intensity, what will be the outcome? . . . However, two things are certain: we have entered a period incomparably more dangerous to the existence of the old society than the period of decennial crises; and secondly, when prosperity returns, England will be much less affected by it than formerly, when she alone skimmed the cream off the world market. The day this becomes clear here, the socialist movement here will begin seriously; not before.[34]

Lastly, the TUC could not remain divorced from the concrete reality of the working-class situation once it was seen as an instrument for revolutionary propaganda and for heightening class consciousness. This recognition waited on the emergence of working-class

[34] *On Britain*, a compilation of works by Frederick Engels and Karl Marx, pp. 518–19.

socialists which in turn was dependent upon the formal expression of a revolutionary ideology in which united trade union action was an indispensable element.

The three factors bore on the insulation of the Congress and Parliamentary Committee in the late 1880s and early 1890s. Trade unionism spread well beyond the skilled trades; the analysis of Engels was validated; and socialists crusaded into the trade union movement in general and the TUC in particular.

13

The reorganization of the Trades Union Congress, 1918–1927[1]

The Trade Union Movement is a term to describe the trade unions which are affiliated to the Trades Union Congress but it is also an ideological concept.[2] In this latter sense it concerns the relationship between trade unions and refers to a process by which working-class unity is achieved. The process has always been apparent in trade union history though only on occasions has it been prominent.

Trade unions emerged and grew in Britain as autonomous sectional organizations, with conflicting interests and powerful self-protective instincts. But they also had common aims which gave rise to a need for united action between trade unions, and common characteristics which facilitated its achievement. These factors increased in importance as trade unionists realized that the principle of united action, which was the basis of their strength in their separate narrow industrial fields, applied equally so in all the spheres of trade union interest. The realization was slow to take effect because greater unity between trade unions meant less freedom of action for them as separate entities. Many trade unionists were unwilling to forgo the intangible advantages of sectional autonomy for the material benefits of greater unity. Yet the ill-effects of uncoordinated action were always present. Trade unions were forever weakening themselves by engaging in bitter demarcation disputes. The problem of survival, more than anything else, brought about greater unity between trade unions. It came in two stages in a slow, sporadic manner. First, trade unions with kindred industrial interests united through amalgamations, mergers, special agreements or federations. Secondly, trade

[1] This chapter is based mainly on unpublished material from the files of the Trades Union Congress. I am most grateful to Sir Vincent Tewson for permission to use the material and to all those TUC officials who have so generously assisted me.

[2] Very few unions of any importance in Britain have remained consistently and deliberately out of the Trades Union Congress.

unions agreed to act together in matters of common interest through a central trades union organization. It is with a phase of the development of this central organization that we shall be mainly concerned here.

The Trades Union Congress did not have an executive committee until 1871 when, at its third meeting, it appointed a committee of five members to organize political agitation against the Trade Union Bill which had been introduced by the Liberal Government. This committee became the Parliamentary Committee of the Trades Union Congress.[3] The Congress was put on a permanent basis,[4] and met each subsequent year (except 1914, the year of the outbreak of war).

The Parliamentary Committee was enlarged in 1872 from five to ten members, inclusive of the secretary; then it increased its size in stages as the membership of the Trades Union Congress expanded, until in 1918 it had seventeen members and a secretary. The functions of the Committee were extended slowly. For a number of years after its formation the Parliamentary Committee considered that disputes between unions were beyond the proper scope of the Trades Union Congress and it played no part in industrial disputes. It confined its activities to lobbying and making deputations to Ministers and was concerned with legal questions, with establishing employers' liability, with removing exceptional legislation affecting workers and with electoral reform.[5] After the turn of the century the services of the Parliamentary Committee were used to effect settlements in interunion disputes arising out of various causes. But the Committee remained aloof from industrial disputes and concerned itself primarily with legislation.[6]

---

[3] The members of the committee were Alexander Macdonald (Miners' National Association), Lloyd Jones (Manchester Fustian Cutters), Joseph Leicester (Flint Glass Makers' Society); George Potter, chairman and George Howell, secretary.

[4] At the fourth TUC, in 1872, the Parliamentary Committee was charged with the job of preparing a code of standing orders for the government of future congresses. Such a code was accepted in 1873 and remained virtually unchanged for forty-seven years.

[5] S. and B. Webb, *History of Trade Unionism*, p. 360. Even the election of such revolutionary characters as John Burns, Ben Tillett and Will Thorne on to the Parliamentary Committee in the 1890s had no effect on its industrial activities.

[6] In August 1919 a deputation from the Parliamentary Committee met the Home Secretary, Edward Shortt, about the National Union of Police and Prison Officers. The Police Bill was about to be made law and the Home Secretary said that under it the Police Federation could not be affiliated to the TUC. 'Why not?' James Sexton asked, 'the Trades Union Congress is not a strike body.' Shortt replied: 'The object of affiliation is, to put it quite plainly, sympathetic strike.' Sexton denied this. 'That is not the function of the Trades Union Congress,' he stated, 'it is purely legislative' (*Police and Prison Officers' Magazine*, 24 September 1919).

Early administrative developments

The limited activities of the Parliamentary Committee were reflected in the administration of the Trades Union Congress. Until 1902 its administrative work was done entirely by a part-time secretary. Early that year Keir Hardie had complained about the inefficiency of the Trades Union Congress office.[7] This complaint, and the poor health of the secretary, Sam Woods,[8] prompted the Parliamentary Committee to appoint a clerical assistant to Woods on 15 October 1902.[9] At the same meeting of the Committee the secretary was instructed to buy a rotary duplicator, to type the minutes of each meeting, then circulate them to members of the Committee.

Exactly one year after his appointment the clerical assistant was dismissed. A vacancy was then advertised in the national press 'for a shorthand typist with experience of bookkeeping' at a salary of £150 per year. There were 1000 applications for the job, out of which a short-list of twelve was compiled; ten turned up for an interview, 'two of whom retired after the explanation given to them, that there was no prospect of promotion in this office'.[10] On 10 November 1903 W. J. Bolton was appointed as clerk.[11] In the following month the secretary was authorized to buy a typewriter, though the minutes of the Parliamentary Committee remained handwritten until 19 January 1905, and not until 18 October 1905 were they consistently typed.

Several changes in the office of the Trades Union Congress occurred in 1905. A subcommittee of two, called the Finance Committee, was appointed in January 'to go thoroughly into the question of the book-keeping of the office, etc.'. It reported on 15 February and recommended that 'a ledger with index and separate accounts, and a Receipt-book with duplicate receipts replace the system at present in the office'. Sam Woods was retiring from the secretaryship through ill-health and the Parliamentary Committee considered that the next encumbent should 'devote the whole of his time to his duties'. This

[7] Parliamentary Committee Minutes, 29 April 1902. The complaint concerned the distribution of circulars and information to Labour Members of Parliament.

[8] In January 1903 Woods was given leave of absence for one to three months because of ill-health.

[9] Minutes of the Parliamentary Committee, 15 October 1902. The assistant was given £156 per year and was required to work each weekday from 10 a.m. to 1 p.m., and 2 p.m. to 5 p.m., and from 10 a.m. to 12 noon on Saturdays.

[10] Parliamentary Committee Minutes, 10 November 1903. Women and men under twenty-four years of age were rejected.

[11] He stayed at the TUC until 1943; he was then the head of the International Department.

was submitted to the Trades Union Congress in September 1905 along with the recommendation that the secretary should be appointed 'without re-election'. Previously he had stood for re-election each year. The recommendations were referred back by the Congress whereupon the Congress Grouping Committee later in the week submitted three separate motions—that the secretary should devote his whole time to his work but could be an M.P.; that he should remain in office so long as his work and conduct gave satisfaction to the Parliamentary Committee and Congress; and that these two conditions should come into operation in 1906. With hardly any discussion the three motions were accepted. And with a majority of only 18,000 out of a total vote of 1,522,000, W. C. Steadman, of the Barge Builders and a member of the Committee since 1899, was elected to become the secretary of the Trades Union Congress. The following year he became the first full-time secretary of the Trades Union Congress.

The next stage in the development of the Congress administration resulted from the initiative of Harry Gosling, a member of the Parliamentary Committee.[12] In his presidential address to the Trades Union Congress in 1916, he said: 'We must not be satisfied until organized Labour is as important in its greater and more national aspects as any of the Departments of State, with its own block of offices and civil service, commodious and well-appointed.'[13] A number of delegates, including a young and loquacious Ernest Bevin, expressed their interest in the suggestion, but a debate on the matter was not permitted.[14] Before the Congress Gosling had read his speech to the Parliamentary Committee and so impressed them with his suggestion that they agreed to set up a sub-committee 'to investigate and report'.[15] As a result a Staff Development Committee was appointed on 27 September 1916; two weeks later it recommended that joint offices with the Labour Party be taken, that a joint scheme for a central Trade Union building be eventually drafted, that a joint periodical and joint literature be published, that independent statistical work be carried out, and that imperial and international relationships be developed.[16] In February 1917 it was agreed to defer carrying out all the recommendations until the question of joint

[12] General Secretary of the Amalgamated Society of Watermen, Lightermen and Bargemen. From 1922 he was the full-time president of the Transport and General Workers' Union.

[13] *TUC Report*, 1916, p. 62.

[14] No discussion on the presidential address is allowed at any TUC.

[15] Parliamentary Committee minutes, 29 August 1916.

[16] Parliamentary Committee minutes, 11 October 1916.

offices with the Labour Party was settled, but that in the meantime an assistant and an additional clerk should be appointed. And there the matter rested until after the Trades Union Congress had accepted the recommendations by general assent in September 1917. Even then the Parliamentary Committee continued to proceed casually. Fred Bramley was appointed as an assistant in the Congress office on 19 February 1918, just over a year after such an appointment had been recommended.[17] In July 1918 it was agreed to establish an international department, much to the disapproval of the General Federation of Trade Unions, whose province international trade unionism had been; no additional staff was taken on for the task. Arrangements were made to have Trades Union Congress and Labour Party offices in adjoining houses at Eccleston Square, and these were occupied before the end of 1918.

It was June 1919 before the Parliamentary Committee took any further steps. Then it approved a report of its Office Subcommittee which recommended that a general information and statistical department be formed, that a monthly journal be issued from July, that two shorthand writers and typists be obtained, that Bramley be appointed assistant secretary with responsibility for the research department, and that Bolton be made confidential secretary and be put in charge of foreign correspondence and translations.

The Parliamentary Committee was quite content to appoint subcommittees, receive reports, and make minor administrative changes. And trade unions were prepared to allow the Committee to act in this nonchalant manner. Indeed, whenever trade union leaders had been concerned about the relative ineffectiveness of trade union action they had attempted to form bodies distinct from the Trades Union Congress, as for instance when they formed the General Federation of Trade Unions in 1899.[18] Not until October 1919 was serious trade union attention directed towards the possibility of reorganizing the Trades Union Congress to provide trade unions with a central co-ordinating body to meet the needs of a rapidly expanding movement and a disruptive industrial situation.

[17] Bramley was an organizer for the National Amalgamated Furnishing Trades Association and a member of the Parliamentary Committee from 1916–1917.

[18] The idea of a federation of trade unions distinct from the TUC had been canvassed on many occasions before the GFTU was established on 24 January 1899. It materialized on this occasion mainly because of the severe defeat the engineers had suffered in 1897. Its objects were far-reaching but it never received the support its promoters hoped for. After the First World War it was shed of its functions and was regarded thereafter as an organization, an inadequate one at that, to finance trade unions during industrial disputes.

The Joint Board

Early attempts were made to coordinate the activities of the Trades Union Congress and the Labour Party.[19] A Joint Board, consisting of representatives of the Parliamentary Committee, the General Federation of Trade Unions and the Labour Representation Committee, was formally established on 29 November 1905. This culminated out of a number of meetings between the Parliamentary Committee and Labour Members of Parliament from around 1902 which were called to discuss the Taff Vale decision, a trade union Bill, and the problem of unemployment. On 30 April 1902 the secretary of the TUC had been instructed to arrange an annual meeting between the Parliamentary Committee and Labour M.P.s, because of Keir Hardie's complaint about the Congress office, mentioned above. Then began many *ad hoc* meetings. Sometimes only the Parliamentary Committee and the General Federation of Trade Unions met; at other times Labour Members of Parliament and/or the executive of the Labour Representative Committee were invited to attend. The formal arrangements between them resulted from a series of meetings about unemployment held between November 1904 and June 1905. At the conclusion of one held on 19 May 1905 to consider the Unemployment Bill which had been introduced into the House of Commons, it was resolved to set up a joint subcommittee to consider and draw up amendments to the Bill and to wait on responsible Government Ministers. The Joint Board was a continuation of this joint subcommittee.

The Joint Board started without either a constitution or defined functions. Its activities depended on the initiative of its members.[20] In November 1906 the Board was summoned by wire to consider whether it could assist in settling an industrial dispute on the Clyde. A deputation was despatched with plenary powers. The following January a deputation from a conference of General Labourers' unions

[19] The Co-operative Union had its own separate arrangements with the TUC. A joint committee of trade union and Co-operative representatives had been formed in 1893 to arbitrate upon disputes which may have arisen between Co-operative Societies and trade unions, though an informal arrangement to do this had operated for some years before. The joint committee, in an amended form, continued to meet in the period under review here. No formal arrangements for the joint determination of policy were made.

[20] Its first members were: D. C. Cummings, P. Curran, A. Henderson, MP, D. J. Shackleton, MP, J. K. Hardie, MP, Allen Gee, J. J. Stevenson, J. Ward, W. C. Steadman, J. R. MacDonald and I. H. Mitchell. Cummings (TUC) was elected chairman and Mitchell (GFTU), at the February 1906 meeting, was made responsible for summoning meetings of the Board.

met the Board to ask its help to prevent the establishment of new unions in their field. The Joint Board agreed to help, suggested that some of the existing labourers' unions should amalgamate, and offered to assist in promoting amalgamations. At this meeting the Board was called the 'Central Joint Labour Authority of the country'. A wide range of questions were discussed by the Board such as joint offices for the TUC and the Labour Party,[21] the establishment of a Labour newspaper, and the elimination of overlapping between the Labour Party Conference and the Trades Union Congress.[22] Trade unions went to the Board with complaints about other unions. Then, on 25 February 1908 the Labour Party raised the question of framing a constitution for the Joint Board. A draft constitution was circulated and accepted by the constituent bodies.

The Joint Board operated with relatively little interruption until 1914 and 1915, when two substantial complaints were made against it. The first complaint, made by the Miners' Federation, was that the presence of the General Federation of Trade Unions on the Board was unnecessary as trade unions were already represented by the Trades Union Congress. The second, made in April 1915, concerned its suitability to deal with inter-union disputes. A motion was carried by the Board which stated that its composition should remain unaltered, that its functions should be confined to consultative and advisory purposes 'and that new machinery be set up for the purpose of settling disputes, to be composed of Trade Union representatives only'. The objections to the Joint Board, however, were deep seated; indeed the Labour Party wanted it to be abolished altogether and to be replaced by monthly meetings of the Parliamentary Committee and the Labour Party Executive.[23] After this the Joint Board

[21] The Parliamentary Committee replied that they could see little advantage in having offices in one building though it would consider a scheme for one large central building devoted exclusively to Labour purposes (Parliamentary Committee Minutes, 18 April 1907).

[22] The Labour Party executive committee had proposed that certain items be deleted from the TUC agenda but the Parliamentary Committee declined to do it as none of the subjects was outside the scope of their usual work (Parliamentary Committee Minutes, 16 May 1907). A joint meeting of the two committees considered the question on 19 December 1907. J. R. MacDonald wanted the work of the two bodies to be strictly defined. Shackleton opposed the suggestion by stating: 'The Labour Party is naturally antagonistic to every Government: the Parliamentary Committee are in a somewhat different position, and are of the opinion that it would weaken the power of labour generally to give up their right to approach Ministers year by year with the different resolutions passed at Congress.'

[23] Minutes of Joint Meeting of Parliamentary Committee and Labour Party Executive, 16 October 1917.

ceased to count as a coordinating body, and by October 1919, it had gone by default.

Reorganization of the Trades Union Congress

The final impulse for a reorganized Trades Union Congress arose out of the experiences of the railway strike in 1919. The National Union of Railwaymen, which called the strike on 26 September 1919, was a member of the Triple Industrial Alliance.[24] This was the first occasion since the formation of the Alliance in 1915 that one of its constituent unions had engaged in national strike action. The railwaymen took unilateral action and did not even consult the other members of the Alliance, thus revealing its essential weakness which later events emphasized more clearly. The Triple Alliance was no more than an agreement to act in collusion and it could be broken as quickly and easily as any other voluntary agreement. It had no separate existence from the unions which comprised it, no organization, no central coordinating staff. Its obvious defects as a consolidating union force compelled those who were concerned about the matter to think of other ways of achieving their end.

The interests of the National Transport Workers' Federation were closely touched by the railway strike. Other transport workers had to decide whether they would handle diverted goods and whether they would extend the strike. So, with the consent of the railwaymen, the executive of the Federation summoned a conference of all unions likely to be involved in the dispute. They met on 1 October and elected a committee of eleven to mediate in the dispute, which it did with remarkably successful results.[25]

After its experience of the strike the mediation committee felt convinced of two things: that there should be a national policy relating to war wages and bonuses, and that the powers of the Parlia-

---

[24] In 1912 the Miners' Federation decided to enter into relations with other trade unions with a view to taking joint action for mutual assistance. It approached the National Union of Railwaymen and the Transport Workers' Federation and obtained their agreement at a conference in April 1914, to act in collusion. The upshot was the formation in 1915 of the Triple Industrial Alliance, a formidable potential industrial fighting force representing about 1,350,000 workers. The Alliance arose partly out of the deficiencies of the Trades Union Congress and partly out of the Miners' Federation's dislike of the General Federation of Trade Unions.

[25] The eleven members were: H. Gosling, R. Williams, J. R. Clynes, Arthur Henderson, J. Muir, E. Bevin, J. O'Grady, J. T. Brownlie, J. W. Bowen, T. E. Naylor and R. B. Walker. Later the number was increased to fourteen by the addition of Frank Hodges (Miners' Federation), C. W. Bowerman and G. H. Stuart-Bunning, secretary and president of the TUC.

mentary Committee should be increased to make it the central co-ordinating body of all future trade union activities. A deputation from the mediation committee made these points to the Parliamentary Committee and pressed for a Special Congress to examine them. The Parliamentary Committee accepted the proposals and set up a 'Trades Union Joint Action and War Wages Sub-Committee' with authority to consult with anyone else who they considered could help them.[26] It was instructed to 'discuss the proposal for the setting up of a central coordinating body for Trade Union activity in relation to Trade disputes'.[27]

The subcommittee was handicapped by lack of imagination and an inability to think beyond the confines of its most recent experiences. It examined the constitution of the Triple Alliance; concluded that it was defective because it had no full-time secretary and properly organized administrative department; and proposed that a department of the Parliamentary Committee without these defects should be established. Fortunately, early in its deliberations, it had the good sense to seek the advice of others. It asked for representatives to consult with it from the Railway Dispute Mediation Committee[28] and the National Provisional Joint Industrial Committee (Trade Union Side).[29] The subcommittee and these additional representatives formed the Trade Union Co-ordination Committee and met for the first time on 11 November 1919.

It was at this stage that the real job of reorganizing the Trades Union Congress was tackled. Hardly a week had passed before Ernest Bevin submitted a memorandum for the 'Suggested Reorganization of the Trades Union Congress'.[30] The document reflected an acute emphasis on the industrial solution of trade union problems. And although Bevin's ideas were not accepted in their entirety they formed the genesis of the final reorganization.

The Parliamentary Committee called a Special Congress for 9 and 10 December 1919, to discuss a number of topics and receive an interim report from the Co-ordination Committee.[31] The report

[26] Parliamentary Committee Minutes, 8 October 1919.

[27] Minutes of the first meeting of the subcommittee, 23 October 1919.

[28] These representatives were: E. Bevin, Frank Hodges, R. Williams, J. T. Brownlie and J. R. Clynes.

[29] This was a committee of the National Industrial Conference which the Government had summoned on 27 February 1919 to examine ways of securing industrial peace. It appointed A. Henderson, W. Bradshaw, W. F. Purdy, J. Hindle and G. D. H. Cole to meet the Parliamentary Committee subcommittee.

[30] It is dated 19 November 1919. A copy is reproduced in an appendix at the end of this chapter.

[31] The interim report had been accepted by the Parliamentary Committee on 24 November. Clearly the pace was quickening.

mentioned the need for closer unity between trade unions and stated that the body to fulfil it should be developed out of the existing organization of the Trades Union Congress. 'At present', it stated, 'the Standing Orders do not permit the Parliamentary Committee to undertake the work which is required. . . . We accordingly suggest that the whole functions and organization of the Parliamentary Committee demand revision, with a view to developing out of it a real co-ordinating body for the industrial side of the whole Trade Union Movement.' A motion was submitted that the Parliamentary Committee be instructed:

1. To substitute for the Parliamentary Committee a Trades Union Congress General Council, to be elected annually by Congress.
2. To prepare a scheme determining the composition and methods of election of the General Council.
3. To make arrangements for the development of administrative departments in the offices of the General Council, in the direction of securing the necessary officials, staff, and equipment to secure an efficient Trade Union centre.

The motion went on to propose the establishment of joint research, legal and publicity departments with the Labour Party and the Co-operative Movement.

The idea of a strong trade union centre was not acceptable to all the delegates. Frank Hodges (Miners' Federation) and John Bromley (Associated Society of Locomotive Engineers and Firemen) moved the reference back of the report and, though defeated by just over a million votes, secured almost 2 million votes to support them. The interim report was then accepted and the Co-ordination Committee was left to get on with the job of working out the details of the reorganization in time for the next Trades Union Congress.

Grouping schemes

Alternative grouping schemes for the election of the General Council were prepared for the Co-ordination Committee by G. D. H. Cole.[32] Both were drawn up on the assumption that the nominations for the seats allocated to a group could only come from unions in that group, but that the election would be by the whole Congress. In one

[32] Cole was a co-opted member of the Co-ordination Committee because of his position as the secretary of the trade union side of the joint committee set up by the National Industrial Conference. He did part-time work for the Labour Party and was associated with the Labour Research Department.

scheme Cole reduced the number of groups to the minimum consistent with some sort of community of interest and point of view within each group. There were eleven groups in this scheme with provision for a Council of twenty-one or twenty-four seats. The second scheme divided the unions into seventeen groups with seats allocated for a Council of twenty-two or thirty. Cole advised a periodical reorganization of the allocation of seats to suit the changed membership of unions. The second scheme for a Council of thirty was accepted by the Parliamentary Committee without amendment and was submitted, with other recommendations, to the TUC in September 1920.

The other recommendations were that a subcommittee system should be established to improve the efficiency of the General Council, and that the standing orders of the TUC should be amended to extend the powers of the General Council. The Parliamentary Committee report on Trade Union Co-ordination was moved at the 1920 Congress by Harry Gosling, the persistent advocate of efficient trade unionism, and debated by a few prominent trade union leaders. To allay the apprehension of some of the delegates at the Congress that the proposals might interfere with the freedom or autonomy of individual unions the Parliamentary Committee agreed to begin the motion to amend the standing orders with the words: 'Subject to the necessary safeguards to secure the complete autonomy of the unions and federations affiliated to Congress, the Standing Orders of Congress be amended as follows. . . .'[33] The main criticism of the proposals came from J. R. Clynes,[34] who considered that all they did was to increase the size of the Parliamentary Committee from sixteen to thirty members and stipulate a form of representation which would not allow the best men available to be elected on to the Committee. Clynes wanted a remodelled central trade union authority which encompassed the Labour Party. An amendment from the National Federation of Women Workers that women should be represented on the General Council, was accepted by the Parliamentary Committee and Congress. Then the whole scheme was endorsed by 4,858,000 votes to 1,767,000.

To provide the representation for women a women's group was formed and the size of the General Council was increased from thirty to thirty-two members. The seats, apart from the two for women, were then allocated among the groups as far as possible according to membership. They were finally allocated as follows:

[33] *TUC Report*, 1920, p. 316.
[34] President, National Union of General Workers.

Name of Group	Membership	No. of seats
Shipbuilding	146,314	1
Printing and Paper	184,482	1
Textiles (other than cotton)	175,400	1
Clothing	176,854	1
Leather	125,330	1
Food,etc.	189,008	1
Agriculture	138,000	1
Public employees	119,958	1
Non-manual	124,300	1
Iron and steel	247,327	1
Cotton	392,060	2
Mining and quarrying	983,415	4
Railways	625,000	3
Transport (other than railways)	465,663	2
Engineering	603,057	3
Building	428,280	2
General labourers	1,381,034	4
Women		2

The allocation into groups and particularly the manner of distributing the seats were bound to be the subject of criticism by some unions. The Parliamentary Committee gave unions until 1 February 1921 to appeal against the operation of the scheme. Thirteen unions were switched to other groups after appealing against their allocation, but more fundamental objections made by a few unions, including those affiliated to the National Federation of General Workers, were rejected.[35] There was an inherent difficulty in allocating the general workers' unions to a single group which could only be overcome if those unions agreed to be treated as single trade organizations for the purpose of allocation. All objections were removed by the time the TUC met in September 1921. There the unions submitted nominations for the General Council seats allocated to their respective groups, the whole Congress voted on the nominations and elected the first General Council.

To some extent the criticisms which Clynes made against the Co-ordination Scheme were justified. Much the same faces were seen on the new General Council as on the Parliamentary Committee. The new method of representation made the General Council representative of industries, but it drew very few men of marked ability into its

[35] As well as wanting a say in the affairs of all the groups where they had large memberships the general workers' unions wanted to double their representation on the General Council.

ranks.[36] The new standing orders widened the field within which the General Council could operate, but they gave it no real power to lead in industrial disputes or intervene in interunion disputes.[37] Indeed the standing orders had been devised to avoid giving offence to the affiliated unions. Yet the election of the General Council made a break with the past. It marked the beginning of a fresh and definite phase in the history of the Trades Union Congress.

Trade unions after the First World War were restive; conscious of their new strength through increased numbers and their vital wartime role, and impatient with political action, they felt that they controlled their own destiny and that it lay in industrial action. 1920, the year during which the Co-ordination Scheme was drawn up and accepted, was a year of belligerent gestures from the unions constituting the Triple Alliance. It was a year during which trade unions threatened a General Strike and formed a Council of Action to compel the Government to change its mind about military interference in the Russian–Polish war. So near in time to war it was not unnatural that trade unionists should use the terminology of war in relation to their own activities. Some of them wanted a 'General Staff of Labour' to coordinate their belligerency. The new General Council had all the appearance of being such a body; and when emotions are roused it is often appearance which matters.

In so far as the role of the General Council as a 'general staff' had any material significance it was dependent on the whims of its affiliated unions; it could plan but it could not direct, or lead on its own initiative; it had no identity which was distinct and separate from those unions. It was possible for this role to disappear by default, or for it to vary considerably in its significance. Had the Trades Union

[36] Ernest Bevin did not go on the General Council until 1925 but this could have been from choice.

[37] The Parliamentary Committee was appointed to watch over legislation which concerned affiliated trade unions, and was largely restricted to this function. The General Council was an industrial body. Its duties were as follows: '(a) The General Council shall keep a watch on all industrial movements, and shall attempt, where possible, to co-ordinate Industrial Action. (b) It shall promote common action by the Trade Union Movement on general questions: such as wages and hours of labour and any matter of general concern that may arise between Trade Unions and employers or between the Trade Union Movement and the Government, and shall have power to assist any Union which is attacked on any vital question of Trade Union principle. (c) Where disputes arise, or threaten to arise, between Trade Unions, it shall use its influence to promote a settlement. (d) It shall assist Trade Unions in the work of organization and shall carry on propaganda with a view to strengthening the Industrial side of the Movement, and shall co-operate with other Trade Union bodies for the attainment of any or all of the above objects. (e) It shall also enter into relations with the Trade Union Labour Movements in other countries with a view to promoting common action and international solidarity.'

Congress been confined to this one function it is doubtful whether it would have survived when the clamour for aggressive industrial action on a large scale had passed.

The formation of an administration

It was the aim of those most intimately concerned with the reorganization of the Trades Union Congress to make it administratively efficient so that it could provide affiliated unions with services they could not give themselves. Harry Gosling had advocated this early in his campaign for improvements and he was supported by the other members of the Co-ordination Committee. But it became the appointed task of Fred Bramley to realize the aim. Bramley did not possess a detailed knowledge of administrative methods; given the state of the TUC at that time such a knowledge would have been of little use anyway. He pressed for simple but fundamental innovations which were necessary to form the foundation upon which a large and stable organization could subsequently be built. From his appointment to the Congress staff in 1918 until 1923 Bramley was first an office assistant, then assistant secretary and then secretary of the Co-ordination Committee. During much of that time C. W. Bowerman, the general secretary of the TUC, was little more than the titular head. In 1923 Bowerman retired and Bramley took his place as general secretary.[38] W. M. Citrine of the Electrical Trades Union became the assistant secretary and brought to the TUC the qualities which were to be increasingly needed. He had a meticulous concern for detail, order and method. Citrine's interventions ensured that the administration expanded along the correct lines. In 1925 Bramley's leadership was prematurely ended by illness, then death, and Citrine became the acting general secretary until September 1926 when he was elected unopposed to the vacant post.[39] By then the conception of the Trades Union Congress General Council as the 'general staff' of Labour had been dissipated. But it had a stable administrative machine capable of expansion without any serious changes in its structure.

From 1919 the administration of the TUC was based on the

[38] Bowerman had been general secretary since 1911. There were six candidates for the vacant general secretaryship: J. Doonan (Miners' Federation), H. H. Elvin (Clerks and Administrative Workers' Union), W. H. Hutchinson (AEU), Robert Williams (T and GWU), M. F. Titterington (Stuff and Woollen Warehousemen's Society), and Bramley. The voting took place at the TUC in September 1923, on the single transferable vote system. 4,319,000 votes were returned. The quota required was 2,160,000 and on the fifth count Bramley got 2,811,000 votes and was elected.
[39] Fred Bramley died on 10 October 1925, aged fifty-one years.

development of the committee system[40] and the employment of specialist trade union officials to serve the committees.[41] The specialization led to the creation of departments within the administration. Three types of committee were developed: there was a systematic establishment of six standing committees, each representing given industrial interests; there was a continuation and an expansion of committees with a functional basis; and there were committees set up jointly with the Labour Party.

The Co-ordination Committee suggested in a report to the Parliamentary Committee in June 1920 that the members of the General Council should be divided into five industrial groups and that each group should be represented by a subcommittee and be served by a specialist full-time official. It wanted each sub-committee to accumulate a special knowledge of industries it represented and to establish working relationships with any related federations or other outside trade union bodies. 'Ultimately,' the Report stated, 'it will be necessary for each Sub-Committee to develop special departments in the offices of the General Council.'[42]

The manner in which the industries were grouped indicated that the Co-ordination Committee envisaged the subcommittees and their departments as readymade organizations to take charge of industrial disputes. Group A, for instance, consisted of Mining, Railways and Transport, identical to the composition of the Triple Industrial Alliance.[43] At the first meeting of the Group A subcommittee on

[40] At the 1920 TUC Bevin had justified the increase in the size of the General Council over the Parliamentary Committee by stating that without the extra numbers the General Council could not develop a committee system.

[41] Mention should be made here of a minor, but unsuccessful, attempt by the Co-ordination Committee to ease the burden of work on the General Council and its officials. Quite late in the development of the Co-ordination Scheme, on 27 April 1921, a small subcommittee of the Co-ordination Committee, consisting of E. L. Poulton, Harry Gosling and Fred Bramley, recommended the appointment of a full-time chairman for the General Council. They gave a number of justifiable reasons for their recommendation, all related to the volume of work and responsibilities of the job. They assumed that after the election of the General Council these factors would increase in significance. The subcommittee enumerated details about the proposed post including the one that there should still be a separate and part-time president of the Trades Union Congress. The Co-ordination Committee and the Parliamentary Committee agreed with the proposal and it appeared on the agenda of the 1921 Trades Union Congress. A number of prominent delegates at the Congress, however, disapproved of the idea and sensing that they might be defeated if the issue were put to the vote, the Parliamentary Committee withdrew the motion. The proposal was dropped altogether.

[42] Report to Parliamentary Committee, 10 June 1920.

[43] The other Groups were: Group B—shipbuilding, engineering, iron and steel, building; Group C—cotton, other textiles, clothing, leather; Group D—glass, pottery, distribution, agriculture, general workers; Group E—printing, public employees, non-manual workers. A women's group was added after the 1920 TUC.

5 October 1921 the question of taking over the functions of the Triple Industrial Alliance was discussed but no formal arrangement was made as the Alliance shortly became defunct.[44] Later, in December 1924, the functions of the Group subcommittees were defined more explicitly. 'Broadly', a report stated, '. . . all important matters affecting Unions in a given Group should be dealt with by that Group in the first instance, and recommendations should be made on the various subjects for submission to the General Council.'[45] The report singled out trade disputes as one of the matters to be dealt with in this way.

The suggestion of creating industrial subcommittees was accepted by the Parliamentary Committee and endorsed by the TUC in 1920. The cost of establishing and operating the subcommittees was detailed in a memorandum by Fred Bramley, the assistant secretary. The 1920 Trades Union Congress had agreed to increase the affiliation fee from 30 shillings for every 1000 members, or part thereof, to one penny per member. The estimated income in 1921 under the new rate was £27,000. Of this, it was estimated that £10,000 would be spent on the subcommittees and their administrative development. Six secretaries were to be employed at salaries of £500 per annum, and they were to have twelve typists. Arrangements were made to consult with trade unions and federations about their appointment. After the first General Council was elected in 1921 the subcommittees were set up and the first appointment was made on 30 September 1921 when A. S. Firth was 'temporarily engaged as Secretary of the Five Groups—'.[46] The Co-ordination Committee then decided to make no further appointments until they had seen how the work of the committees developed.[47]

The policy of caution which was adopted in implementing the Co-ordination Committee's recommendation in part neutralized it, and prevented a subsequent expansion of the work of the subcommittees. No further specialist appointments were made to assist the subcommittees, and Firth remained as secretary of the five groups until 1927, when he was appointed as the assistant general secretary.

[44] When the question was raised there was talk in the press that the Alliance was winding up.

[45] *Final Report* of the Functions Committee of the General Council, 15 December 1924.

[46] Minutes of the Co-ordination Committee, 30 September 1921. Firth had been employed to assist Arthur Greenwood on a Cost of Living Inquiry but in January 1921 he had been given the temporary job of helping to prepare for the election of the General Council.

[47] A separate secretary was appointed to serve the group formed for women trade unionists.

The essential secretarial work of the subcommittees was done, but there were no persons to develop their work, in a sense to create work for them. Consequently they depended for their existence solely upon the interest which the member unions took in them. Their work varied considerably over time and in form and was never sufficiently important to warrant an increase in staff to serve them. There was thus a circular relationship between the employment of specialist officials and the development of the subcommittee system. In 1924 when a memorandum on the work of the subcommittees was compiled it was found that many trade unions had either neglected the subcommittees altogether or had just not bothered to submit any questions to them. Group A dealt primarily with mining subjects; it did not replace the Triple Industrial Alliance for when the miners wanted to consolidate trade union forces in 1925 they formed a separate Industrial Alliance. Group B was the most active and examined such matters as excessive overtime, juvenile education, apprenticeships and factory legislation. The other groups did comparatively little work.[48]

The second type of committee consisted of those which were set up for special purposes. The Parliamentary Committee had for many years elected committees to examine problems such as the management of the TUC office, but such committees usually lapsed, either on the completion of their allotted tasks or by default. The committees on interunion disputes were a permanent feature of Parliamentary Committee activities, due to the recurring nature of the problem, but they changed in personnel from one dispute to another and were in no sense a part of an administrative expansion.

The development of functional committees was not a specified part of the Co-ordination Scheme, though it figured in Bevin's memorandum. It arose largely out of the impetus towards administrative efficiency which the Co-ordination Committee created. It enabled work to be done in specialized fields which the General Council was not competent to do itself. The development involved the continuation on a regular basis of committees already in existence and the creation of a large number of new committees. It became less of an *ad hoc* affair and was orientated towards functions which closely and permanently affected the interests of the TUC. The series of subcommittees on interunion disputes was replaced in November 1919 by a Disputes Committee of three. Later a panel of seven members

[48] The women's Group was not assessed. This Group was always treated separately from the others. Since the early 1930s, the subcommittees have hardly ever met though they have continued to be elected each year up till the present.

was established from which three persons were chosen for each hearing. Citrine stated that by 1925 the work on interunion disputes alone was sufficient to keep one administrative official regularly employed.[49] The Office Committee which was elected intermittently until 1919 lost its function late in 1919 to the Co-ordination Committee, but it was re-established on 1 February 1922 to discuss staff problems. By the end of 1922 it also dealt with finance and was called the Office and Finance Committee. It became the Finance and General Purposes Committee in 1926 and was to be the most important subcommittee of the General Council.

There was a gradual increase in the number of new committees so that in 1924 there were seven subcommittees of the General Council, excluding the Group committees, and nine joint committees with bodies other than the Labour Party. Some of these resulted from a better organization of the work of the General Council, others from an extension of its functions. The administrative difficulties concerning office methods and staff which the growth of these committees created preoccupied Bramley and Citrine and prompted the General Council in September 1924 to set up a committee to investigate committees. The new committee was designated the Functions Committee and its terms of reference were 'to enquire into the whole question of Committees, having regard to their functions, personnel and appropriate work in the light of past experience and bearing in mind the new duties conferred by Congress'. Before it was dissolved in October 1926 this committee left a permanent mark on the administration of the TUC.[50]

As new committees were formed they were entrusted to the care of one of the full-time officials so that by 1925 there had developed personal and not functional departments within the office of the TUC. There was one exception to this development which should be described first. After the war some trade unions were disturbed about the operation of the second Trade Boards Act, 1918, and they wanted a means of meeting together and discussing common problems. The general secretary of the National Union of Boot and Shoe Operatives urged the Parliamentary Committee to take up the question of establishing a central authority to deal with trade boards and not to leave the matter to an unofficial body.[51] This the Parliamentary Committee

[49] Report to General Council on Office Organization, May 1925.
[50] At its most influential stage it had Ernest Bevin, Walter Citrine and Arthur Pugh amongst its five members. Its activities ranged well beyond its terms of reference.
[51] In a letter read to the London members of the Parliamentary Committee, 4 November 1920.

did. It convened two conferences of affiliated unions interested in trade boards and out of them, in 1921, were established a Trade Boards Advisory Council consisting of representatives of these unions and the Parliamentary Committee, and a Trade Boards Department under the direction of the TUC to give effect to the decisions of the Advisory Council. J. J. Mallon became the honorary secretary of the Advisory Council and part-time secretary of the department; he had a full-time assistant, J. V. C. Wray, who looked after the administrative work of the department.

The committee work was allocated to the full-time officials by the general secretary. Some of it he kept for himself and the assistant general secretary, and each of them had what was called a department, though obviously this was a loose term because they were both concerned with the work of the whole office. In his first memorandum on office organization, written when Bramley was ill, Citrine said that the time required for attention to committees was so great that there was little opportunity to do ordinary administrative work. He stated that the secretary dealt with twelve committees in addition to such specific duties as questions of general policy, general correspondence, preparation for General Council meetings, minutes of meetings, Congress reports, memoranda and deputations to Ministers. The group secretary, A. S. Firth, also had a department: a mixture of unrelated tasks. In addition to his group work, he looked after six committees, one of which, the Committee for the Co-ordination of Trade Union Effort, had such wideranging functions as the promotion of amalgamation between unions, closer contact between trades councils and federations of unions, and propaganda and educational activity necessary for closer unity.[52] There was no logic in the distribution of committee work. Of the remaining full-time officials, Wray had a number of committees added to his Trade Board work and W. J. Bolton was in charge of the Finance Department and the International Department. The Women's Department in 1925 had no secretary and was relatively inactive. Citrine was diffident about making clearcut recommendations for he was acting for Bramley and he did not know in detail what Bramley's plans were. He did suggest, however, that a department should be established to deal with the organization of trade unions and related matters. This suggestion was accepted. An Organization Department was formed in June 1925 and H. V. Tewson became its secretary. A Stationery and Directory Department

[52] This particular committee had been established on 1 March 1922 at the instigation of Group B subcommittee to organize resistance and to combat attempts to reduce wages in any trade or to lengthen the working week.

was also established to deal with the post, to address envelopes, to keep addressograph records and to maintain stocks of stationery.

As soon as Citrine became the acting general secretary he made his presence in the office felt. Members of the staff were given detailed instructions relating to committee procedure, correspondence and administration in general. A division of labour was effected among the clerical staff as clerks within departments were detailed to specialize in the work of particular committees. The secretary's and assistant secretary's departments were merged into one and the group secretary's department disappeared through a reallocation of committee work. But there still remained a lack of uniformity between departments. Not all of them were clearly based on functions so that there was some overlapping and conflicting of interests.[53] Uniformity, however, was intended and all new departments were to be based on functions. The administration was rationalized as far as the resources of the TUC permitted at that time.

The third type of committee consisted of those which were set up jointly with the Labour Party. Ever since the Labour Party had been formed there had been discussions of one kind or another about having closer working arrangements with the Trades Union Congress, but nothing had materialized.[54] Then in 1919 the Co-ordination Committee recommended the establishment of research, publicity and legal departments under joint control. This recommendation, because it involved two separate organizations, was the subject of more memoranda, put under greater scrutiny and implemented after more delicate negotiations than any of the other recommendations made by the Co-ordination Committee.

The discussions took a long time to get under way. Although Labour Party officials were members of the Co-ordination Committee the Labour Party was not officially represented on it. Representatives of the Labour Party and the Co-operative Union were invited to a meeting on 20 May 1920, but the meeting closed without discussion as only one Parliamentary Committee member was present.[55] All the signs were that the pace would be slow. No recommendations about joint departments were included in the Co-ordination Committee report which was accepted by the Trades Union Congress in September 1920.

[53] The Organization Department, for example, dealt with the organization of all kinds of persons, including women workers, while the Women's Department dealt with women as a class.

[54] See above pp. 162–3.

[55] Representatives of the Co-operative Union played no part in the subsequent discussions.

The first detailed plan for coordination between the Labour Party and the TUC came from the Labour Party, early in November 1920. It contained the Labour Party's conception only and was received with some annoyance by Bramley because he thought it should have come from the joint subcommittee. The memorandum contained positive proposals for discussion. This was a step forward, but the pace remained leisurely. The memorandum was not discussed until 25 May 1921. Then Arthur Henderson, the secretary of the Labour Party, said that since the discussions had begun the Labour Party had agreed on coordination on a larger scale than hitherto.[56]

The memorandum was based on the premise that there should be the maximum cooperation between trade unions and the Labour Party to devise a common policy and effect joint action. The Labour Party wanted to prevent overlapping—it expressed concern at the tendency of the Parliamentary Committee to formulate unilateral policy on political matters—and it wanted to provide joint services. It proposed, therefore, that there should be a National Joint Council of Labour consisting of representatives of the Labour Party, the Parliamentary Labour Party and the Parliamentary Committee. The functions of the National Joint Council would be:

1. to consider, at the request of any of the three groups on the Committee, questions affecting the Labour Movement as a whole;
2. to control the joint department of research, information and publicity. . . .

It proposed also that there should be one department to conduct the research, information and publicity work of both the Labour Party and the Parliamentary Committee and that the Labour Research Department, an independent research body, should be merged into the new department. Under the Labour Party plan the National Joint Council was to control all existing departments and services which were of common utility to the Labour Party and the Trades Union Congress.

Another subcommittee was appointed at the meeting on 25 May to examine the scheme. Six days later it successfully presented its own draft of a scheme to a Joint Co-ordination Committee meeting. The fresh draft differed from the Labour Party one in an important respect. The idea of having a National Joint Council to speak and act for the Labour Movement as a whole was accepted, but its powers were circumscribed. It was given no control whatever over the pro-

[56] Minutes of Joint Co-ordination Committee, 25 May 1921.

posed joint departments; it was simply intended to operate as a joint committee in general, national labour matters. The proposal for one joint department was rejected; instead separate departments were to be established for research, publicity, legal advice, and international affairs, with provision for the formation of other departments if necessary. Each joint department was to be governed by its own joint sub-committee of the General Council and Executive Committee of the Labour Party, though what was termed 'the general control of the work of the Joint Departments' was to be the responsibility of the chairmen and secretaries of the two national bodies.[57] A full-time official was to be placed in charge of each department. It was to be the duty of each department to undertake '(a) the work required of it by the General Council of the Trades Union Congress and the Executive Committee of the Labour Party, both individually and jointly; (b) such work as may be necessary for the National Joint Council; and (c) special work for affiliated organizations'.

All the pressure to get a scheme formulated and implemented seemed to come from Arthur Henderson. He pressed the Parliamentary Committee to name a date to discuss his own scheme; then shortly after the revised scheme had been endorsed by the Co-ordination Committee he got the approval of the Labour Party Conference for it; and on 12 July 1921 he circulated another memorandum to the members of the Parliamentary Committee, called 'Co-ordination— Next Step', in which he suggested questions for the consideration of the National Joint Council, proposed arrangements for the composition of the joint departmental committees and the staffing of the joint departments, and named the Labour Party nominees for the National Joint Council and each of the joint committees. This was too much for Bramley. At the top of his copy of the memorandum was added the note: 'No attempt to submit same to joint committee. They just make plans and ask us for endorsement.' The Parliamentary Committee had endorsed the revised scheme on 15 June but they were unable to implement it until it had been accepted by the TUC in September. In October the new General Council submitted their nominees for the National Joint Council and the joint committees,[58] but continued to discuss details of the scheme until 4 January 1922, when it was jointly and finally ratified.

Once the joint committees were manned steps were quickly taken

[57] The ultimate control lay in the hands of the full national committees of the two bodies.

[58] The first members of the National Joint Council were: Arthur Pugh, Robert Smillie and Harry Gosling for the General Council, and C. T. Cramp, J. R. MacDonald and Sidney Webb for the Labour Party.

to shape the departments. The Labour Party already had staff employed on research, publicity and international matters and these men were transferred to work for the joint departments. As neither the Trades Union Congress nor the Labour Party had anyone employed on legal matters, the formation of a Legal Department was a completely new venture. This induced the National Joint Council to recommend that it be postponed until the other departments were firmly established.[59] The joint committee for the Legal Department was not summoned and the Department was never formed. The Research, Press and Publicity, and International Departments functioned from 1 January 1922. The Labour Party library also came under joint control.[60]

The three joint departments expanded as their functions increased and this in turn resulted from the drive of their full-time heads.[61] The correlation between the appointment of specialist officials, the success of committees and the formation of departments, which was shown in the case of other TUC committees, was amply demonstrated by the joint committees. In the one case where no official was appointed to take charge of a committee, namely the legal committee, it became defunct without even having met. At their inception the joint departments employed five administrators and ten clerical workers; in 1925 they employed nine administrators and seventeen clerical workers. Their staff in 1925 was greater by five than the whole administrative staff of the TUC.

TUC officials were not satisfied with the joint departments. Their lack of enthusiasm for them was apparent in the early stages of negotiation and they seemed to be willing to carry on only in deference to Congress decisions on the matter. When the reorganization of Congress had taken effect and an expansion of the General Council's own administration was taking place, Bramley resented having to share the control of the joint departments with the Labour Party. He had other objections too which he outlined in a brief memorandum, undated but obviously written sometime during the first five months of 1925 when a case for withdrawing from the joint departments was being prepared.

The case, elaborate and detailed, was drawn up by Citrine on the basis of the points Bramley had made, and issued to the General Council on 14 May 1925 as a Report on Joint Departments. Firstly,

---

[59] Minutes of the first National Joint Council, 18 November 1921.

[60] This was a part of the Research Department.

[61] These were: research, Arthur Greenwood; press and publicity, W. W. Henderson; international, W. Gillies.

the report stated that the specifically trade union services provided by the joint departments were excessively costly; that the General Council was consuming the whole of its income and could neither fulfil its functions efficiently nor extend them.[62] Secondly, that dual control prevented an effective supervision of the work of the departments and that it had not been possible to exercise discipline over the staff. The heads of the departments had hardly ever consulted with Bramley. Thirdly, some friction had resulted between the General Council and the Labour Party over the right of heads of departments to continue in their posts after they had become Members of Parliament. The General Council was opposed to them holding two posts. Fourthly, it was argued that the operation of the departments had been made more difficult by the anomalies in the salaries paid to the joint department officials and the General Council staff, which favoured the former.[63] Lastly, the officials of the TUC, believing firmly in the effectiveness of trade union action, wanted the Congress distinguished from the Labour Party, strengthened and widened by its own services for research, publicity and administration. 'We need have no quarrel with the Labour Party', Bramley wrote, 'but we must recognize our separate spheres of work.' He stated that the experience

of the Labour Government when in office made it quite clear that the policy of the TUC General Council could not permanently remain in the present association with that of the Labour Party. . . . The Labour Party cannot have it both ways. If when in office we are to be detached from the Labour Movement, we cannot be treated as an integral part of that movement when Labour is out of office. During the period the Labour Government was in office we were not taken into consultation at all by the Prime Minister.[64]

Bramley said that he did not have five minutes' conversation with MacDonald during his premiership.

The case for withdrawing from the joint departments was accepted by the General Council and, after discussions with representatives of the Labour Party, fresh arrangements were made to operate from the end of March 1926. The three joint departments ceased to function as

[62] In 1924 the General Council had an income of about £18,500 to cover all its expenses; the grant given by the TUC to the three joint departments for the period 1 April 1924–31 March 1925 was £6500.

[63] In 1924–25 each head of department received £575 a year, whereas Citrine, the assistant general secretary of the TUC, received only £475 a year. The salaries of others displayed anomalies too.

[64] Undated memorandum. Bramley claimed that the Home Secretary (Arthur Henderson) in the first Labour Government treated the TUC like an association of employers.

such. The International Department reverted to Labour Party control; the staff of the other two departments was shared between the TUC and the Labour Party, and the TUC set up its own research and press and publicity departments. The joint committees for the departments were abolished. Only the library and the telephone operator remained under joint control. The TUC thus went a stage further in its process of unilateral development. The principal constitutional link between the TUC and the Labour Party was the ineffectual National Joint Council. The physical contact between the two, however, became closer after 1926.

Joint premises

The conception of a large central Labour Headquarters which had been discussed periodically since 1907 by the Parliamentary Committee became more of an administrative necessity and less an attempt to act on a grand scale for its own sake, once the reorganization of the TUC had been achieved and the joint departments with the Labour Party formed. The nearest the TUC and the Labour Party came to fulfilling the conception, until 1927, was by occupying adjoining offices in Eccleston Square, though this was not for the lack of ideas or trying.

A scheme for a National Labour Memorial of Freedom and Peace was launched in January 1918 as a war memorial, but it failed for lack of funds. By 1921 only £15,808 had been subscribed to the Memorial Fund so it was wound up.[65] Late in December 1920 the London Labour Party, the London Trades Council and the London Co-operative Society laid plans to build common headquarters in London. These were expanded later to incorporate the plans of the National Labour Memorial of Freedom and Peace. This larger scheme was to consist of trading premises and offices for the London Co-operative Society and a café; offices for the Parliamentary Committee of the Trades Union Congress and for the Labour Party; suites of offices for trade unions, trade union federations, the London Trades Council and the London Labour Party; large and small meeting rooms; and, eventually, hotel accommodation. The London Co-operative Society intended to finance the project by raising money in the form of investment. The trade slump, particularly its impact on trade union funds, caused this scheme to be dropped.

While discussions about separating the joint departments were

---

[65] £9000 of this had been given by the South Wales Miners' Federation, and another £3000 by other miners' organizations.

going on in 1925 the General Council decided to obtain more suitable offices for its own use, though it agreed to consult with the Labour Party and decide whether joint offices would be desirable. At this time the Transport and General Workers' Union was erecting its own headquarters in Smith Square, London, and Ernest Bevin suggested that the TUC and the Labour Party should either take over part of his union's offices, or build their own on an adjoining site. Bevin's offer of accommodation was accepted in December 1925. The conception of joint premises, though less grandiose than had been intended, was finally realized in 1927 when Transport House was occupied.

Summary and conclusion

The principal changes in the organization and administration of the Trades Union Congress occurred between 1918 and 1927 and constituted a distinct phase in trade union development. At the beginning of the period the TUC was strong in numbers, but weak in almost every other respect. It held no authority over its affiliated unions, either constitutional or moral; it was narrow and restricted in its activities; unable to give guidance, to coordinate or to provide material assistance where unions could not help themselves; and it was palpably inefficient in the use of its limited resources. At the end of the period the TUC was weaker numerically; it had engaged in an unsuccessful industrial dispute of major proportions, but it was strong in a new and lasting respect. Its constitutional authority had changed little. On the other hand its activities were as wide as its members cared to define them. By itself this factor was unimportant for if an organization is inefficient it matters little how wide its activities are. But the TUC was now consciously striving for efficiency and to get it all the known conditions were being applied. It had laid the foundations of an effective administration and had built the essential superstructure.

The reasons for the changes are clear. In the first place there emerged a few determined and ambitious trade union leaders whose skills were complementary. There was Harry Gosling whose fanciful idea about a trade union centre started the final movement towards reorganization. He displayed a dogged persistence in support of his idea. Ernest Bevin gave the idea a realizable form. Gosling and Bevin worked together closely in other matters during these years and it is not easy in fact to isolate their contributions. Bevin may have wielded more influence than appeared on the surface. These two had other jobs to do. The fulfilment of the idea had to be the task of a full-time official of the TUC. After Bevin and G. D. H. Cole had worked out a scheme it became the dedicated task of Fred Bramley to implement it. He wanted a strong and efficient Trades Union Congress for various reasons, prominent amongst which was the desire to lead it himself. Without the ego and drive of Bramley, Gosling's idea might have remained just an idea. Later in time and in demand were Citrine's qualities as an administrator.

A feature of the changes in the TUC was the role played by a few individuals in bringing them about. Yet, with all their complementary qualities, they would have been ineffectual had not the economic and social condition of the country obtruded the need for a strong Trades Union Congress, and created the climate of opinion to make it possible. The whole period was marked by industrial unrest, a belief in the effectiveness of industrial action and a desire to use it on a grand scale.

In the matter of reorganizing the Trades Union Congress, as indeed in all sociological problems, there were a number of inter-dependent factors of unequal weight yet each vital for the correct solution. As already mentioned, the trade union leaders who desired a reorganization acted at a propitious time. But unless they had used technically adequate methods the opportunity to reach a permanent solution might have been wasted. As it happened, the methods used were adequate. Their basic feature was that they contributed towards the division of labour in administration and therefore increased specialization.

The Parliamentary Committee was replaced by a larger General Council more representative of industrial interests. This ensured that the General Council could divide up into specialist subcommittees covering all the main industrial interests of the TUC. The General Council thus delegated the work of deliberating on specific matters to committees more suited in size and composition for deliberation. Its principal function was to receive reports and recommendations and to make decisions on the basis of them. The subcommittees could only deliberate effectively on the basis of information. Collecting and collating information about complex problems was not an easy task which a subcommittee consisting of busy trade union leaders could undertake. It was possible for a subcommittee to delegate such a task to one of its members, but it was unlikely that it would be performed effectively for a number of reasons. Subcommittee work was dependent on a supply of memoranda on the matters under discussion. The only sure way of getting them, certainly of getting fully documented ones, was to employ full-time officials for the task. That is, to extend the division of labour still further. On a limited scale this way was used. Full-time officials were allocated to serve subcommittees. The need for this specialization was reflected clearly in the results. Where an official had a manageable number of subcommittees to look after, the subcommittees flourished regardless of their subject; where an official was overburdened, as was the secretary of the Group Committees, some of the subcommittees functioned ineffectively or ceased to function altogether; where a subcommittee did not have the services of a full-time official at all, as with the joint legal committee, it was a committee in name only. The move towards efficient administration then necessarily involved an expansion of the specialist staff. As this occurred subcommittees were redistributed, reorganized or dissolved to enable the officials to perform related tasks. When this happened functional departments developed. The very existence of departments created an impetus towards expansion for in each department the same process of specialization tended to take place; moreover each head of a department had facilities for 'empire building', even though on a small scale, which were denied him in a simple uncomplicated monolithic organization.

By 1927 the TUC had the making of a trade union bureaucracy akin to the civil service. By comparative standards its scale was small, but it was sufficient to have an impact on the nature and effectiveness of trade union action. Within the limits of trade union traditions and practices, the decisions of the General Council came more and more to be based on information supplied by specialists. The ambit of administrative decision-making spread so that minor and routine decisions were made quickly, and often more effectively. From this stage the TUC was able to accumulate authority amongst trade unions which had no constitutional basis but which was derived from its knowledge and integrity. It thereby contributed more positively than ever before to the Trade Union Movement.

Appendix

London Nov: 19th 1919

SUGGESTED RE-ORGANIZATION OF THE TRADES UNION CONGRESS

by: [Ernest Bevin]

I hold the view that Congress should develop the Industrial side of the Movement as against the 'deputizing' or 'Political' conception, and to this end, I suggest:

1. THE ABOLITION OF THE PARLIAMENTARY COMMITTEE as such, and the SUBSTITUTION of a GENERAL COUNCIL which shall be representative of the various groups of Economic interests affiliated to Congress.
2. The GROUPS should be divided as follows:

(*a*) MINING.
(*b*) RAILWAYS.
(*c*) TRANSPORT—all forms other than Railways.
(*d*) METAL, CHEMICAL and allied PRODUCTION.
(*e*) ENGINEERING ETC: to include metal and woodwork manufacture such as Engineering, Shipbuilding, and all forms of manufacture by conjunction of Metal and Wood.
(*f*) BUILDING.
(*g*) DOMESTIC TRADES MANUFACTURING SECTION: such as, Clothing, boots, etc.
(*h*) DOMESTIC DISTRIBUTIVE.
(*i*) GENERAL WORKERS AND MISCELLANEOUS.

The CONSTITUTION of the COUNCIL should be two from each GROUP, making a Total Membership of 18 (EIGHTEEN). The qualification of a person to represent a group shall be that the body nominating shall have a PROVED MEMBERSHIP in the group, and they shall be subject to election by the whole Congress.
THE DUTIES OF THE COUNCIL should be:

1. To watch all Movements; to attempt where possible to co-ordinate Industrial Action when more than one Union, or one Body of persons in a Trade is affected.
2. To conduct enquiries where disputes exist between Unions or groups of Unions with the view to preventing internal struggles in the Movement.
3. To assist in the co-ordination of DEMANDS on general question, such as MINIMUM WAGES and HOURS OF LABOUR.
4. To carry on PROPAGANDA with the view of strengthening the Industrial side of the Movement.

I further suggest that the Council should, by means of sub-committees who should report to the Council, develop the following DEPARTMENTS:

(*a*) RESEARCH & INVESTIGATION; (which means incorporation of the work now carried on by the Fabian Research Department).
(*b*) TO WATCH THE POLICY of all Industrial Councils and to offer proposals to the various Unions to strengthen the workers' control over Industry.
(*c*) To CO-OPERATE with the CO-OPERATIVE MOVEMENT to devise the best means of Distributing FOOD, etc., during National Upheavals.
(*d*) To establish INTERNATIONAL DEPARTMENTS co-ordinating all the various International organisations.

(e) To establish a LEGAL DEPARTMENT which could be at the disposal of all the TRADES UNIONS dealing with Industrial Legislation.

(f) To establish a Committee for the purpose of assisting when any affiliated Union is attacked on a vital principle and needs the assistance of the rest of the Movement.

The COUNCIL should also have power to appoint ADVISORY COMMITTEES from the groups to advise the General Council which should be presided over and officered by Members of the GENERAL COUNCIL.

I would further suggest that a report of the work of each Sub-Committee or group, should be submitted to ANNUAL CONGRESS, in their order.

FINANCE: I suggest that the whole cost of this work should be met by a LEVY OF ONE PENNY PER MEMBER per annum, which would yield approximately £20,000 (twenty thousand pounds) per ANNUM.

I support that TWO members of the LABOUR PARTY EXECUTIVE COUNCIL shall sit upon the General Council and vice versa, but who shall have no vote, they to act as liaison officers between the two bodies in order to strengthen and co-ordinate the efforts of both.

14

The centenary of the British Trades Union Congress, 1868–1968

The occasion of the centenary of the British Trades Union Congress in 1968 draws attention to the unique position which the British body holds among central trade union organizations. In no other country has a central union organization survived for so long without either being displaced from its role as the prime national representative body for organized labour or experiencing permanent splits in its ranks. Of course, the length of the TUC's life can be explained in part by the fact that Britain was the first nation to industrialize and give rise to the necessary and sufficient conditions for trade unionism. The ability of the TUC to survive, however, cannot be explained by this fact. In most countries, except where central union organizations have not been protected and perpetuated by the use of state power, ideological divisions have produced two or three or even four competing bodies. In Britain there has rarely ever been the possibility that this might happen.

A discussion about the character of the British Trades Union Congress raises questions concerning the nature of the British environment and the relationship of trade unions to it. Trade unionism is a universal phenomenon arising out of particular structural conditions. It has no ethnic, national or religious boundaries. Indeed it transcends these factors provided the class situation is appropriate. But the factors which go to determine different cultures and variations within a common culture influence the form which trade unionism takes. It is then an examination of such factors which will explain the peculiarities of the British form.

It is also the case that various parts of a superstructure are causally related to each other. The characteristics of the Trades Union Congress are derived from those of the trade unions which comprise it. It is for this reason that it is meaningless to suggest, as many have done, that the British TUC should model itself on, say, a Scandinavian pattern, or that it should draw on the experiences of other central union organizations over the issue of control over wage negotiations. Institutional forms are not readily transferable as British trade unionists themselves discovered when they attempted to build unions in tropical Africa on the British pattern. Only the name was transferable; the forms it described were either adapted to indigenous conditions or disappeared as irrelevant.

Central trade union organizations have common elements. They all consist of differentials of power, of skills and of values which interrelate with each other but where they differ is in the distribution of these elements and their relationships with each other. Take the British TUC in the context of the British labour movement and juggle around with the distribution of power between unions by making interunion solidarity a necessity or by destroying the historically determined character of the movement as the German government did in the 1930s or as war has done in other countries, and a new type of central organization would result, perhaps resembling the Scandinavian or German models. Or, alternatively, alter the distribution of occupational skills by making non-manual work predominant in the place of semiskilled manual work so that unions of clerical and administrative workers determine the decisions of the TUC and a new attitude to organization would emerge. Or, again, change the skills of employers in the class conflict either by breaking down the size of industrial units or by intensifying the trend to monopoly capitalism and the nature and degree of interunion solidarity would also change. In other words, the form of a central union organization is determined by a particular set of historically evolved relationships between the elements of power and skill and values. Two central organizations, then, can only be similar if these relationships are precisely the same in two situations.

The existence of two or more central organizations in a common situation occurs as a result of a contradiction in the situation of organized labour. Any incompatibility between emerging forces and existing institutional forms will result in divisions between unions, but these need not necessarily be institutionalized. For example, the British TUC is becoming increasingly representative of white-collar workers who are under-represented in the controlling body and unable to influence policy in the direction of their interests. Whether or not white-collar workers feel the need for their own central organization will depend on the extent to which the TUC can satisfactorily make internal adjustments. The less flexible it is, the more will white-collar workers look elsewhere for representation. In the past, the TUC has been able to adapt itself to the needs of a changing occupational and industrial structure. Control by craft unions gave way under the pressure from organized unskilled and semiskilled workers; the significant influence of the cotton textile workers was superseded by that of the miners which in turn was replaced by that of the general unions. A classic case of a fracture-creating contradiction was in the United States in the 1930s, when the American Federation of Labor, dominated by craft unions, was confronted by the spread of mass production industries which employed mainly unskilled and semiskilled workers. The craft unions could maintain their domination only by refusing to organize mass production workers or by admitting them as second class members, but neither of these courses could be pursued successfully because these workers were being impelled to take collective action by forces over which the American Federation of Labor had no control. The American Federation of Labor's inability to cope with the spread of trade unionism resulted in the rise of the Congress of Industrial Organization in 1935. In so far as the British trade union movement has had a comparable experience, it was following the London dock strike in 1889. There was then an equivalent spread of collective action but without any serious, permanent disruptive consequences. The British labour movement had a resilience which was absent in the American one, and its contradictions were less intense.

The ability to survive is not by itself a positive attribute, though doubtless in a centenary year it will be highlighted as one. Better, perhaps, to have a short life but a principled one than a life made possible by compromises and concessions. In other words, existing is not an end in itself: concrete achievements and the choice of means to them have a bearing on the utility of existence. More than this, in the case of trade unions, means and the character of achievements determine in part the ability to take action in the future. Trade unions derive impulses from a concept of struggle which has to be fed on actual struggle and which in turn must be based on achievement. The future of the British TUC rests heavily upon its past. An examination of the causes of its longevity will, therefore, explain much about the course the TUC can take in the future.

The TUC's main relationship is with the Government of the day, whatever its political complexion. It aims to influence government decision-making on matters which are considered to be the concern of the trade unionists. It acts as a pressure group for organized labour. The means used for this purpose are the conventionally accepted means for bringing pressure on Governments. The TUC submits memoranda to government departments, as it does, for example, each year to convey its views about the budget to the Chancellor of the Exchequer. It sometimes uses Members of Parliament to take up issues but largely prefers to deal with the Government directly and for this purpose the TUC sends deputations to Government ministers, waylays the Minister of Labour and waits on the Prime Minister. It protests, asserts, demands, then retires until the matter is either raised again through the Government's action or inaction or dropped because other decisions have had to be made. Sometimes the TUC makes public pronouncements on issues of policy and leaves it at that in the belief that due notice will be taken by policy-makers and their advisers and in order to show the world at large just where organized labour stands. In addition to these continuing but *ad hoc* measures, representatives of the TUC sit on government committees with representatives of other interest groups or simply with employers and civil servants. Such committees may be standing ones or those which are set up for a specific purpose such as committees of inquiry and Royal Commissions. In all its activity, the TUC uses its power and exerts its pressure in order to influence government decisions. It is concerned with modification, adaptation, amendment, clarification of public policy issues. It is engaged in an essentially pragmatic approach to social change.

This approach involves more than tackling issues as they arise with conventionally acceptable devices of protest. It also entails treating issues according to circumstances at the time. This is what is meant by TUC leaders when they say that unions 'must not blink at the facts', must 'face harsh realities'. Thus collaboration with a Government is not a matter of principle but of expediency. It can be given and withdrawn as circumstances vary. The TUC accepts constraints on its own actions in the same way. In one set of economic and political circumstances it can agree that legislative control over incomes is necessary while in another set it rejects such a move as *unnecessary* or *unrealistic*. At one time it wants unrestrained wage advances while later, with a change in the situation, the TUC advocates wage restraint. The consistent element in this approach is inconsistency. Virtually any policy can be justified, as can any change of policy. Action is not determined by consistent and precise principles for these might cause it to be taken in the face of actually existing circumstances or through other than conventional means of protest. This is not to say that TUC action is unprincipled. There is no doubt that the TUC always acts in what it considers to be the best interests of trade unionists, but this is the kind of principle which can embrace a range of different acts and is never really an inhibiting factor. In an election period, for instance, *all* political parties justify their conflicting, sometimes contradictory, policies on the grounds that they are acting in the best interests of the community.

The TUC accepts the basic features of capitalism and aims for adjustments within it. It does not regard a qualitative change in the relations to the means of production as a prerequisite for the fulfilment of trade union objectives. It does not, therefore, challenge property rights and the distribution of power which goes with them. The TUC, in its policy-making deliberations each year, has its aggressive moments during which it sees the futility of perpetually trying to adapt and repair a defective distributive system. At the ninety-ninth TUC in 1967, for instance, a majority of the delegates approved a motion which advocated an extension of public ownership and a use of planning mechanisms. But these moments pass all too quickly into moods of acquiescence or cynicism or false optimism. In any event they do not result in action by the General Council of the TUC, which is responsible for applying policy decisions. The most that happens is that more strongly worded memoranda are written or more feeling is put into the representations made to the Government by delegations.

Pragmatic action is not adopted by the TUC because of disillusionment with other methods or because of an increasing involvement of trade unions with the capitalist system. It is not a case of the TUC seeking the means of survival for it was never without them. From the outset the TUC has been involved with whichever establishment has held power, seeking to use its power in order to influence, trying to infiltrate so as to be better placed to exercise influence.

The first meeting of the TUC was held from 2 to 6 June 1868 at the Mechanics Institute in Manchester. It was called by the Manchester and Salford Trades Council with the intention of assuming 'the character of the annual meetings of the British Association for the Advancement of Science and the Social Science Association, in the transactions of which societies the artisan class are almost excluded'.[1] It was proposed that 'papers, previously carefully prepared, shall be laid before the Congress on the various subjects which at the present time affect the trade societies, each paper to be followed by discussion upon the points advanced, with a view of the merits and demerits of each question being thoroughly ventilated through the medium of the public press'. This meeting made no demands on unions, required no sacrifice of autonomy and presented no challenge either to employers

---

[1] From the original circular, reprinted in Musson, *The Congress of 1868*, p. 33 (see pp. 138–9).

or the government. In this sense it was unlike all earlier attempts to bring unions together in a horizontal unity.

The situation of 1868 and after distorted the main Congress purpose of relieving the profound ignorance which prevailed in the public mind with reference to the operation of trade unions. A Royal Commission of Inquiry into trade unions had been appointed in February 1867 arising out of the publicity given to the assaults upon non-unionists in the Sheffield file trades. There was a strong feeling that repressive legislation would be introduced to reinforce an already repressively interpreted common law. Trade unions had no legal identity and had no means, therefore, of protecting their funds. This was a serious legal deficiency, particularly for the relatively large amalgamated unions. Unions, moreover, could not take strike action without risking criminal proceedings being taken against them for 'threatening', 'intimidation' or 'molestation' in the course of picketing. Even 'black looks' at a strike-breaker were enough to warrant an arrest. The legal position of unions dominated the discussion at the first TUC and set not only the tone, but the purpose, of subsequent meetings. The TUC from an inauspicious beginning and only partially representative of the trade union movement, became a united, representative body in the early 1870s with the prime purpose of securing an alteration in the law relating to union action. A Trade Union Bill had been introduced by the Government in February 1871 which with one hand granted full legal recognition to unions and with the other still left trade unionists liable for criminal prosecution for peaceful picketing. Pressure on the Government managed only to secure a division of the Bill into two, a Trades Union Bill and a Criminal Law Amendment Bill. The TUC became involved in the agitation for the repeal of the second after it became law. It acted as the forum for assessing the feeling of trade unionists about this contentious issue.

The TUC started then with a limited objective which was attainable within the framework of the existing system of society. When this objective was attained in 1875 with the repeal of the Criminal Law Amendment Act, some union leaders considered the TUC to have completed its usefulness. Other union leaders saw the TUC as having a watchdog function for unions in relation to the Government. They set it a series of minor objectives such as securing amendments in the Factory Acts. The situation after 1875 was an anticlimax for the TUC and in a sense it had to start afresh justifying its existence and providing a rationale for the Parliamentary Committee which controlled its activities in between annual meetings. In practice, it combined its initial function as a debating society with a limited watch-dog one. For many years after 1875 the TUC could have slipped into obscurity without any loss to the trade union movement. That it did not do so was, in part, due to the fact that the annual meeting fairly quickly became an institutionalized ritual.

It was not inevitable that the TUC should have started with a confined, limited, objective. Once the initial meeting had been called it could have been diverted to more aggressive activities or it could have acquired longer-term revolutionary aims. The political environment of the early TUC's was a highly volatile one. The first meeting in 1868 followed the successful agitation of organized labour for political reform. The period between the formation of the National Reform League in February 1865 and the passing of the Reform Act in the summer of 1867 was characterized by organized agitations and mass demonstrations with undertones of class disaffection. An address issued by the League in May 1865 stated that 'The Working Classes in our Country, the producers of its wealth, are in a degraded and humiliating position . . . the men who have fought her battles, manned her ships, tilled her soil, built up her manufactures, trade and commerce . . . are denied the most essential privileges of citizens.'[2] At one conference jointly sponsored by the League and trade unions it was resolved that unless the working class was enfranchised it would be necessary to consider calling a general strike. The membership of the executive of the Reform League and the International Working Men's Association overlapped and to many upper and middle class observers so did their policies.

The agitation for the repeal of the Criminal Law Amendment Act after 1871 resembled that which preceded the Reform Act in its intensity and direction but it was different in that it occurred against the background of successful working-class action for reform and of evidence that working-class voters had aided the return of a Liberal majority to the House of Commons. The extended franchise had, it seemed in the early 1870s, given trade unionists an additional weapon in their struggle.

Yet neither the methods of struggle nor the aspirations implicit in political struggles by the working class penetrated the fabric of the TUC as continuing factors. The reason for this was that the environment of the TUC was a complex one containing powerful consensus-making, disarming pressures as well as conflict-generating ones. It was not enough that conditions gave rise to class agitation; the movements arising out of unrest had to be given direction and purpose in

[2] Gillespie, *Labour and Politics in England, 1850–1867*, p. 252.

order to make achievement possible. The nature of the direction and purpose could extend or curtail, distort or misdirect, encourage or discourage social movements.

The leadership of trade unions in the period from 1865 to 1875 was influenced by a new set of factors. Some of the unions, such as the Amalgamated Society of Engineers, formed through amalgamations, were large by contemporary standards and were stable organizations in that they possessed sufficient resilience to enable them to survive both trade depressions and attacks by employers. Their interests lay in survival, preservation and stability. In other words, institutional preservation became a motivating factor in trade unionism. Action was considered not only in terms of its impact on employers or the government but also in terms of its effect on union organization. For such unions class collaboration was often more productive than class antagonism. Moreover, involvement in the system was a surer means of survival than rejection of the system.

The transition of some of the union offices from lay to full-time, and the consequent professionalization of union leadership, accompanied the growth of amalgamated unions. It was in the interests of full-time officials to perpetuate their organizations, to conserve funds, to remain solvent. They pressed strongly for full legal recognition of unions in order to protect union funds; they deprecated strike action because it dissipated union resources. The activities of Robert Applegarth, general secretary of the Amalgamated Society of Carpenters and Joiners, and William Allan, the general secretary of the Amalgamated Society of Engineers, epitomized this new type of union leader who saw merit in pedestrian achievements and wanted a share, no matter how small, in the material progress of mid-Victorian Britain. Their limited aspirations and willingness to work within limits consistent with the preservation of capitalism were recognized by political leaders. Cracks, hairline ones, appeared in the social structure and gave union leaders access to government officials, enabled them to serve political parties and to have intellectual middle-class friends. For the first time in the history of trade unionism, union leaders were drawn into the political power game, though only as hand-servants at first. But even the role of hand-servant had a politically demoralizing effect.

The TUC first elected a Parliamentary Committee in 1871. Its chairman was George Potter, once the reputed militant editor of the *Beehive* but in 1871 a mellowed, sober companion to the leaders of the large amalgamated unions who had acquired control of the journal. But even before Allan and Applegarth had acquired control of the

Beehive, Potter had entered into a secret agreement with industrialist leaders of the Liberal Party whereby in return for financial assistance he was to 'publish *a series of special articles* upon political subjects of the deepest interest, and circulate them widely among working-class voters, to guide them at this important crisis in sustaining the LIBERAL PARTY'.[3] The crisis was over the manner in which the newly enfranchised workers would use their votes in the general election of 1868.

The first secretary of the Parliamentary Committee was George Howell of the Operative Bricklayers' Society. Howell had been involved in much more shady dealings with Liberal leaders than had Potter. When Howell had been secretary of the National Reform League he had been in the pay of G. G. Glyn, the banker and Liberal Party Chief Whip, and Samuel Morley, the industrialist and prominent Liberal politician.[4] He had manipulated the machinery of the Reform League in favour of Liberal candidates and against working-class candidates. Even after he became secretary of the Parliamentary Committee of the TUC he made an approach to Glyn for a favour. 'Surely', Howell wrote, 'there would be a chance of some good appointment where my qualifications would be a fair test.' William Allan, who was the treasurer of the Parliamentary Committee, was openly committed to the Liberal Party. Even Robert Applegarth, who became perhaps one of the keenest British supporters of the International, was on Howell's list of speakers for the official Liberal Party and was ever ready to help the causes of Liberal manufacturers.

The position was that the leading members of the Parliamentary Committee up till 1875 were ideologically committed to the Liberal Party and supported it either secretly or openly in election campaigns, but at the same time they were compelled at least to pay lip-service to the demands of trade unionists for increased working-class representation in the House of Commons. In addition, these same union leaders were drawn into the agitation against the Liberal Government for the repeal of the Criminal Law Amendment Act, despite their own attachment to the Government. Their position illustrated the contradiction which has always dominated the Trades Union Congress. From the outset union leaders with national organizational responsibilities coveted connections with the political establishment but had in some measure to satisfy the demands of ordinary members which conflicted with those of the establishment. The contradiction belonged to the situation. It did not develop or grow out of it.

[3] Harrison, *Before the Socialists*, pp. 192–3.
[4] *Ibid.*, chapter 4, 'The Reform League and the general election of 1868'.

The situation containing this contradiction has in part already been explained. It arises when organizational survival becomes a factor which influences action and this is all the more likely when the organizations are run professionally in a hostile environment. Aims and methods have to be accommodated both to organizational needs and the dominant ideology and, therefore, are distorted from the forms necessary to satisfy consistently the demands of members. This distortion is an inevitable consequence of the fact of organization but it appears in varying degrees. The extent to which officials give prominence to the preservation of their organizations in determining the action they take depends upon the nature of other determinants of their action. For instance, if a trade union official analyses situations and, therefore, decides upon action through the use of a theoretical framework which is dynamic in conception, he is more likely to advocate a course of action to alter things than if his theoretical framework for action is static in conception and related to the preservation of the *status quo*. If, moreover, his theoretical approach is expressed in formal ideological terms so that he has a consistent and constant guide to action, he is even more likely to act irrespective of organizational needs. In other words, the only real protection a trade union leader has against distorting the prime purpose of trade unionism is the acceptance and use of a revolutionary ideology. Without this he is as a pawn in a struggle to keep things as they are.

Members of the Parliamentary Committee or General Council of the TUC have very rarely been anything but stodgily conservative in their approaches to trade union issues. There is relatively little evidence that any of them have been motivated to keep the system as it is by the possibility of gaining financially from it, in the manner of Howell. Accusations were made against Henry Broadhurst, who succeeded Howell as secretary of the Parliamentary Committee, that he accepted shares from Brunner-Mond as a reward for supporting Sir John Brunner in an election in 1887, but the accusations were not substantiated. There have been suspicions about others since Broadhurst but the evidence against them has always been circumstantial. In any event it is not necessary to malign personal characters in order to make the point. Some union leaders no doubt hoped to gain from the distribution of political patronage and their expectations may have influenced their attitudes to political questions. In the main, however, they have regarded the offer of conventional honours such as peerages and knighthoods and lucrative part-time appointments on the boards of nationally owned undertakings as recognition of union service and not as evidence of self-aggrandisement. Nonetheless, the opportunities for union leaders to become involved in the distribution of conventional rewards are wide and varied and this may play some part in directing their actions. The behaviour of union leaders in this respect is consistent with their general acceptance of the capitalist system. They are socialized to accept the framework of the system and this affects their actions.

Collectively, the leaders of the TUC have consistently sought either compromise solutions or solutions which unequivocally supported the Government. Advice from TUC leaders invariably takes into account responsibility to the public or community as if these are identifiable in reality and possess a single common interest to which all classes and groups contribute. Responsibility of this kind is regarded as being synonymous with statesmanship, the prime virtue of the British establishment. When either the Parliamentary Committee or the General Council have advocated action of a onesided kind in favour of the interests of trade unionists, it has been because the pressures from the rank and file could not be ignored without a serious rejection of TUC leadership. In other words, the policy of compromise or class collaboration has usually been rejected only for tactical reasons of leadership. The conversion of TUC leaders to progressive class policies has always followed, never preceded, agitations from delegates at the annual meetings of the TUC.

The Parliamentary Committee, according to the standing orders which were adopted by the TUC in 1873, had the function of watching over 'all legislative measures directly affecting the questions of labour, and ... initiating, whenever necessary, such legislative action as Congress may direct, or as the exigencies of the time and circumstances may demand'. In effect it acted as the TUC in between the annual congresses. The TUC had no regular source of income until 1892 and, apart from a part-time secretary, no administrative staff. The secretary was allocated a clerical assistant in 1902. From 1906 the post of secretary became a full-time one and he was appointed without having to seek re-election annually. No other assistance was employed until 1918. So for fifty years the Parliamentary Committee acted without any real administrative supports and guidance. The TUC had no bureaucracy to act either as a buffer or a link between the Parliamentary Committee and its affiliated members. For most of the time it was not a continuously operating administrative unit.

The absence of a permanent administration had a bearing on the internal power structure of the TUC. It was the function of the annual Congress to make major policy decisions while their application was left to the Parliamentary Committee which met intermittently

in between Congresses. Whether or not the Parliamentary Committee carried out the decisions of Congress was determined mainly
by the Committee and its secretary. The Committee could stall,
evade or take contrary action as it pleased so long as it could produce
arguments sufficiently cogent to convince delegates of its sincerity
at the next Congress.

Following the reorganization of the TUC between 1919 and 1926
when the basis of a subcommittee system served by full-time administrators was laid, decisions of the TUC were acted on more promptly.
A continuing administration curtailed the freedom of the Parliamentary Committee to ignore the annual Congress decisions because the
administrators had to take up work if only to justify their employment. The heads of departments in the reorganized TUC continually
fed material to the General Council (as the Parliamentary Committee
was renamed), on which decisions were necessary. In one important
respect, the creation of a specialist administration increased the power
of the General Council in relation to the delegates at the annual Congresses. Increasingly, the General Council based its decisions on
detailed, reasoned advice which was not always available to delegates
and which was used as debating weapons.

The Parliamentary Committee and General Council were formally
under the control of the Congress. They were elected annually by the
Congress. The methods and bases of election were altered. First the
elections were by a show of hands; then, in 1895, unions used their
block votes. First nominations came from the Congress as a whole,
then, from 1907, they were submitted on a group basis. Under the
reorganization scheme, nominations were made according to a
rearranged group basis and were voted on by Congress as a whole.
This last method is still used. None of the alterations in the methods
and bases of election, however, had a marked effect upon the personnel selected. The only significant result of the 1895 alteration in the
TUC standing orders was the elimination of John Burns, then a
socialist, from the Parliamentary Committee. Both Burns and Keir
Hardie were excluded from the TUC as delegates, at the same time
because they were neither full-time officials nor working at their trade.
The changes in 1920 increased the size of the Parliamentary Committee from sixteen to thirty members, yet of the new members only
one, George Hicks of the Amalgamated Union of Building Trade
Workers, could be described as an active socialist. Acknowledged left-
wing union leaders normally were elected to the executive of the
TUC only when there were no means of excluding them. The socialist
leaders of the 'new' unions of unskilled workers, John Burns, Ben

Tillet and Will Thorne secured election to the Parliamentary Committee during the phase when socialist measures commanded a majority of the TUC votes in the early 1890s. In 1895, however, TUC opinion changed and Ben Tillet lost his seat until 1921. Since the reorganization of the TUC, rarely has a left-wing leader been elected to the General Council on a competitive basis. He has either been returned unopposed because the number of nominations in his industrial group equalled the number of seats allocated to that group or he has stepped in to fill a vacancy in between annual Congresses. A. F. Papworth, then a member of the Communist Party and the Transport and General Workers' Union, joined the General Council in 1944 because he was one of three nominations in the Transport group for three seats. Frank Cousins filled a vacancy in 1956 caused by the death of the general secretary of his union and afterwards was re-elected without a contest. The position of Will Paynter, a Communist and general secretary of the National Union of Mineworkers, was different in that when he obtained a seat on the General Council in 1960 there was no contest in the Mining and Quarrying Group, but the following year when there was a contest and Congress was able to vote he was defeated and never returned to the General Council. The list of union leaders who have not secured election to the General Council because of their left-wing politics is a long one.

The domination of the General Council by conservative elements has been largely possible because the annual Congresses have had little control over the composition of the General Council. Each of the industrial groups is represented by a given number of seats. If the unions in a group, from which nominations must come, agree amongst themselves to nominate only as many candidates as there are seats, then the matter is taken out of the hands of Congress and there is no contest. In each of the twenty-two Congresses between 1945 and 1967 there were no contests in an average of more than eleven groups out of the nineteen or twenty which existed. The highest number of contested elections was in 1947 when there were eleven, while the lowest number was six in the years 1959, 1960, 1961, 1964 and 1967. Where there were elections the results were usually determined beforehand by at least tacit agreement among the leaders of the largest unions. Either a union would agree to support another's candidate in return for support for its own, or agreement would be reached between unions on political grounds. For this reason it was by no means the case that the candidate of the largest union in a group would get elected. From 1946 to 1956, R. J. Jones, the secretary of the North Wales Quarrymen's Union, a tiny appendage of the Transport and General Workers' Union with less than 6500 members, held one of the three seats in the Mining and Quarrying group. During that period, Arthur Horner the unquestionably able Communist general secretary of the National Union of Mineworkers, which had between 500,000 and 600,000 members, was consistently defeated in opposition to Jones. The tenure of Jones was significant only in that he was passed over when, in terms of seniority, he was due to be president of the TUC after Charles Geddes in 1955. A number of others have held seats on the General Council simply as a means to keep politically unacceptable men off it.[5] The elections in the main have been annual rituals.

Both the Parliamentary Committee and the General Council have been self-perpetuating oligarchies. The advent of John Burns, Ben Tillet and Will Thorne to the Parliamentary Committee in the 1890s made virtually no impact on the course of its deliberations. The possibility of a newcomer upsetting the General Council nowadays is even more remote for the General Council has its conservatism and oligarchic control protected by the bureaucratic form of organization introduced and developed by the then Walter Citrine who was general secretary of the TUC from 1926 until 1946. The General Council is now so divided into subcommittees, with a ranking order of priority and filled by members largely in order of seniority, that it is difficult for any newcomer, let alone one who belongs to a minority, to make an early impact on the Council. The Council in full session is largely a body which receives reports from its subcommittees. By the time the newcomer has intruded into the inner councils it is often sadly the case that he has mellowed or become cynical or become so conditioned by the General Council environment that he is unable to defy its traditions and penetrate its conservatism. Such was the case with George Hicks, Ernest Bevin, Jack Tanner and Will Lawther.

The constant and predictable element in the TUC is the General Council. The variable and unpredictable element is the behaviour of delegates. Within the TUC itself the General Council's main task is handling, curbing, restraining, moderating the militancy of the delegates in order to produce policy decisions which it considers to be consistent with its statemanship. As each General Council member is a leader of a trade union the question arises why there should be differences between them and the delegations they lead. Firstly, each person elected to the General Council is representative of an industrial group, not a trade union. He is, therefore, in so far as his union is concerned, on the General Council in his individual capacity, free to take decisions independently of his own union's policy. The General Council thus is a body of individuals unrestrained by mandates from their own rank and file members. They can, and often do, act contrary to their unions' wishes. This was the case over the issue by the General Council of the anti-communist circulars 16 and 17 to affiliated unions and to trades councils in 1934 and 1935. The anti-communist attitude of some General Council members was not a reflection of their union policies. Similarly, in the periods when the General Council has advocated wage restraint, some members have walked out of meetings to pursue wage claims in accordance with their union policies. As the members of the General Council, with but a single exception, are traditionally full-time paid officials of unions they are already subject to environmental influences which separate them from their rank and file.[6] Once they are freed from the democratic policy-making mechanisms of their unions and sit as a group of individuals they are more likely than not to become instruments of their relatively abstracted environment with its bureaucratic controls.

The TUC consists of affiliated unions, not individual trade unionists, so the internal contradiction is reflected in policy differences between the General Council and individual unions. For most of the year the General Council makes its decisions and goes about its business in its own formal manner while the unions respond to the day-to-day pressures on them, determine their own policies and pursue them with little reference to what the General Council is doing. Occasionally issues arise which compel constituent parts of the TUC to consult, but in the main the significant confrontation occurs at the annual Congress. The meeting is the principal image-creating activity of the TUC. It formally determines the policy and is widely publicized. The arguments in debates are reported but the crucial determinants of the image are the votes on policy issues. The General Council's main concern is with the image and, therefore, with the way in which unions vote.

By and large unions determine their policies at policy-making conferences which are held every one to three years. Union delegations at each TUC meeting are usually required to vote as their respective unions have decided but this is often difficult to do because economic and political conditions may change to make policy decisions inappro-

---

[6] The single exception occurs because the Transport and General Workers' Union insists on including a lay member of its executive as a nominee for the General Council.

priate in some degree between the period when the decisions are taken and the TUC meets. Union delegations, therefore, frequently have the task of reformulating or interpreting their union policies. This task is rarely performed during the debates at the TUC because union delegations contain diverse views which, under the block vote system, have to be represented by single votes. Each union, moreover, tries to present a united front with selected speakers expressing its policy. The consequence is that vital policy discussions take place in private before the Congress meets at delegation meetings. When the Congress debates policy the attitudes of most unions are known and fixed and all that really matters is the counting of the votes.

The General Council, then, is understandably more concerned with pre-Congress delegation meetings than with debates. If it is convinced that sufficient unions of sufficient size support it, then it will virtually leave the debate to the opposition minority. Where there are known differences of policy between numerically important unions and the General Council, its members, in so far as they support its policy, turn their attention to their union delegations. They have been known to use arguments but where these failed, a variety of devices have been resorted to. In the years of Labour Governments, appeals to loyalty to the Labour movement have been in constant use against left-wing opponents. Where these appeals have failed, some General Council members who have been chairmen of delegation meetings have used their authority over procedural matters to question the competency of delegations to determine or revise policy. When everything else has failed, the opinion of delegation meetings has been flouted and union block votes have been cast to meet General Council requirements. Because the policy-making functions of delegation meetings are rarely formulated in union constitutions, their authority is frequently determined by the needs of immediate situations. Where the rules are vague, the delegation chairmen have the authority to interpret them. The Amalgamated Engineering Union has a history of procedural wrangles about the policy-making rights of delegations which has been marked by bitterness and legal action. At the 1966 TUC lay members in two unions sought legal injunctions to restrain the leaders of their union delegations from voting for General Council policies. The problem is a perennial one.

When the General Council has failed to get its own policies accepted, its reactions have varied according to the relevance of the TUC decisions for its all-the-year-round business and the strength of the pressures on it. In other words, when the decisions have affected the image of the TUC and nothing more, the General Council has worried little about Congress defeats. To a large extent, this has also been true for foreign policy issues such as unilateral nuclear disarmament and the Vietnam war. The General Council has also been able to carry defeats on political issues, on issues which have been declarations of political faith, with relatively little concern. In the 1890s, when the political declarations of the TUC became markedly more socialist, the activities of the Parliamentary Committee remained unaffected. A TUC resolution on public ownership or workers' control does not affect the day-to-day operation of the Congress administration. At the most, a General Council deputation may have to put a case to a Minister with which it may disagree. The General Council can sometimes ignore Congress instructions on political matters as the Parliamentary Committee did on a number of occasions in the 1890s. The pressure for General Council action is greater when the issues concern the organization or administration of the TUC but even then resolutions can be dealt with in a dilatory fashion. Complaints about the inefficiency of the administration of the TUC began to be made in 1902 and the issue was raised at Congress on a number of occasions afterwards but no real steps were taken about the matter until 1918.

The situation is different when the issues concern immediate relationships with employers and the Government. The General Council could not ignore the changing mood against wage restraint which began in 1950 and resulted in the rejection of General Council advice at the TUC that year. There was not an over-night conversion. At the 1951 Congress the General Council still advocated 'moderation' and in 1955 opposed a motion which rejected any form of wage restraint. But by 1956 the General Council felt able to support the attack on wage restraint led by Frank Cousins, though it made no verbal commitment in the debate. The attitude of the General Council to Congress deliberations in general was put by George Woodcock, the General Secretary of the TUC, when he said:

> The General Council do not as a rule welcome motions on the Congress agenda. Our general attitude to motions is that if they tell us to do what we already intend to do they are redundant, and if they try to tell us what we do not intend to do they are offensive.[7]

The essential point to consider in an examination of the power position within the TUC is the power situation of the TUC itself. The internal contradiction has been perpetuated and not resolved in either organizational changes or fission, because the pressures for resolution

[7] *TUC Report*, 1962, p. 298.

have been weak. On the one hand, the TUC has never been considered to have enough power to warrant its use as an essential medium for union action, while on the other hand the individual unions have never been bound or even restricted in their activities by TUC decisions. These two aspects are causally related.

The conditions in which unions operate are continually making greater unity necessary and are producing more unified action. Unions are a response to a capitalist environment and changes in it produce changes, with timelags of course, in union organization. Such environmental changes are increases in the size of markets and, therefore, business organizations; increases in the degree of monopoly; changes towards capital-intensive methods of production; greater interdependence between economic units; alterations in the lines of demarcation between occupations and categories of work such as manual and non-manual and an increasingly influential intervention in economic affairs by Governments. These factors create acute exigencies for people who live by selling their labour power; they compel workers, such as those in non-manual employment like bank clerks or teachers or airline pilots, to organize collectively; they compel existing unions to collaborate or federate or amalgamate; they produce needs for centrally organized class action. In other words, they create the need for unity over different ranges and in various forms. If this need is not met, then the power of collective action is reduced.

Unions are always made conscious of the need for solidarity and attempt to achieve it, but they are hampered and frustrated by forces which are divisive in their impact and which derive from the same environment as that which produces solidarity. Union organizations reflect the competitive free market mechanism. Workers with common group interests compete for job opportunities with those in occupationally related groups; the interests of those in contracting and expanding industries are pitted against each other. Whenever the market creates a diverse interest, it will in some way divide workers against each other in their struggle against the conditions which that mechanism creates. This is the secondary contradiction which determines the character of the whole trade union movement. Trade unions are institutionalized expressions of vested occupational interests; their main concern, therefore, is with the protection and improvement of the interests they represent not only against employers but against each other.

The operation of the secondary contradiction can be seen in a historical study of interunion relations. The dominant force is for solidarity because it is derived from the main structural contradiction between social relations and forces of production. The history of British unions, therefore, shows a process involving the merging of local unions into national ones; the amalgamation of national unions with similar industrial or occupational interests; the amalgamation of unions with a general class interest; and the formations of federations between unions on an industrial and a local and national class basis. Many of these moves for solidarity have failed or have been shortlived because of divisive forces. Others have persisted but have been contained by these forces. The TUC is an example of containment.

The TUC is a loose federation of trade unions for particular purposes. It does not impinge on the autonomy of individual unions. It has strictly limited control over its affiliated members for the only sanction it possesses is expulsion, and this has no adverse material consequences for unions. In central class struggle situations, this loose form of organization is deficient, for it cannot mobilize working-class forces against the owners of the means of production. This deficiency has been recognized from the inception of the TUC. Before 1868 most attempts to create horizontal, interunion unity sprang from particular conflict situations. The prime need was for a general controlling strike-organizing body. Each attempt was defeated partly because it was dependent on the success of a particular strike movement, partly because both employers and the Government attacked it as a threat to their power and partly because the degree of centralization involved was greater than that which even the individual unions themselves possessed. When the TUC was formed it was as a debating society, not a strike body. It made no demands on individual unions. Although by 1874 the TUC was involved in the agitation for the repeal of the Criminal Law Amendment Act, it was recognized that it was not strong enough for the task. The Congress in that year debated the possibility of reforming itself into a federation with wider powers. In 1879 the TUC voted to do this, but the trade union movement was then seriously weakened by depression and employers' attacks. The membership of the TUC in 1879 was less than half of its 1874 figure.

Then in 1897 the TUC set up a committee to consider the best means of federating trade unions. The committee produced a scheme which involved the formation of a parallel organization and left the TUC untouched. As a result, the General Federation of Trade Unions was formed in 1899 but this, too, was handicapped by the forces which pitted unions against each other. A concern over the weakness of both the TUC and the General Federation of Trade Unions caused the Miners' Federation, the National Union of Railwaymen and the National Transport Workers' Federation to form the Triple Alliance in 1915 to coordinate joint action on 'matters of a national character or vitally affecting a principle'. The declaration of the Triple Alliance in 1919 and 1920 caused the Government and employers some anxiety, but it was in reality an alliance only of honourable union intentions bound by words and was not equipped to overcome interunion differences in the face of common problems. It had no separate organization and no administration and specifically made no intrusion on the autonomy of the three organizations. The Triple Alliance collapsed in 1921.

In the meantime, the TUC was reorganized in an attempt, by the principal architects at any rate, to form it into a 'general staff of labour' in the event of outright national conflicts with employers and the Government. The reorganization, however, added no power to the TUC over its affiliated membership nor did it increase the confidence of unions in the ability of the General Council to give direction in a conflict. When the Miners' Federation was faced by an attack on miners' wages in 1925 it did not turn to the TUC but approached a number of unions in transport and heavy industry to form an Industrial Alliance. The mining situation reached crisis dimensions before the Alliance could be formed, so the Miners' Federation approached the General Council for assistance. From this point, the authority structure underwent a change which has persisted to 1968. In order to obtain direction and collective backing in the event of a clash between the miners and the Government in 1925, the General Council summoned a special conference of trade union executives on 30 July, not a specially convened meeting of the TUC. That is, in order to get a decision which committed the trade union movement, it went to the union executives who alone had the constitutional authority to commit unions to action. The General Council did the same on the eve of the 1926 General Strike. On every occasion since then, when a crisis involving the trade union movement has occurred, the General Council has sought the backing of union executives rather than the TUC.

After 100 years, the power situation of the TUC has basically remained almost unchanged. Neither the General Council nor the Congress has the power to compel unions to take a particular course of action. In so far as these bodies have power, it is derived from the ethic of solidarity. The TUC has evolved a 'common law', based on the Bridlington Agreement of 1939, to regulate interunion relationships but this depends upon the ethic of solidarity. The TUC has no right to intervene in the affairs of individual unions except in two respects. Under rule 11(c) of its Standing Orders, the General Council can intervene in an industrial dispute 'if . . . there is a likelihood of negotiations breaking down and creating a situation in which other bodies of workpeople affiliated to Congress might be involved in a stoppage of work or their wages, hours and conditions of employment imperilled . . . to use their influence to effect a just settlement of the difference'. A union which ignores the advice of the General Council can be reported to Congress and, presumably, expelled. The second respect concerns the conduct of affiliated organizations. Under Rule 13(a), the General Council can summon a union to appear before it 'if at any time there appears to the General Council to be justification for an investigation into the conduct of any affiliated organization on the ground that the activities of such organization are detrimental to the interests of the Trade Union Movement or contrary to the declared principles and policy of the Congress'. Both rules are applied cautiously, in a way unlikely to create offence to unions. The intervention of the Government in industrial relations and the growing centralized power of employers has confronted the General Council, however, with the need to make decisions on behalf of the trade union movement. It has sought authority for these decisions from conferences of union executives as a means of overcoming the weakness of the TUC. The actual power situation has changed in so far as the General Council now acts as the executive for the trade union movement as a whole rather than just for the TUC. The General Council, acting on behalf of a conference of trade union executives, has no constitutional power to discipline recalcitrant union members but the executives which make the decision do have this power. The General Council, therefore, has greater authority as the executive of conferences of trade union executives than as the executive of the TUC. This, however, amounts to only a marginal accretion of power.

The TUC is a part of the centralization of trade union activity, which in turn is the institutionalized expression of solidarity. As has been stated above, the contradiction from which the trade union movement get its momentum is continually extending and intensifying solidarity. Trade union activity in consequence is becoming more centralized. The number of unions affiliated to the TUC is continually declining even though new unions seek affiliation in most years. More significantly, the membership of the TUC is becoming increasingly and highly concentrated in a small number of unions within the TUC. In 1967 ten unions out of the 169 affiliated to the TUC had 5,381,072 members while the remaining 159 shared between them only 3,406,210 members. The process of centralization, though inexorable, is a slow one. It depends for its speed on trade union crises. Individual unions merge with others usually only under the threat of extinction through insolvency but lesser and different pressures can force them to concede some autonomy. For many unions, government control is equivalent to insolvency and when this is interpreted in crisis terms, further centralization may take place. The TUC may be given powers to control some union activities in order to restrain Government intervention. Or a different form of organization may be created out of the TUC. The only sure thing is that in some way solidarity will increase.

When examining the power situation of the TUC, it is necessary to separate illusion from concrete reality. The trappings of TUC involvement in political decision-making have become more numerous and apparent. The TUC *appears* to be exercising more power now because it consults and is consulted by the Government, because the General Council has easy access to the Prime Minister, because the TUC is represented on numerous government bodies, because in general the TUC is accepted by the established power-holders in Britain. These trappings, however, are a façade and create an illusion of power. What the TUC can do does not depend on its bureaucratic involvement in society. Indeed, it can be argued that this involvement is a handicap on the use of power. Certainly, involvement is not power. The power of the TUC is much less than, and never can be more than, the collective power of unions, and this without doubt depends on their ability to exploit their economic strength. The concrete reality of power involves the class-conscious use of economic strength and, in a capitalist society, this strength varies with the level of employment. In so far then as the TUC has any real power in 1968, it is determined by the employment situation. A sudden change in the level of employment would alter its power situation irrespective of the extent to which the TUC was involved in the formal decision-making apparatus.

The power of the TUC has varied along a relatively constant trend. It has been high during wartime and periods of peacetime full employment, and low during periods of unemployment. Occasionally non-economic factors may temporarily intrude into the power situation. Universal suffrage was such a factor in the period between 1868 and the First World War. This was the period when political parties competed for the electoral allegiance of the newly enfranchised workers by promising, and in some cases making, concessions to the unions in the belief that the unions influenced the voting behaviour of their members. Political parties still compete for the votes of trade unionists but no longer believe that they have to make concessions to unions in the process. Capitalism in Britain is going through a crisis which may lead to the corporate state. Before this state can be reached, and as a condition for reaching it, the power of unions has to be arrested by legislative measures. The arresting process has begun. But the attempt to control unions in which the present Government is engaged is creating the very pressures which will force unions to strengthen themselves and, perhaps, the TUC as well. The TUC will have the complacency of the years following its centenary disturbed by the crisis of British capitalism.

PART IV

15

Unions in developing economies: the validation of a method

So far in this book the differences between the principal methodologies have been discussed without precise conclusive evidence one way or the other. There is good reason for this. Neither approach has been subject to the test of laboratory conditions. Neither has been through the testing process of validation. Often it is only over time and with hindsight that the usefulness of one method compared with the other can be seen. Fortunately, however, this is not always the case. Although the precision of the natural sciences cannot yet be achieved, it is possible in some situations to examine the consequences of the application of one method or the other. Some such situations have occurred in developing countries. The variable has been the development of trade unionism. The laboratory has been the changing traditional, subsistence cultures of Africa and Asia.

Trade unions are highly developed phenomena in Western industrial countries. They differ in their structures in that in some of the countries they are more centralized than in others; their functions and methods vary. But in some essential ways they are comparable: they are large, relatively stable, self-financing organizations in which policy determination and administration are mainly undertaken by the members. According to the methodology used in this book these organizational characteristics are a consequence of specific environments in Western industrial countries. Every organization is moulded by its environment. If the environment changes then so must the organization. An organization which does not respond to environmental changes must inevitably lapse. This does not mean to say that trade unionism is the product of the specific qualities of an environment; it arises, as has already been pointed out, from the existence of a certain structural condition, the buying and selling of labour power on the open market and this can be present in markedly different environments. What it does mean is that the forms trade unionism take are the product of environmental influences and therefore cannot be transferred from one environment to another without impairing their effectiveness.

The growth of trade unionism in Africa and Asia has been dependent upon the presence of the necessary conditions, the buying and selling of labour power, in those areas. Until the end of the Second World War the growth was imperceptible, except perhaps in India. Then as the process of industrialization was speeded up and free labour markets were extended trade unions were formed. But the unions did not emerge from African and Asian environments unaided. With slight exceptions the countries in these continents were colonies of metropolitan Western capitalist states. Their political and industrial development was controlled and guided to meet metropolitan needs. Their unions, because they were political bodies, were, therefore, subject to control and guidance. In every case they were fashioned from a Western industrial model for this was the form the colonial administrations knew about and what they were familiar with they thought they could control. So in British controlled territories the British model of trade union was transplanted. The British model was a relatively autonomous organization, hierarchical and pyramidal in shape with a branch membership base, dependent for its operation on membership participation, and loosely connected with other unions in federations or a central congress. The same process took place in French controlled areas. In French West Africa, for instance, the trade unions were adjuncts to the metropolitan organizations, reflecting all the religious and political ideological differences which were present in France but not in West Africa. These transfers were encouraged by the missionary zeal of trade union officials from the metropolitan countries who were frequently given the task of advising on union development. It was believed that Western industrial organizational forms had a universal validity. If, however, the analysis used here has any validity then an empirical investigation of unions in Africa and Asia should reveal them to be defective in the ways in which Western industrial environments differ from those in Africa and Asia. If the investigation showed unions with Western industrial forms flourishing in developing economy environments, then the analysis would need to be questioned seriously and, perhaps, rejected. This test can be applied to the transfer of any institutions, for example, parliamentary democracy, or a two-party system, or university education.

The causal explanation of the state of trade unionism in developing economies will vary with the conceptual approach. A structural and dialectical approach involves identifying the main environmental determinants of union forms in Western industrial countries and isolating and assessing their presence in developing areas. The extent to which they vary will indicate the problems which unions in developing areas, with unchanged forms, face. This approach also involves identifying the elements in the African and Asian environments which have the biggest moulding impact on organizational development, and from this obtaining some notion about the form which an indigenous trade union would take. At no point is it relevant to judge or assess unions in developing areas by the standards of British or French or American unions, for to do this is to assume that these standards have a general relevance. It may be found, for example, that a Nigerian union is administratively inefficient according to British standards. To condemn it for its inefficiency implies that the administration is being wrongly handled and attention, therefore, is directed at such matters as the competence of personnel, the existence or quality of equipment. Solutions are sought through training courses for union officials and the provision of cars, typewriters and the like. But if the logic of the analysis outlined here is followed the first question which would be asked about an administratively inefficient union would be whether an administration of the kind envisaged is appropriate for the conditions of Nigeria and whether, therefore, it could ever be efficient in the British meaning of the term.

The chapters in Part IV do not provide detailed evidence about the extent and impact of trade unionism in developing economies. This evidence can be found in the growing body of literature on the subject.[1] They are based, however, on the knowledge acquired from documentary and field research that where alien union models predominate trade union movements are weak and ineffectual. This knowledge tends to support the conclusions reached through the analysis here. The time sequence in which the chapters were written may be of some interest. Chapter 18 was written in 1959 as part of a wider study from documentary material only. This research provided hypotheses which were the basis for field work in various parts of tropical Africa between 1960 and 1965. Chapter 17 was written as a preliminary result of field work in East Africa alone in 1961. Chapter 16, which is an assessment of methods used in the study of trade unionism in tropical Africa, was written in 1967–68 at the end of the field work and after subsequent reflection. There has been no need to question the initial hypotheses.

[1] See William H. Friedland, *Unions, Labour and Industrial Relations in Africa: an annotated bibliography* (Cornell Center for International Studies), New York, Ithaca, 1965.

HIR

16

The study of trade unionism in tropical Africa[1]

The growth of interest

The phenomenon of trade unionism in tropical Africa has only recently become the subject of serious social inquiry. In the main, academic attention has been focused on labour as a commodity rather than as a social movement. Through the activities of the National Institute for Personnel Research in Johannesburg and the Commission for Technical Co-operation in Africa South of the Sahara, labour research interests have been primarily concentrated on productivity, efficiency, labour turnover, selection, control, and training. The volume of such work has been small compared with similar work in western industrialized countries, but it has been large in comparison with that concerning the collective action of African labour.

The reason for this bias was twofold. First, the interest in the efficiency of indigenous African labour arose out of the needs of expanding industrial sectors after the Second World War. African labour with increasingly complex skills was demanded, both to meet the expansion and to satisfy the political insistence on Africanization. Secondly, because it was generally assumed that indigenous labour had to be committed to European industrial values relating to pace of work, motivation, and discipline, a marked emphasis was placed on achieving this commitment. Here the impulse came from South Africa and was transmitted to tropical African territories either through South African owners—of the mines, for example—or through the use of South African managers, or simply through emulation. Both agriculture and manufacturing industry were dependent upon the efficient technical utilization of African labour, especially after political independence, which accelerated the development of competitive industry.

[1] This chapter is primarily concerned with the former British-controlled territories of tropical Africa.

Trade unionism has never been given the same prominence, either as a negative or a positive force, as has labour utilization.[2] It was usually assumed, before political independence, that African unions were weak and ineffectual in both industrial and political terms, and that they were playing little or no part in independence movements. The more politically important a phenomenon appears to be, the easier it is to get research funds. In consequence African trade unions did not appear significantly on research agendas until long after Africa itself had attracted attention. Although trade unions in western industrial countries, particularly the USA, were the subject of intense research interest, this did not spill over to Africa, even out of curiosity about comparative developments.

The lack of interest in African unions before colonial ties were broken is partly explained by the limited extent of trade unionism in Africa. Trade unionism is collective action by people who sell their labour power in order to protect and improve their living standards. The necessary condition for trade unionism, therefore, is the buying and selling of labour power on a significant scale, which in turn is the core element of industrialization. But this, in Africa, has proceeded slowly. Until the end of the Second World War, apart from the settler territories of South Africa, Southern Rhodesia and Kenya, which had always depended upon the existence of a supply of indigenous labour, industrialization existed only in isolated mines and plantations. Wage and salary earners comprised a tiny proportion of the total population. After the war industrialization increased in all tropical African countries, but even by the late 1950s it was still a marginal activity. In 1958 the number of wage earners as a proportion of the total population in British-controlled territories ranged from less than 1 per cent in Nigeria to approximately 10 per cent in Kenya and Zambia. In all the French-controlled territories in 1955 and 1956 there were only approximately 836,000 wage and salary earners out of a population of 30 million.[3]

If the necessary condition for trade unionism is the buying and selling of labour power, then everyone who sells his labour power is a potential trade unionist. But this is not a sufficient condition for such a person actually to become a trade unionist. The sufficient conditions for trade unionism in tropical Africa vary between cultures and even between countries within a single culture. Broadly, they relate to the

[2] See Willie Smith, 'Industrial sociology in Africa', *The Journal of Modern African Studies* (Cambridge), vi, no. 1, 1968, for a discussion of works on this topic.

[3] Colonial Office returns (London, HMSO, 1958), for the British territories. The French figures were estimated by the International Labour Office in 1958 for internal use.

freedom and facility to organize collective action; but these have never been generally and uniformly present. Many workers have been free only to sell their labour power. Once having done that they have lost the freedom to regulate or influence its use, either through the action of governments or through the excessive power of employers. Other factors have prevented or inhibited the emergence of trade unions of the western industrial type, such as the high level of illiteracy, the lack of organizational resources, or the attempt to maintain traditional tribal methods of control in industrial situations.

The consequence of the absence of sufficient conditions has been that in all tropical African countries until they obtained political independence, and in most even until the present, the number of trade unionists has constituted a small proportion of the (small) total labour force and, therefore, a minute fraction of the total population. In the British-controlled territories of Nigeria, Ghana, Sierra Leone, Kenya, Zambia, Malawi, Uganda, and Tanzania, it was estimated that in 1958, out of about 2,404,000 wage and salary earners, only about 370,000 were members of trade unions. In the French territories there were about 268,000 trade unionists in a labour force of 836,000.[4] The actual number of trade unionists might indeed have been lower because of the tendency to inflate union membership figures. Clearly, then, social scientists might have been justified in ignoring such small African unions.

The growth of interest in trade unions

Before the 1950s there were occasional brief pamphlets and articles, of varied quality, about African unions. They were written either by visiting, participating European trade unionists, or by social scientists employed in African universities who happened to be on the spot. One of the earliest was an 84-page booklet by W. S. Mare, *African Trade Unions* (London, 1949), which described various facets of union organization and activity in simple, elementary terms. In the same year a very slim pamphlet by R. E. Luyt called *Trade Unionism in African Colonies*[5] was published by the South African Institute of Race Relations. Little else appeared for several years, even at this simple descriptive level, until the Fabian Colonial Bureau published a more general pamphlet by Walter Bowen, *Colonial Trade Unions* (London, 1954). This covered industrial relations in the West Indies,

---

[4] Colonial Office returns (London, HMSO, 1958), for the British territories.
[5] South African Institute of Race Relations, New African pamphlets, no. 19, Johannesburg, 1949.

East Africa, West Africa and Malaya. In its appendix suggesting further reading, the only non-government items were an International Labour Office report on the West Indies and the pamphlet by Luyt. In the same year R. B. Davison published an article called 'Labour Relations and Trade Unions in the Gold Coast';[6] this gave an account of the legislation which had been introduced by the British administration to regulate the formation and administration of trade unions and to settle industrial disputes in Ghana. The year before, Davison had written a paper on 'The Study of Industrial Relations in West Africa' (Ibadan, mimeo., 1953) for the annual conference of the West African Institute of Social and Economic Research. Davison, who had been a trade unionist, was employed at the University College of Ghana. His work was largely descriptive, but it reflected an intellectual quality which so far had been missing in the small amount of literature.

More typical of the general standard up to the mid-1950s was an address on the Copperbelt unions delivered at a joint meeting of the Royal African Society and the Royal Empire Society, in June 1955, by R. W. Williams, a British MP and legal adviser to the National Union of Mineworkers in Britain. Williams had been sent to Zambia by the Miners' International Federation to investigate an industrial dispute in the copper mines. His address tended to be impressionistic, reflecting the British conception of trade unionism and a marked political purpose.[7] A number of articles of a similar character and purpose were published in the *Free Labour World* (Brussels) by the International Confederation of Free Trade Unions and in the *World Trade Union Movement* (Paris), the organ of the World Federation of Trade Unions. None of these ranked in any sense as studies but, in a limited way, they provided material for the social analyst. The Inter-African Labour Institute occasionally published factual, descriptive articles about trade union and labour legislation in its *Bulletin*.[8] This Institute was established in Bamako in 1952, under the aegis of the Commission for Technical Co-operation in Africa South of the Sahara, and later transferred to Brazzaville in 1956. It reflected the primary interests of its founder members, the senior officials of labour departments in British, French, and Belgian territories south of the Sahara, who were not concerned with

[6] *Industrial and Labour Relations Review*, vii, no 4, July 1954, 592–604.

[7] R. W. Williams, 'Trade unions in Africa', *African Affairs* (London), liv, 217, October 1955.

[8] For example, 'Labour in Africa', in *Bulletin* (London), iii, no. 1, January 1956, and 'Some recent developments in trade union legislation in central Africa', *ibid.*, iv, no. 2, March 1957.

the causes and growth of trade unionism, but largely with its containment and manipulation. But it now forms part of the Organization of African Unity.

The results of research usually take several years to appear. Projects have to be launched and completed and their findings published. The initiation of serious research interest in Africa followed the recognition of African nationalist movements which were capable of challenging colonial control in the middle of the 1950s—especially after Ghana's independence in 1957 set in motion a chain reaction which was to affect almost every African colonial territory. Africa was now seen by social analysts primarily as a continent of rapid political change. Trade unions, however, were either still ignored or treated as part of general political movements; as for example, by Thomas Hodgkin in *Nationalism in Colonial Africa* (Muller, 1956). In the main, the methodological approach of the author determined the emphasis given to trade unions in the treatment of social, economic, or political change in Africa. There were those who believed, with Thomas Hodgkin, that an understanding of any particular segment or aspect of social behaviour could only be explained by reference to its whole environment; they gave more prominence to trade unions than those who believed they could isolate and insulate segments or aspects in an analytically meaningful way.

The results of the development of an intellectual interest in tropical African trade unions began to show towards the end of the 1950s. B. C. Roberts published an article on overseas labour relations in 1957.[9] Then the following year J. I. Roper's *Labour Problems in West Africa* (London, 1958) appeared in the new Penguin African Series, describing unions in West Africa against their cultural and economic background. It was relatively short and necessarily superficial, but it was amongst the first to provide a book-length treatment of tropical African unions. The International Labour Office *African Labour Survey* (Geneva, 1958) was a lengthy, descriptive volume in which every aspect of labour, including industrial relations, was treated. The scope of the volume determined its length, not the intensity of its analysis. It covered more countries than Roper's book and included more data, but in the main it was just as superficial in its treatment. In the same year A. L. Epstein produced the findings of a study which had begun in 1953; although his *Politics in an Urban African Community* (Manchester University Press, 1958) concerned the whole political environment of Africans on the Zambian

[9] B. C. Roberts, 'Labour relations in overseas territories', *The Political Quarterly* (London), xxviii, no. 4, 1957.

Copperbelt, he attributed a vital role in this environment to trade unionism. He produced a study in depth which was qualitatively superior to previous work on African unions, and still ranks with the best that has followed, in that it assisted an understanding of the causes and motivation of trade unionism in an African environment. Trade unions on the Copperbelt were also the subject of a historical and descriptive article, after the style of R. B. Davison, published in South Africa by P. K. Lomas.[10]

With the growing popularity of the subject among the social scientists, the output of studies of African unions increased after 1958, though not nearly as fast as in other fields.[11] The increase was simply sufficient to justify an examination of the methodology used by the writers. The trade union investigator faces all the methodological problems which are inherent in the analysis of social behaviour. The data are complex, sometimes to a perplexing degree, and are not amenable to controlled investigation. Furthermore, especially in Africa: (1) the selection and collation of the data are subject to the bias of the investigator, and (2) the material itself is often unreliable for objective analysis.

Problems of methodology: (1) Cultural bias

Every investigator of social behaviour carries with him the influence of his social environment; this acts as a subjective determinant of his decisions on how much of the data is relevant and how much is not, and on the priority to be given to the relevant data. The influence is especially important in questions of economic and social class. The British investigator of British trade unions is often a person of middle-class background with a set of values which in some ways are alien or incomprehensible to the subjects of his investigation. He does not automatically understand the traditions and practices of trade union-ism. The investigator of African trade unions may have the additional handicap of a stronger cultural bias, unless he is an African.

Apart from those African union leaders who have occasionally contributed brief articles to international union journals, very few Africans have written on trade unions. An African trade unionist, J. Benibengor Blay, wrote *The Gold Coast Mines Employees' Union* (Ilfracombe, 1950); but 254 pages out of a total of 297 consisted of

[10] P. K. Lomas, 'African trade unionism on the Copperbelt', *South African Journal of Economics* (Johannesburg), xxvi, no. 2, June 1958.
[11] See Friedland, *Unions, Labor and Industrial Relations in Africa* for a list of publications up to 1964.

appendices recording such items as petitions, interviews with the Chamber of Mines, and a lengthy report of arbitration proceedings. But only one African, T. M. Yesufu, has produced a detailed study, *Industrial Relations in Nigeria* (Oxford University Press, 1962). All the other authors have been western interpreters of the African situation. This is not, of course, an automatic handicap. The ethnic origin of a social scientist is relevant only to his cultural bias. If a British, American, or German model of trade unionism is being used as a standard for assessing the development of African unions, then a cultural bias is introduced which handicaps the study. Such an approach involves two assumptions about trade unionism which are of doubtful validity. First, it assumes that trade unionism is at most a western phenomenon rather than a universal one. In other words, trade unionism is seen as the product of certain societies as a whole rather than a set of conditions, especially the buying and selling of labour power, which can be present in any society. Secondly, it assumes that the form of trade unionism experienced in the west can be transplanted to African conditions despite the environmental differences. In other words, there is an underlying assumption that organizational forms have an existence, therefore a cause, apart from the environments in which they operate.

There is evidence of cultural bias in many of the studies of African unions. P. K. Lomas, for instance, stated in 1958 that

> examples of successful African trade unions are difficult to find. The reason for this is very apparent. Trade unionism is an institution that has spontaneously and gradually developed out of the peculiar economic and social conditions of highly industrialized western societies. These conditions are not yet present in Africa; in consequence attempts to foster the growth of trade unions among the indigenous workers frequently end in failure due to impediments and disabilities resulting from the differences between local social and economic conditions and those obtaining in the environments where trade unions flourish.[12]

Lomas went on to analyse correctly the causes of the failure of African unions in terms of the differences between Western European and African environments. He failed, however, to see trade unionism as a general phenomenon of collective action which can be distinguished from its various specific forms. His analysis simply amounts to a statement why a particular type of organizational structure could not survive in Africa. What he did not recognize was that the failure of trade unionism in Africa at that time was the failure of an imposed western

[12] Lomas, loc. cit., pp. 114–15.

form, not the inability of Africans who sold their labour to act collectively.[13]

A similar inability to understand the qualities of African environments and, therefore, to explain African trade unionism is evident in the work of B. C. Roberts. Discussing British colonial labour policy in 1957, he stated:

> It does not follow that different fundamental principles ought to be applied to overseas territories simply because they are at an earlier stage in their economic and social development. . . . Whatever the shortcomings of British Colonial policy might have been, there can be no possible doubt that the governments of both parties have been absolutely right to foster free trade unionism and a pattern of industrial relations based in principle on ideas pioneered and tested in Britain and the Western world.[14]

This belief was the basis for Roberts's analysis of trade unions in *Labour in the Tropical Territories of the Commonwealth* (G. Bell, 1964) and in his later work. He does not expect unions in Africa to be the same as those in Western Europe, but only because he considers the areas to be in different stages of development. 'The critics of colonial trade unions', he writes, 'have, in effect, assumed that these *new* organizations should have started from a state of development that has only been reached elsewhere in the world after considerable experience and when certain conditions have been fulfilled.' Roberts goes on to ask questions about possible alternative courses of development, but concludes

> that if unions are allowed to develop freely within an appropriate framework of law they will succeed in defining the limits of legitimate behaviour as unions in the older political democracies have done. There is certainly no reason to assume that unions in the tropical Commonwealth territories are less capable of arriving at a satisfactory *modus vivendi* with the state than unions in other parts of the world.[15]

In this statement the meaning of the key terms, 'appropriate', 'legitimate', and 'satisfactory', are related to British standards of behaviour.

In a jointly written book, *Collective Bargaining in African Countries* (Macmillan, 1967), Roberts and L. Greyfié de Bellecombe explicitly raise the question of transplanting institutions from western industrial to African environments but do not give an explicit answer. Granting that there is 'some truth' in the arguments against the suitability of the collective bargaining model in Africa, they add that their purpose

---

[13] Lomas, ibid.   [14] Roberts, *Political Quarterly*, xxviii, 1957.
[15] Roberts, *Labour in the Tropical Territories of the Commonwealth*, p. 88.

is to describe and analyse what exists, in whatever form, without taking sides.[16] However, in so far as these authors support arguments against transplanting institutions it is because they have insufficient evidence to disprove them. In other words, their attitude is not determined by methodological objections. In any case, by adopting an empirical approach they do not rule out the possibility of transplanting British institutions to Africa and, therefore, make their methodological position clear. This position markedly influences the subsequent treatment of collective bargaining in Africa in the book.

Very few analysts of trade unions in Africa have gone beyond the position of Roberts and de Bellecombe to admit the inappropriateness of the western model, with the implication that indigenous forms of stable union organization could have developed out of the African industrial environment, as, for instance, the Histadrut grew out of the unique Palestinian conditions. Charles A. Orr takes such a minority view:

> Neither European systems of labour relations nor European organizational forms have proved to be quite appropriate for African labour. The same may also be said of the American preoccupation with anti-communism, a preoccupation which was not felt by African workers and which, therefore, could not do much to help build the African labour movement.[17]

This statement may either be a simple observation, which can be confirmed or otherwise by empirical data, or it may reflect an approach which stipulates that viable unions must draw their qualities from the environments in which they operate. The latter view would be a step towards reducing the western cultural bias; the implications for research are further discussed in the concluding section of this article.

Problems of methodology: (2) The reliability of data

The reliability of the material for objective analysis is of special concern to analysts of African unions. There are two main sources of information, documentary material and field work, both of which vary considerably in their reliability.

Documentary material is the most commonly used source for original data and most of it comes from government departments. Government documents about trade unions are mainly annual

[16] Roberts and de Bellecombe, *Collective Bargaining in African Countries*, pp. xvii–xviii.
[17] Charles A. Orr, 'Trade unionism in colonial Africa', *The Journal of Modern African Studies*, iv, no. 1, 1966, 78.

reports from Labour Departments, special reports of committees of inquiry into exceptional issues such as strikes, and fact-finding bodies. The reports of committees of inquiry, usually appointed by colonial administrators, cover the major industrial relations issues in all the former British-controlled territories in Africa since before the Second World War. They make up a long list, and provide a reliable index of the main issues which have confronted governments. There is no doubt of the importance of these official documents; they are usually the only source of historical material apart from local newspapers. It would be difficult to study trade unions in the former British African territories without using them.

A more recent source of documents is the International Confederation of Free Trade Unions. Since 1949, when the ICFTU was formed, it has taken a special interest in tropical Africa. Following a visit by an ICFTU mission to West Africa in 1951, a Trades Union Information and Advisory Centre was established in Accra early in 1953, which reported to the head office in Europe. At the same time a resident ICFTU official in East Africa reported on the situation there. Various fact-finding missions consisting of representatives from union centres affiliated to the ICFTU reported on 'trouble spots', while emissaries were sent out to investigate particular situations. Reports of the British Trades Union Congress also give some information on the growth of unions. In the 1950s more than half of the trade union movements in tropical Africa seeking affiliation to the ICFTU were in British-controlled territories, in which the TUC played a paternalist role. Documentary evidence of union activity has rarely been available from the unions themselves because so few of them have been able to meet the cost of publishing informative reports. Either unions have not published reports at all, or they have published the roughest outline of their activities. The exceptions in this respect were the unions in Ghana during the Nkrumah period, which produced long and detailed annual reports. But there are virtually no union records extant which cover the period of union formation.

This paucity of documentary material was stressed by Roger Scott in his preface to *The Development of Trade Unions in Uganda* (Nairobi, 1966): 'Because of the almost total absence of published records, apart from press reports, the book depends heavily upon interview material and unpublished files.' Scott also used Labour Department reports extensively. B. C. Roberts was similarly compelled to rely on government documents for his description of the development of trade unions.[18] S. C. Sufrin, in *Unions in Emerging Societies* (Syracuse

[18] Roberts, *Labour in the Tropical Territories of the Commonwealth*, part 1.

University Press, 1964), depends upon the reports of commissions of inquiry into industrial disputes. However, the predominance of documents from government sources raises a serious problem for the investigators of African unions, though it is not one which seems to have troubled these authors.

The issue arises because Labour Department reports reflect, by and large, the views of governments which were primarily concerned with protecting investments from the metropolitan country and with maintaining the existing state of affairs. The reports of investigating committees with independent chairmen fall into the same category, for rarely is a person chosen by a government to conduct an inquiry on its behalf who cannot be trusted to produce conclusions which are largely acceptable to the government concerned. In consequence the trade unions were frequently criticized as irresponsible, unrepresentative, and led by political agitators or self-seekers. The problem is first to recognize the bias. Those investigators who use government sources uncritically, reproducing both the interpretations and the factual data, appear to believe that impartial observation in the social sciences is possible and that government officials and advisers practise it. They do not recognize that environment affects action. So, for Scott, Roberts, and Sufrin there was no problem. Having decided that governments, even colonial ones, and their advisers could be impartial in industrial relations, they proceeded to rank interpretations and empirical data as possessing equal validity. The consequence has been to reduce the relevance of their work for explaining reality.

There is, of course, bias in all the sources available to the analyst, as has been recognized by Ioan Davies, in *African Trade Unions* (Penguin, 1966), and by Jean Meynaud and Anisse Salah-Bey, the authors of *Le Syndicalisme africain* (Paris, 1963), which was translated into English as *Trade Unionism in Africa* (Methuen, 1967). The reports of the International Confederation of Free Trade Unions were particularly unbalanced where the question of Communist influence arose, while the British TUC disliked any organizational form which did not conform to its own standards. Detecting bias in all sources and taking account of it are necessary for scientific precision in the social sciences.

The investigator of African unions, however, has difficulty even with empirical data, for he cannot rely on the accuracy of statistical information. Population statistics are especially unreliable in Africa, often arbitrary, as was illustrated by the periodic revisions of the census in Nigeria. Statistics relating to the size, composition and employment of the labour force tend to be both incomplete and arbitrary, especially for migrant workers, and those geographically dispersed within and across national boundaries; the task is often made more difficult by the lack of census-taking resources. Trade union statistics are probably the most unreliable of all because they are frequently inflated, either through inefficiency or deliberately by union leaders in order to acquire status and power. There is evidence of union members who have never been crossed off the books when they died, left their jobs, or simply stopped paying their dues. The figures should clearly be treated as approximations.

The second main source of data, field work, also varies in its reliability. Field work is a systematic on-the-spot investigation involving interviews, questionnaires, and observation. It usually entails some involvement in the situation, perhaps simply by living in it, in the manner of anthropologists. A. L. Epstein used the techniques he had learnt as a social anthropologist to gather material for *Politics in an Urban African Community*. He studied the social life of the community in detail and depth in order to focus attention on its politics, but went beyond anthropology by placing his material in its historical and sociological context. Epstein never gives the impression of studying a subject isolated from its environmental context, as a classical anthropologist might have done. W. A. Warmington broke new ground with a case study of the Cameroons Development Corporation Workers' Union *A West African Trade Union* (Oxford University Press, 1960). Warmington says that most of the material was collected incidentally, in a rather haphazard way, while he was on a survey of plantation labour in the Southern Cameroons. But the finished work, less analytically sophisticated than that of Epstein, adds considerably to the knowledge of the way in which the British-model union operated in an alien environment.

Both these books indicate how the detail obtained from field investigations should be fitted into a structural context. They point to the value of field work, not to its sufficiency. The mere collection of data, as many narrowly conceived anthropological studies have shown, contributes little unless it takes place within a conceptual framework which itself aids understanding. The research of W. H. Friedland into the evolution of trade unions in Tanganyika, undertaken during 1958–60, is indicated by his brief survey in *Unions and Industrial Relations in Underdeveloped Countries* (Bulletin 47, New York School of Industrial and Labor Relations at Cornell, January 1963). Friedland examines union development in a wide economic and historical context and distinguishes between the environmental determinants of organizations in different societies. He does not go so far as to acknowledge the possibility of an organization which differs profoundly from that in western industrial countries, but he does see that the defective operation of the western model in developing countries is due to environmental differences. His definition of underdevelopment at the outset emphasizes the factors which distort African unions from the western model. The documentary material in Robert's *Labour in the Tropical Territories of the Commonwealth* is supported by data from visits to the territories concerned, not from field studies; but no matter how the data was collected its use was predetermined by Roberts's static, descriptive approach. Reliably collected data loses much of its reliability by being placed in a static framework.

The interpretation of field work

Evidence obtained from questionnaires and interviews, always limited in validity because of their static nature, narrow scope, and dubious relevance to reality, becomes even less reliable when there is no documentary support, as happens so often in Africa. Questionnaires and interviews are usually resorted to when there is insufficient documentary data, so that this method is most commonly used to get information about African unions, not employers' or government organizations. Where both kinds of material are available, the problem is how to use hearsay evidence, prejudiced interpretations, and faulty memorized details, alongside detailed documentary data. If all are given the same validity ranking, then the final analysis can be no more valid than the least reliable of the data employed. The difficulties involved are illustrated by Roger Scott's research into trade union development in Uganda. The core of his work amounts to potted histories of the most important unions in the country. The Railway African Union, the National Union of Plantation Workers, and the Uganda Public Employees Union, are given a chapter each, with one on general unions and another on company unions in the textile and tobacco industries. The material is concentrated, and therefore the selection of data is important. If Scott's interview material on African unions was unreliable, then his whole work must have been adversely affected. Frequently such evidence is difficult to check, and only a general caution can be given. However, since I was personally involved in the development of the National Union of Plantation Workers—and figure in Scott's narrative—I can provide some sort of check on the material in that chapter. The question at issue here is not whether or not the incidents described took place, but whether the interpretation of the data assists in understanding them.

The impression Scott gives is that the development of the National Union of Plantation Workers was *dependent* upon the interplay of personalities, whose ability and integrity are assessed in western industrial and cultural terms. This interplay was between African full-time officials and their executive members, between African officials and Asian and European advisers, and between European advisers on the one hand and Asian and European employers and Labour Department officials on the other. It is suggested that the success of the union, even its ability to survive, depended upon the inability of a European adviser to stay long enough to ensure that his advice was carried out, the misuse of a union car by his successor, the uncompromising tactics of another European adviser, which made him unpopular with both employers and Labour Department officials, the involvement of the union general secretary in a car crash, the regional bias of two successors and the activities of 'ambitious individuals outside the union leadership [who] seem to have coveted the prestige enjoyed by the established leaders'.[19] The interview material seems to consist mainly of criticisms and countercriticisms of people who felt themselves attacked, threatened, abused or ignored. This could hardly have been otherwise; since Scott thought that personal animosities were important, his questions were likely to have been about personalities. When a Tanzanian union official was unable to make an impression on Asian and European employers, Scott explains that this was partly because he was an African; at no point does the author explain this inability in power terms. He interprets other situations in personal terms, without adequately examining the action which gave rise to them. Such explanations are irrelevant, because they gloss over the structural determinants of action. For example, the cause of the unpopularity of one European adviser among the employers was the growth of union power in the face of the employers' opposition. The relevant question here is what caused the change in the power situation.

Even Scott shows, within the period covered by his descriptive study, that the interchange of personalities really changed nothing. The environmental obstacles to the establishment of the European model remained unaltered. The union officials were career-oriented in that they regarded union posts as steps to more lucrative ones in industry or politics, and therefore had no ideological commitment to

[19] Scott, *The Development of Trade Unions in Uganda*, p. 114.

trade unionism. But there was a special explanation for this. In a situation of large-scale illiteracy, the small group of literate Africans was bound to have the character of an élite. Yet union officials were required to be literate in English—which meant that ideologically committed Africans who could not read and write English, even though they might have been literate in their indigenous language, could not occupy the main union posts. The misuse of private union property, such as a car, as if it were common property, may have been the result of a confusion between cultural values. The confidence and arrogance of employers and Labour Department officials stemmed from colonial rule. The temporary penetration by the union into the established colonial power structure, when it obtained recognition and a wage increase in the summer of 1961, was due to an attempt to harness the collective strength of the plantation workers outside the artificial frame of the European model, not to the bargaining or tactical ability of a European adviser. The interplay of personalities no doubt occurred and makes interesting reading; but without a structural analysis it does not aid interpretation.

The most reliable form of field work involves direct observation, either as a non-participant or a participant. The social anthropologist who witnesses and takes notes—as did Epstein, Warmington and Friedland, with some differences of approach—is a non-participant. In the study of African trade unions, however, non-participatory observation has limitations. First, the observer is usually excluded from some important areas of activity, such as negotiations with employers and executive decision-making, and he has to rely on interviews and imagination to cover these areas. Secondly, if he is a white man his attempt at objectivity may cause him to be identified with the white employers and government administrators, thus closing channels of communication with Africans. Of course, identification with the unions may have a similar effect with employers and administrators. A. L. Epstein, for instance, lost the confidence of the Northern Rhodesian mine management because of this. Thirdly, during periods of action a non-participant observer is likely to be regarded as a hindrance and, therefore, cooperation may be refused.

The above disadvantages apply much less to participant observation. An identification with one side or the other matters less if the social analyst is involved in the situation and able, therefore, to witness it. The main methodological disadvantage of participant observation is that the participant may be confined to a restricted area of activity, say to one union among many, or one of many branches in a single union. The duties he has to perform may further restrict his ability as a social analyst to examine the structure of the total situation. I was able to practise participant observation in the summer of 1961, as field representative in Uganda for the International Federation of Plantation, Agricultural and Allied Workers. Because the situation was largely unstructured, and I was not answerable to a local bureaucracy, I was therefore free to choose where to work and collect data. Such freedom is relatively uncommon, even in developing countries. In addition to occupational restrictions, participant observation carries occupational risks. In all tropical African countries trade unionism is a delicate political matter, involving risks of arrest, detention, rustication, imprisonment, or deportation. These risks are as great for a participant observer as they are for a normal participant, but they in no sense detract from the methodological advantages which accrue from involvement.

The conceptual approach

The points made above concerning the reliability of data, and the interpretation of field work, hold good no matter which conceptual approach is used. The more closely the evidence relates to concrete reality, the better is its explanatory value. However, no improvement in the collecting and handling of data can make up for conceptual deficiencies. For example, as suggested above, a more critical view of government sources and a more intensive collection of non-documentary data might have improved Roberts's work on *Labour in the Tropical Territories of the Commonwealth*; but none of this could have removed the deficiencies of Roberts's empirical approach, based on an initial faulty interpretation of reality. This book was destined from the outset to be mundane and merely descriptive.

The point at issue is clearly illustrated by Ioan Davies in *African Trade Unions*. Davies did not visit Africa to collect data; he relied exclusively on documentary sources, both primary and secondary, which were largely the same as those used by other students of African trade unions. Yet this book stands out in marked contrast to most others in its understanding of the determinants of trade unionism in tropical Africa. The core of the discussion is about the development of an African working class, and this is the central point in *African Trade Unions*. The point is historically elaborated and seen in the context of economic development and the changing social structure, of colonialism and the rise of political commitment, and of the contradiction between the labour needs of industrialization and attitudes to race. Only within this context does a description of the two-way migratory character of the labour force and its subsistence, bachelor standards, take on a useful meaning.

Once the African working class is understood, then it is possible to conceive of the possible forms of collective action within it and to compare them with the European-imposed forms. The structure of *African Trade Unions* takes into account the totality of the situation; it embraces economic, political, and social elements but accords economic factors the main causal significance. The discussion in the second part of the book about unions and governments is set, there-fore, against a background of the need to raise the appallingly low African living standards, the lack of economic resources for develop-ment, and the difficulty of obtaining investment capital. The political control of trade unions can be seen clearly as derived from a particular economic plight.

African Trade Unions is more than an illustration of the value of a conceptual framework; it shows how, given this, the explanation could be further improved by using more reliable data. There are places where Davies, not knowing the situation, extrapolates or makes intelligent guesses. It is impossible, however, to offer reliable data for all aspects of African trade unions in a book of only 256 pages. It would have been helpful if the scope of the book had been restricted. A case can be made out for excluding North Africa, because of its different cultural development, and South Africa, because of its different forms of industrialization and political control. Tropical Africa, south of the Sahara and north of South Africa, is a more homogeneous and manageable unit than the whole continent, which Davies included. When the scope is so wide, and inadequately covered by detailed case histories, the problem arises of balance between descriptive background detail and general analysis. There is a temptation, to which Davies has succumbed, to present a number of potted histories, which do justice to neither description nor analysis. Scott in *The Development of Trade Unions in Uganda*, with less justification, has done the same.

This problem is not easily resolved. Jean Meynaud and Anisse Salah-Bey, attempting to cover the whole continent, have divided *Trade Unionism in Africa* into three parts—concerning the back-ground, the politics and the international relations of African unions. Each comprises a large number of relatively short descriptive sections, dealing largely with specific countries or organizations, bound into the general categories by theoretical summaries or assessments. The declared intention of the authors was 'to analyse the stages and lines of evolution of African trade unionism from its beginnings to the middle of 1956'. But this may be ignored, since their aim in practice seems to have been to separate description from analysis, giving priority to the former. The result is, in effect, a guide to organizations, events, and persons. If the book is judged as such, then, though it lacks the authenticity and thoroughness a guide should have, it is useful for reference. The authors use broadly the same approach as Davies but without the same clarity of definition.

Unions in Emerging Societies, by S. C. Sufrin, stands in marked contrast to Davies's work, especially in its highly theoretical approach. It deals with all developing societies in a mere 76 pages, excluding the bibliography and index. There is no empirical base, but the author endeavours to show the relationship between his theory and practice by providing a chapter on 'Pakistan: a case in point'. The book in general represents the conventional American approach in terms of organic unity, or consensus, to the analysis of industrial relations. It implicitly assumes that there is no structural class division between employers and employed, and explicitly assumes that industrialization —and not the social relations arising from the means of production— is the dominant factor in the development of a society. Thus all types of societies, provided they are industrializing, can be treated in the same analytical manner. Sufrin's analysis draws heavily upon a series of 'Inter-University Studies of Labour Problems in Economic Development';[20] he also makes use of the work of Wilbert E. Moore and Arnold S. Feldman, *Labour Commitment and Social Change in Developing Areas* (New York, Social Science Research Council, 1960). Indeed, so much of the short text consists of quotations from these authors, that it is difficult to discover Sufrin's own contribution. In any event, it is of little explanatory significance.

The consensus analysis of American social theorists is primarily similar, in its theoretical basis, to the empiricism of B. C. Roberts, for example; and it also involves an empirical approach to actual situations. It is not surprising then, to find that Sufrin, after analysing the conflicting goals of unions, officials, and members, in the manner of structural functionalism, concludes that

> the role and function of each trade union movement in each under-developed area must be analysed separately if the analysis is to have pragmatic, instrumental value. Peculiarities of social development,

[20] Walter Galenson, ed, *Labour and Economic Development* (New York, Wiley; London, Chapman & Hall, 1959), and *Labor in Developing Economies* (Los Angeles, 1962). Clark Kerr, J. T. Dunlop, F. H. Harbison, and C. A. Myers, *Industrialism and Industrial Man* (Harvard University Press, 1960). Of the two collections edited by Galenson, only one contribution, Elliot Berg, 'French West Africa', relates to tropical Africa.

historical accident, and social structure, form a setting which cannot be neglected. . . . There is no blueprint for the future. It must be lived, and in the living adjustments will be made in means and ends.

Nonetheless, with the merest empirical support, Sufrin considers that his analysis has a 'pragmatic, instrumental value' and goes on to provide an epilogue with advice 'it is hoped . . . of operational value to administrators and policy makers in developing societies'.[21] The analysis of Sufrin is teleological, in the sense that it relates the institutional behaviour of trade unions to certain specific purposes. It bears little relation to the prime causes of trade unionism in tropical Africa or any other developing area, and his advice is not worthy of repetition.

The main requirement of any conceptual approach is that it should enable a dynamic analysis to be undertaken. This requirement is important for the study of all societies; but it has a particular relevance in the case of tropical Africa, where change is not only taking place but is so rapid that it can be seen to be taking place. Trade unions are media through which some of the forces for change operate; they epitomize the cultural clash which is taking place between the mainly subsistence economies and the industrial societies. To treat them as static objects in a static society is, therefore, so remote from reality as to be largely worthless. Descriptive studies and theoretical analyses in terms of consensus are static in conception, for they assume an organic unity and deal only with the end of a causal sequence. A useful approach must be capable of locating the change creating elements in African societies; and it can only do this, given the present state of knowledge about social behaviour, if it gives a priority to economic determinants and traces their operation through a series of primary, secondary, and internal contradictions. Such qualities are relatively uncommon in studies of African trade unions.

[21] Sufrin, *Unions in Emerging Societies*, pp. 48 and 69.

17

The East African worker in transition

The vast majority of East African workers are experiencing the disadvantages of industrialization without having the benefits which we in Western countries know it can create. They are undergoing the transition from subsistence farming to being a landless proletariat in much the same way as the move from rural to industrial life was made by workers in Britain in the eighteenth and early nineteenth centuries. At so many points there are analogies. It is as if there have been few changes in industrial morality over the last two centuries.

But in one respect there is no analogy. The change in Britain was spread over many decades, so that the impact of industrialization was diffused over time. In Kenya, Uganda, and Tanzania this is not happening. There, complex and highly efficient industrial methods and bureaucratic forms are being applied swiftly, providing no time lag for assimilation or for adaptation. The East African workers make the transition to industrialism in a single simple journey in a lorry.

Industrialization in East Africa is largely confined to the tea, sugar, coffee and sisal plantations, to agriculture and to the mining industries. In all of these activities labour is mainly migrant, illiterate, and fresh from tribal societies. It is grossly inefficient but it is cheap and easily replaceable and the industries are adapted to use it. The workers move between the three territories in search of paid employment and they come from the neighbouring countries, such as the Sudan, Somaliland, the Congo, and Mozambique; but they never lose contact with their traditional societies and most of them return home after periods ranging from six months to three years.

Some Africans, like the Ngoni from southern Tanzania, may make this journey only once in a lifetime; while others, such as the Bakiga from the Kigezi district of Uganda, make it frequently. There are various degrees of instability among members of the labour force. The Buganda cycle or walk daily from their banana or cotton holdings to work in the Kampala district of Uganda. But the least migrant of all are the Kikuyu from Kenya who live either on coffee estates or on nearby settlements. For the Kikuyu there is no escape from industrialism; they have to sell their labour power, for either they have no land of their own or what they have is insufficient to maintain them.

Within the social organizations of their tribes the East Africans obtain some measure of security in sickness and old age which they lose once they move permanently away. In paid employment their welfare rests almost entirely with employers. There is an elaborate framework of labour ordinances, established by colonial administrations, which stipulates contractual obligations, prescribes rules to govern recruitment and terms and conditions of employment, and lays down standards for accommodation and food. But the ordinances are neither effectively nor uniformly applied because of inadequate inspection by the Labour departments.

The workers live on camps near the mines, or on the plantations and estates. The provision of houses, food, education, medical facilities and suchlike amenities are the responsibility of employers. I conducted a survey of the housing conditions on one such camp in northern Tanzania. The houses, shaped like beehives, were twelve feet in diameter, windowless, with narrow raised doors. They were numbered as in a British street and I visited each one in turn. In number 268 there were two men, two women, and four children; in number 55 there were two men, three women, and five children. At each house I was given similar details of human congestion. At this mining camp there was one teacher for ninety children who attended school for only two years.

In complete contrast, alongside the camp, stood a gleaming, spotless, highly mechanized aluminium mine structure which was maintained with the utmost care. I saw many rectangular houses on a sugar plantation in Uganda, made of iron or asbestos sheets with no lining, no windows or chimneys. Each house was about the size of a lounge in a moderate British dwelling and accommodated six, seven, or eight men. Some camps had small hospitals, others had dispensaries, but the elderly man I took from a coffee estate to a hospital in Thika had been lying unattended for three days with an acute attack of malaria because the estate manager had provided no medical facilities.

These living conditions in some ways infringed the labour ordinances but they also contravened the traditional standards of the people themselves. Neither the Luo, who mined gold, nor the Bakiga, who worked on the plantations, tolerated overcrowding in their tribal homes. They had strictly regulated living habits. A married couple would live together, but in a polygamous family each wife had her own house. The children were separated from their parents at an early age and, after puberty, each male built a house for himself. The family units of the Bakiga on the hillsides of Kigezi and of the Luo on the plains to the north of Lake Victoria can be seen in clusters of houses. Other tribes live in much the same way.

The overcrowding among wage-earners was explained away in various ways. The men, it was said, were employed as bachelors but had taken wives for themselves in native fashion; some lived polygamously. The congestion of men in a single house was attributed to their desire to live in that way. Employers insisted either that they had satisfied the ordinances and that the workers had brought about the infringements themselves, or that, in any case, if they made improvements the workers would abuse them. These reasons sounded familiar; as did the one by an employer that if he gave his employees a wage increase they would only spend it on drink. They had a nineteenth-century British ring about them.

The majority of the workers in each of the three East African territories earn from between two and six shillings a day, depending largely on whether or not they are provided with food by their employers. They need much of what they earn to pay poll taxes or to make payments which marriage in their traditional societies might involve. What remains is often insufficient to buy any of what we in Western countries regard as basic commodities. 'I have worked for eight years,' one sugar-plantation worker protested to me, 'but I still cannot afford to buy a pair of shoes.' The satisfaction of primary needs has to compete, moreover, with seductive advertising of certain consumer goods. It is almost impossible in East Africa to escape from the repetitive exhortations to drink bottled beer, or to smoke cigarettes of one brand or another. Bare feet and bodies partially covered with tattered clothes are a mark of irresponsible industrialism, not tribalism. Even the women, who can so easily cover themselves attractively with cheap Japanese cotton pieces, reflect the poverty and oppression of industrialism after they have ventured forth to sell their labour.

But it seemed to me that the impact of industrialization on African workers is greatest in the work situation itself. Most of the workers on the plantations and estates are employed on contracts of six to twelve months. They are put to do simple manual tasks which they have to complete otherwise they are not paid. The law states that this should be so. The Uganda Labour Ordinance provides, for instance, that 'it shall be lawful for an employer to require an employee to perform his work on the basis of a daily task which shall be an amount of work which can reasonably be performed in a day of not more than eight hours'. If a worker is aggrieved because he has not been paid, he can appeal to the Labour Commissioner. But nothing in the ordinance explains how an illiterate, penniless labourer can make such an appeal. Workers who voluntarily absent themselves from work can be arrested and prosecuted. In some case the employers enforce their own laws with their own police; and, like nineteenth-century British textile manufacturers, they sometimes impose fines for offences which workers cannot easily avoid committing. For example, the tea pluckers on an out-grower's estate in Uganda were fined from five to ten shillings out of their monthly earnings of thirty shillings if they were caught plucking bad leaf. If they happened to cut their plucking finger they were dismissed.

Although Africans in their traditional environments do not know the meaning of time in the Western sense they are compelled to maintain strict working hours. The manager of a coffee estate near Thika in Kenya always sent latecomers home, even though the workers had a long way to walk to work. I remember sympathizing with a young Kikuyu woman who was so afraid of being late that she set out well before it was light in order to walk the ten miles to work each day. It was always dark when she arrived home.

There are physical as well as cultural factors which make it difficult for African workers to maintain a sustained working pace. Many of them simply do not get enough to eat. Yet these factors are often ignored by employers. The workers, in consequence, are designated as lazy, a concept belonging to Western industrial culture, and are subjected to a discipline which has no counterpart in tribal life, except, perhaps, in cases of tribal domination. Mostly the discipline is left to the discretion of supervisors and managers so that it is applied with varying degrees of intensity ranging from sheer brutality to understanding. An important exception to this practice occurs in the diamond and copper mining industries. There the discipline is applied through the full use of modern management techniques.

New recruits to the mines are given aptitude tests which are recorded, with other details, on index cards. Depending on the results of the tests, the workers are allocated to groups. But so far there has been no retesting and it seems that the management is more concerned with maximizing its output through control than through using its labour effectively. The management has complete control over labour; it knows where every man is at any given moment. If a worker is ill, he must report sick; if he has defaulted, he is listed as being absent without leave. His movement on and off the camps is strictly regulated by passes and police barriers. And everywhere, at work and at home, broadcast systems penetrate with prayers, music, messages, and directives. Although the material living standards are higher in the diamond and copper mines than elsewhere in East Africa I got the disturbing impression that the mining camps are little Brave New Worlds in which a standardized human unit of labour is being produced out of the crude raw material which enters them.

My investigations in East Africa brought me into a close and informal contact with some thousands of workers on plantations and in the mines. They were eager to show me their conditions and to point out their main grievances, and before I left I had some idea of their priorities. They showed most concern over the failure of managers and employers to treat them as human beings: often they complained about abusive treatment. Next, they wanted improved medical facilities, then better accommodation, and, lastly, higher wages. The East African workers I met wanted to remedy their grievances, but often they did not know what to do: they were in a confused, bewildering situation which was not made easier by the advice they were given to improve it.

Through the medium of the Colonial Office and the British Trades Union Congress, the elaborate British-type trade union, with its local branches, its districts and national committee served by full-time officials but run by literate, articulate members, has been introduced to East Africa. Detailed constitutions have been drawn up to protect the rights of members, and fabrics of organizations with officials, offices, typewriters, receipt books, and sometimes motor-cars have been created. Yet, after attempts lasting for many years, the majority of East African workers are still not organized. The unions have large paper memberships but only small sections of these regularly pay contributions. In consequence the unions are financially weak and many would disappear unobtrusively were it not for outside financial help. There is little collective bargaining machinery and few worthwhile collective agreements. With a few exceptions most unions have not been able to obtain real improvements for their members.

Where unions have secured agreements it is due more to the desire of employers to come to terms with African nationalism than to trade union strength. In some instances in Tanzania unions have obtained check-off agreements whereby employers deduct union contributions from the wages of their employees. These unions have achieved some financial stability in this way. But in no case I examined did the check-off system make a union stronger in industrial relations, for every agreement of this kind was accompanied by rigorously restrictive conditions which enabled employers to contain the development of trade unionism in their particular fields. Indeed, one group of employers claimed that because they were collecting union contributions they should also be responsible for recruiting union members and that, therefore, there was no need for union officials to have access to the workers.

Trade union officials in East Africa constitute an élite which may or may not understand and sympathize with the ordinary workers. Few of them have had industrial experience because first and foremost, irrespective of leadership qualities, they have to be literate in English, the language of the employers and the governments. They risk political victimization, for trade unionism is still in some minds synonymous with public disorder or revolution. They have to negotiate with employers, recently autocratic or at the least paternalistic, who as yet have not learned how to negotiate because they lack the facility to compromise. They are confronted by all manner of temptations to exercise power, enter politics, to indulge in what, by their standards, is gracious living. But, above all, they are faced with the unenviable task of recruiting members from the never-ending stream of migrant workers, of obtaining regular contributions from workers to whom such an act is culturally foreign, and also of obtaining patient, disciplined behaviour from workers new to industrial life. In other words, they have the task of trying to create organizations which are the product of Western industrial conditions and values out of an environment where those conditions do not exist and where those values conflict with the traditional ones. The task is an impossible one.

But it is possible, nevertheless, to protect the interests of the East African workers. It is the Western-type structure, not collective action itself, which the workers find difficulty in operating. I discovered through experiments in union organization on a large sugar plantation that no matter how new the workers were to industry, or how transient, they quickly realized the value of collective action and readily subordinated tribal allegiances to make it possible. They were also prepared, in their own way, to make financial contributions to an organization provided they could recognize its existence through a leader or some other visible means. My experiences convinced me that an effective indigenous form of trade unionism could develop in East Africa.

The difficulties which the East African workers are experiencing in industry and trade unions stem from the fact that when they board the lorries for paid employment they are embarking on a journey which takes them not merely to another district but to a different belief system. They leave societies which are organized on a kinship basis and which give them rights and impose obligations as members of a family. Their traditional values have no place for economic individualism, yet it is this which dominates the society they have to work in.

The Western industrial and traditional African belief systems conflict at many points. The conflict is an important one, for it concerns the survival of things and values which are African but it is also an uneven one. The indigenous institutions in Africa, unlike those in Asia, are weak. They have not been sufficiently strong and viable to resist and contain the values underlying Western industrialism, as Hinduism and Buddhism, for instance, have been able to do. They have not, therefore, been able to provide continuity and stability to those involved in the spread of industrialism. The collapse of African institutions under the impact of Western values has left individuals to settle for themselves the issues arising from the cultural differences. It has resulted in a situation which suffers from a deep-seated instability. Instead of reconciling their traditional values with industrialization, African workers give way and seek either personal relief or escape from the problems the concession brings. This produces the excess of individualism which can be seen, particularly in Kenya, in a high incidence of antisocial behaviour. The absence of indigenous institutional restraints has not only exposed the African to the full force of Western industrialism; it has allowed it to be developed with an almost complete disregard of its social cost.

18

Trade union leadership in developing economies[1]

Trade union leadership in all countries demands certain basic qualities, irrespective of the forms the organizations have taken or their stages of development. Before a worker can participate effectively in organizational activities he must be literate. Without the ability to read and write he has no access to the information about the issues at stake and the problems of the environment in which they occur, on which an understanding must be based. He cannot, moreover, develop even the barest minimum of administrative ability which is necessary if he is to exercise any authority in the organization. He must at least be capable of undertaking clerical tasks such as writing letters, drawing up agendas for meetings and writing up minutes, collecting subscriptions and issuing receipts and membership cards, and keeping a record of membership and finance. A trade union official is invariably involved in more than this. Even at the lowest level of the hierarchy he must read reports, digest and disseminate their information to his members. He must be a source of information and a means through which it can be passed in two directions.

An official in a union must possess some organizing ability. He must be capable of persuading uncommitted workers to join his organization and for this he must be able to argue logically, coherently and at length about trade unionism. He has to be able, therefore, to collect and collate facts and to present them verbally in a logical form. In most instances he must have sufficient eloquence to be able to address small and large gatherings of workers. For this he requires contrasting qualities—the ability to discuss and argue exhaustively in committee and the facility to shout single-point arguments to mass meetings.

Some of the qualities needed for committee work will also assist in negotiations with employers. But additional ones will be required,

[1] Written in 1959.

such as patience and a readiness to compromise. When negotiations fail a new set of qualities may be called on, for strike situations may develop. The leaders of strikes must show determination, single-mindedness and sometimes ruthlessness. They must possess the confidence of the ordinary members and the facility to control their behaviour. In all, a trade union official must be a many-sided man.

One further quality warrants mention. Trade union leaders, no matter how they are selected, are representatives of their members. It is therefore their function to give effect to the wishes and aspirations of the ordinary members. In order to do this they must be able to understand their members, appreciate their intentions, interpret their behaviour, and translate their demands into an organizational form. In other words, they must have an intimate and constant relationship with their members. This the leaders can best achieve if they originate from the class of their members.

The degree to which all the qualities mentioned must be present in one man and the standard of each quality, depend on the stage of development of organizations in general, their environment, their size and the positions held by individual officials in them. These factors determine the use of a division of labour and the nature of the problems which have to be tackled. By the stage of development is meant the extent to which bureaucratic methods have been evolved and are used. An early stage of development is one where formal methods of administration have not been devised and where, therefore, the organizations are not run on the basis of efficiency. In such a stage there is little or no division of labour; men perform composite tasks and are not chosen on the basis of their fitness for the tasks. This stage, in the main, has been passed because it is known, or it can be learnt, how to construct administrations. The stage of development depends, however, not simply on the availability of bureaucratic methods but also on their use, and in this respect unions in many countries lag behind business enterprises. Trade unions rarely take the division of labour to its optimum point because of a general reluctance to use specialists.

Given that unions can be and are being based on bureaucratic methods, the larger a union is the more easily can a division of labour be effected. Administration in a large union can be separated from organizing and negotiating and can be subdivided itself. Size is important in this respect because before specialization can be applied there has to be a sufficient demand to utilize the specialist services fully. Thus it would be uneconomic to establish an education department in a union which was so small that the demand for education was negligible. Specialization then occurs most commonly where trade unionists are concentrated in a small number of large organizations. So far as the individual's position in the hierarchy is concerned, the lower down he is the more likely is it that he will have to perform a variety of tasks. The specialists are normally employed in the top levels of the hierarchy. Where there is no hierarchy the individual will invariably have to do a variety of jobs.

When assessing the qualities needed for union leadership the position of unions in each national community has to be taken into account. The leaders of trade unions which are established and integrated into community activities will have different tasks from those involved where the unions are precariously situated. For instance, in Western communities union leaders participate as government advisers, figure prominently as politicians, and play a part in a wide range of social affairs. In countries where unions are struggling to become established the roles of the leaders are less institutionalized and contain a relatively high content of charisma.

Trade unions in the developing countries do not resemble Western unions in every detail but they possess, and endeavour to possess, comparable forms, and the comparisons are sufficiently close for the leaders of them to require similar basic qualities. But thereafter the similarities end. Trade unions in Western industrialized countries are large, established and socially accepted institutions. Their environments are conducive to their operation. This is not so in developing countries where forces operate against the establishment and expansion of permanent union organizations. Contemporary bureaucratic methods may be known but they cannot be applied properly. Illiteracy, migrant labour, conflicting traditional loyalties, poor transport and communication systems, a lack of finance and therefore administrative equipment, antagonistic governments and uncooperative employers, all make the tasks of union leadership more exacting and complex. In developing countries union leaders sometimes have to perform every conceivable organizational role. Their tasks range from the most menial to that of international delegate and political leader. But this is not all. The most prominent factors in their environments restrict the supply of candidates for leadership and retard their quality. In relation to organizational needs there are too few men available to perform leadership functions.

Restrictions on supply

Trade unions, in the main, in Western industrial countries, draw their leaders from their own ranks. Sometimes, as in Britain, they stipulate in their constitutions that such should be the case. An adequate supply of leaders is maintained in these countries because of the combined effects of compulsory education and an inequality of opportunity. Workers are educated to a standard beyond mere literacy and many of those with a high innate ability are then frustrated because of the lack of opportunity. The frustrated ones who possess strong social consciences find an outlet for their ability in trade union activity. In developing countries unions cannot obtain leaders from their own ranks so easily because of the high incidence of illiteracy, the necessity of leaders to converse in an alien language, the existence of caste and tribal loyalties, the extent of victimization by employers and the inability of unions to finance full-time officials. In order to appreciate the severity with which these factors operate it is necessary to examine each one in turn.

Illiteracy

There is a high degree of illiteracy among working people in all developing countries, but its precise level varies according to the educational policies of the controlling governing powers. It is lower in urban areas than in rural areas but it varies considerably between occupations in urban areas. Unions benefit from the concentration of literacy in urban areas because they themselves are largely confined to the same precincts, but they suffer from the disparity between occupations.

In all of the developing countries literacy is regarded as a sign of status. Workers who are literate avoid manual labour whenever possible. In some cases, particularly in India, they may prefer to be unemployed rather than undertake manual work. In other cases the ability to read and write is accompanied by ambitions which go beyond the desire not to do manual work. In such instances comparable social aspirations are manifested. Literate workers then are concentrated in the clerical occupations. And because the Government is the principal employer of clerical labour they are mainly government servants. Some occupations, the manual and dirty ones such as coal-mining and building construction, may have virtually no literate workers.

The consequences for trade unions are serious. Literacy and education should not be confused and it is possible to have one without the other; but education of the kind needed for trade unions must be based on literacy. Occasionally illiterate workers undertake union jobs. In 1956 eight out of the ten union presidents in Dar es

Salaam (Tanganyika Federation of Labour) were illiterate.[2] But normally unions use only literate workers for official posts. Because there is a shortage of suitable candidates there is little competition for union jobs. Unions sometimes are forced to accept candidates whose only qualification is the ability to read and write and who regard trade unionism simply as a means of earning a livelihood. The situation for some unions is worse than for others. Mining unions, for instance, find it difficult to obtain leaders from their own ranks because mining labour is largely both illiterate and migrant. If different unions cater for different grades of labour within the hierarchy of an industry then the union catering for the lowest grade will suffer most from the absence of literate workers. This was seen to be the case in Northern Rhodesia when the Miners' African Staff Association was formed to organize monthly paid African staff workers in the copper mines. Whenever an African gained promotion he had to leave the manual workers' union, the African Mineworkers' Union. This union was continually being depleted of its literate and able members.

Employers who wished to damage a trade union could do so by promoting literate workers to positions which precluded them from taking part in trade union activity. This was done in Ghana early in its development as an independent state. The movement of literate workers away from trade union activity has not been caused by employers alone. It has been characteristic of developing new politically independent countries for they provide widening opportunities. The attractions have been greatest for those already installed as union leaders, for posts have been open to them which have been far more lucrative and secure than anything unions could offer; and the courses of promotion have been far less hazardous. The total situation caused a premium to be placed on ability. So union officials and potential union officials have been attracted away to work for the Government or private industry. Many Nigerians who trained in Britain for union posts in the early 1950s were lost to trade unionism in this way.

Moreover, wide political opportunities existed in these countries. Political posts may also have been insecure, but they were better paid than union jobs and carried with them greater status and potential power. In some instances union leaders became members of Governments. This was so in India and Pakistan. Unions could not afford to lose their officials in this way for they had a limited, inadequate, supply of replacements from their own members.

[2] ICFTU, *East Africa Office Report*, September 1956.

Fluency in an alien language

A further restriction on the supply of leaders was created by the need for literacy in an alien language. Most of the countries in Africa and Asia have been or are now governed by an alien power. And in each case the major commercial and government activities have been transacted in the language of the governing country—English, French, Dutch or Portuguese.

It so happens that the educational systems in developing countries have been largely confined to teaching in the language of the dominant alien power. There has occurred little literacy in the vernacular languages. The degree of literacy in an alien language required for effective trade union action, however, is high and attainable only by a small minority. And this has usually to be combined with a fluency in one or more vernacular languages. Union officials have to be able to conduct negotiations with European employers and make representations to European governments. They must also be able to address their members in their own languages or dialects. In Bombay, for example, union leaders have to speak Marathi, Hindi and English. Marathi is used to address most of the workers in Bombay; Hindi is used when trade unionists from various parts of India collect together; and English is used in labour courts, in the office of the Registrar of Trade Unions, and in negotiations.[3] The linguistic demands are comparable in all multilingual communities. In Ceylon a union official would need to know English and Singhalese and possibly Tamil if he were concerned with plantation workers; while if he were in Malaysia he would be called on to speak Tamil, Malay and English.

The rise and success of nationalism in Africa and Asia will reduce the need for fluency in a European language. Vernacular languages are being used more extensively and may eventually replace the European languages as official means of communication. In India, for instance, Hindi is replacing English as the official language. But it is unlikely that the European languages will be wholly displaced so long as Europeans retain commercial interests in these countries.

Caste and tribal loyalties

Any social system which has a traditionally fixed pattern of authority may enforce loyalties which prevent the emergence of other than traditional leaders. The most obvious case is in the operation of the caste system in India, which divides the population into rigid social groups with little social intercourse or movement between them. The

[3] See *The Economic Weekly*, special number, July 1958, p. 878.

development of modern industry, the concentration on economic efficiency and the growing emphasis on economic individualism in India have tended to interfere with caste traditions. Men of various castes have been thrown together in industry and have had to evolve satisfactory work relations. But to some extent workers have been able to divorce their industrial activities from their social lives and have been able to preserve the essential elements of the caste system. The degrees of status which the system accords to different castes have been maintained. This means that low status castes continue to look to high status castes for leadership and that members of the high castes refuse to accept the leadership of members of low castes. There are exceptions to this generalization, and they are increasing in number, but they are still insufficient to disturb the generalization. Representative leadership, therefore, cannot operate, because the potential supply of leaders is concentrated in the high status castes. This is borne out by a survey of trade union leadership in Bombay in 1958 which discovered that whereas Brahmins, the highest caste, barely figured at all among the membership of trade unions they constituted 60 per cent of the leadership. Even where caste divisions are weakening, members of low castes are unlikely to attain official union positions because they constitute the main body of illiterates. It should be emphasized, however, that because of the long-established use by Indian unions of officials who originate from outside the trade union movement representative leadership is relatively uncommon, and therefore the full effects of caste on leadership cannot be seen. It is possible that the Brahmin leaders in Bombay belong to the group of 'outside' leaders and have not been chosen for leadership simply because of their caste positions.

Tribal social systems also can have a restrictive effect upon the supply of union leaders. Tribalism can act in two ways. First it can cause workers to refuse to accept representative leadership or indeed any form of leadership which falls outside the traditionally accepted pattern of authority. This factor is reinforced by the determination of those with traditional authority to prevent the rise of alternative forms of leadership.

In the early years of the copper-mining industry in Northern Rhodesia the authority of tribal elders was extended into industry. The elders represented the African miners before the employers and performed other community functions too. Their existence was due in part to a tribal practice and in part to the desire of the colonial authority and the mining employers to prevent the emergence of trade unions. The authority of the elders weakened once the workers discovered that their grievances had no tribal basis. Then the African miners formed trade unions. For a time, from 1948 until 1953, the tribal elders and trade unions operated side by side. Then in 1953 tribal representation was abolished at the instigation of the African Mineworkers' Union. The mining employers have continued to pay some attention to tribal elders and in some cases deal with workers through their elders who may sit on works committees.[4]

The second way in which tribalism may affect the supply of leaders is through the existence of a dominant tribe or powerful intertribal rivalries. Workers may be willing to accept representative leadership, but may be unwilling to accept it from any but their own tribes. They may, of course, be encouraged to retain their tribal allegiances by Government authorities or employers who exploit tribal rivalries to prevent the growth of a unified representative movement.

A dominant tribe is present in Kenya. In Kenya before the Emergency the Kikuyu constituted a high proportion of the wage-earning population and controlled the labour movement. It would have been difficult for members of other tribes, no matter how able they were, to obtain representative union posts. Tribalism may be practised, not through the preferences of the workers, but through the attachment of existing representative leaders to their own respective tribes. That is, the existing leaders may endeavour to influence the selection of others. It is in this way that tribalism was practised in Kenya during the period of the Emergency. Restrictive regulations were imposed on the Kikuyu, Embu and Meru tribes during the Emergency and their members were removed from positions of influence in the trade union movement. Smaller tribes such as the Luo moved into the vacuum. A member of the Luo tribe, Tom Mboya, became the general secretary of the Kenya Federation of Labour in 1953. Subsequently other members of the Luo tribe have obtained trade union posts. The ICFTU Mission to Kenya in 1958 reported that:

> At recent elections in the Dockworkers' Union in Mombasa, a new General Secretary, President, Vice-President and Treasurer were elected all belonging to the same tribe. The new General Secretary, Mr Dennis Akumu, has no trade union experience at all; he was an organizer in Nairobi for Mr Mboya's political party, and did not know of his election until afterwards.[5]

Later Mboya accused five officials of the Kenya Federation of Labour, including the president, of promoting tribalism. Dissension

---

[4] ICFTU Mission to Central and East Africa, *Report*, 1958.   [5] *Ibid.*

resulted and although the accusation was denied the five officials were eventually dismissed from their posts. [6]

In general an African will try not to offend his tribe. There are various reasons for this. It has been stated that an African's loyalty to his tribe derives from his fear of witchcraft which could be used to harm him.[7] It may be that he wants to retain links with his tribe because it provides him with a social security system. If he falls out of work or has to retire because of an accident, sickness or old age, he relies on his tribal system to protect him. An African who offends his tribal authorities by accepting the leadership of a man from another tribe may incur the displeasure of the practitioners of witchcraft or may cut himself off from social security provisions. Existing representative leaders are not excluded from these pressures. For example, during the state of emergency which was declared on the Northern Rhodesian copper-belt in 1956 a number of African union leaders were arrested and rusticated. During their period of rustication some of the union leaders offended the chiefs of the tribe of the president of the African Mineworkers' Union, Lawrence Katilungu. Although the union made formal attempts to get the men released, Katilungu himself was both reluctant to have them back and unable to press publicly for their release because of their offence to his tribe.[8]

African communities normally consist of a large number of tribes of varying sizes and significance. The Northern Rhodesian copper-belt, for instance, is served by about seventy different tribes. Under these conditions, unless there are clearly dominant tribes, the effects of intertribal rivalries are often difficult to disentangle. The same is not so in multi-racial societies. In these societies the racial divisions are usually clearcut and are marked by lingual and cultural differences. The effects of racial factors upon the leadership of unions varies, depending upon whether the races have evolved common institutions or not.

In Africa, by and large, trade unions have been confined to Africans, Europeans or Asians. Where distinct unions have been formed race differences have not influenced union leadership. In West and East Africa, however, the growth of nationalism has reflected itself in a reluctance of African union leaders to work with European advisers. This attitude has particularly concerned representatives from the metropolitan countries. In Kenya, for example, there was opposition to having an Englishman as a field representative of the ICFTU. It is in

[6] *African World*, February 1959, p. 42.
[7] John Bond, 'The barrier of African Mysticism', *Optima*, March 1958, p. 7.
[8] ICFTU Mission, *Report*, July 1958.

multi-racial unions that the problem of leadership selection occurs and for various reasons there are not many such unions. In French West Africa in the early postwar years, French wage-earners played a considerable part in the trade union movement and in some cases joined in unions with Africans. But in recent years the place of the European has become insignificant, except in the Force Ouvrière, the only important union with a joint European–African leadership. [9] A small number of non-racial unions have been formed in British settler territories. The Civil Clerical Association in Kenya organizes all races, while the Typographical Union there organizes Asians and Africans. In Southern Rhodesia an attempt is being made to encourage the development of non-racial unions but this in effect means only that Africans can be admitted to existing European unions. It is unlikely that these unions would permit such an influx of Africans into their ranks as to disturb the authority in them which Europeans possess and allow the rise of African officials. The inexperience of the Africans is sometimes given as a reason to justify the continued domination by Europeans. For example, when a Liaison Officer visited Southern Rhodesia on behalf of the Miners' International Federation in 1958 he reported:

> Some four years ago in Southern Rhodesia the European Union altered their constitution to cater for all classes of labour. They are seeking to have all men paid in accordance to the category they are employed in, and not their colour. Africans are now eligible to join the European Union, and in this respect both patience and skill will have to be exercised to prevent unqualified Africans from taking control of the Union before competent to do so. [10]

The same situation exists in the Northern Rhodesian Mine Workers' Union. This union has deleted the word European from its title and can admit African workers as members provided they are members of the grades which the union organizes. This union, however, exercises considerable influence over job classification in the copper mines and it can and does prevent Africans from becoming eligible for membership. Assuming that Africans could eventually become members it is inconceivable that the European mine workers would permit the rise of Africans as representative leaders within the union. In general in Africa multi-racial unions will tend to have leaders who are representative of the dominant race within the unions.

The situation in Asia has marked differences from that in Africa.

[9] Elliot Berg, 'French West Africa' in *Labour and Economic Development*, ed. Galenson, p. 208.
[10] Report to MIF, 1959.

The multi-racial societies in Africa are in the process of political change whereas those in Asia have qualities of permanence. This is not only because the distribution of political power is changing less rapidly than in Africa; it is also because each ethnic group has preserved its linguistic and cultural characteristics. The effect which this situation has on the supply of union leaders depends upon the attitude with which the ethnic groups view each other and upon the composition of the ethnic groups in the labour force.

The most highly organized workers in Malaysia are of Indian origin and their leaders are mainly Indians too. But the predominance of Indians among leaders of unions is not entirely due to ethnic factors. Before the 1948 Emergency the Chinese were the most politically and industrially active of the races and the control of the trade union movement was largely in their hands. When the Emergency was declared many of the Chinese leaders escaped to the jungle and took with them union funds and most Chinese workers contracted out of trade union action. As a result the Malaysian trade union movement disintegrated. The unions which were formed later consisted almost completely of Indians who distrusted the Chinese because of their behaviour in the emergency. And the Chinese workers never re-entered the unions in sufficient numbers to restore the pre-emergency leadership pattern. So far as the unions in Malaysia are concerned the future supply of leaders depends on the extent to which Chinese and Malays enter the labour force and the speed with which Emergency experiences are forgotten. It also depends upon the degree of success in creating a Malaysian nation out of the different races.

A problem exists in Ceylon arising from the tensions between the Singhalese and the Tamil-speaking Indians who have settled in Ceylon. The Tamils do not possess full citizenship rights and understandably exercise influence through their own pressure groups. As they constitute the majority of the plantation workers and are relatively highly organized they can and do confine their allegiances, in the main, to members of their own ethnic group. A fully representative leadership cannot arise in Ceylon, then, until these tensions have been reduced. It can be said that this holds in general.

Victimization

This can take two forms in developing countries. It can occur in industry or be applied for political reasons. The supply of union leaders in all countries has been restricted whenever workers have been victimized because of their union activities. Sometimes the fear of victimization alone has been sufficient to discourage workers from becoming active trade unionists.

Victimization in industry can take one of three forms. It can be applied through a simple refusal by an employer to permit a worker facilities to engage in union activities. This could entail an inability to get time off without the risk of dismissal. The employer might permit unions within his factory or establishment but only at the cost, measured in terms of finance or promotion prospects, to trade unionists. Or he might not countenance trade unionism at all and would dismiss the workers who practised it. Thus it might not be possible for part-time officials to come from the ranks of the unions.

Industrial victimization has been widely practised in developing countries and because unions there have been weak, it has not been effectively countered and suppressed. In Western industrial countries an initial countermeasure was made when unions removed some of their active members from the influence of employers by paying their wages. These men were able to act independently of employers without risking their livelihoods. Many unions in Africa and Asia, however, have not been able to afford to finance full-time officials, either because they have been too small or because they have been unable to collect subscriptions. Nor, because of their lack of organization, have they been able to use the strike weapon as a protest against victimization as some Western unions have done. Indeed strike action, for whatever reason, has sometimes resulted in further victimization against union officials. After a strike of building workers in Tanganyika in 1956, for instance, two officials of the Building and Construction Workers' Union were not given their jobs back although the ordinary members were reinstated.[11] Incidents of this kind have been numerous: so much so that dismissal has been an accepted hazard in union activity.

Political victimization has had the effect of restricting the supply of candidates for union leadership and of reducing the number of active leaders at particular times. Political victimization means simply that for undertaking union activities men have been arrested and either imprisoned or rusticated. It is a characteristic of politically unstable countries and territories subjected to alien domination. It is often applied in circumstances which tend to confuse the motives of the governing authorities and sometimes it appears that political crises are used as excuses to remove union leaders when the real reasons are industrial. Some involvement in political action by union leaders is almost inevitable, either because the Government is the

[11] ICFTU Mission, *Report*, 1958.

largest employer of wage labour, or because unions recognize that only through legislation can they achieve their objectives. Their actions in stable Western countries would be regarded as politically legitimate, but in developing countries which are either independent with unstable governments or under alien rule they are often regarded as being subversive.

The effect of political victimization on the potential supply of leaders undoubtedly exists, but it cannot be measured. The prospect of sudden arrest and of rustication or imprisonment without trial is unpleasant. Its significance is increased when the other features of union activity such as industrial victimization are considered. Its effect on the existing supply of leaders, however, can be observed and measured. Trade union leaders in most countries in Africa and Asia have suffered from the arbitrary use of Government powers at one time or another.

The trade union movements which have suffered most have been those in which the Governments have declared states of emergency to exist, for in this way the ordinary processes of law have been by-passed or suspended. Arrests and imprisonment have been permissible on the barest suspicion and without trial. When the Mau Mau terrorist campaign began in Kenya in 1952 the arrest of union leaders was widespread. Successors to the arrested persons were also subject to arbitrary arrest. The culmination to this process came early in 1954 when Operation Anvil was undertaken and the majority of union leaders in Nairobi were taken to detention centres. Most of the arrested leaders were still detained in 1956.[12] Some of those who were not arrested were intimidated and assaulted.[13] The removal of union officials to detention centres in remote parts of the country may have helped to disrupt the Mau Mau campaign, but as most of the union officials were simply detained and gradually passed through the screening process before the Emergency ended this effect is unlikely. Their removal, however, undoubtedly weakened and almost destroyed the trade union movement. In 1956 the Kenya Federation of Labour had nine affiliated unions; five were inactive and the remainder were barely functioning. The ICFTU Mission which went to Kenya in 1953 had reason to believe that the Emergency was being used to weaken the trade union movement.[14]

The situation in Malaya was not wholly comparable. When the

[12] Report to the Executive Board of the ICFTU by its East African Representative, July 1956.
[13] ICFTU Mission to Kenya, *Report*, July–August 1953.
[14] *Ibid.*

Malayan emergency was declared many union leaders voluntarily left their unions and joined the rebels. But during the course of the emergency arbitrary arrests were made on the basis of suspicion and the trade union movement was depleted of some of its officials. It was not necessary to have disturbances of the dimensions of those in Kenya and Malaya to justify the arrest of union leaders. Political instability is often reason enough. In countries where political opposition parties are forbidden trade unions are the only organisations through which opposition can be expressed so, understandably, union leaders are regarded as political figures. In Vietnam political opposition is stifled and there are camps for the 'rehabilitation' of political offenders.[15] Trade unionists are frequently jailed and even the leaders of the Christian trade unions, which receive most favour from the Roman Catholic President of Vietnam, are occasionally arrested.[16] After the institution of military control and the proclamation of martial law in Pakistan in October 1958 trade union activities were severely circumscribed and strikes became illegal. Ten strike leaders were convicted of organizing a strike in February 1959 and were sentenced to heavy terms of imprisonment. Eight of the men were given six years' imprisonment and five stripes each; the other two each received five years' imprisonment.[17] The unions in Singapore suffered less than those in Malaya during the emergency but were affected by Government action in 1956 when the Government engaged in an anti-Communist campaign. Seven of the leaders of the left-wing Middle Road unions were arrested and imprisoned in September and October 1956. One of the arrested men was Lim Chiong Siong the secretary-general of the Factory and Shop Workers' Union, the largest union in Singapore. The arrested men were not released until June 1959 when the political party their union supported, the People's Action Party, won the general election.

Trade union leaders in the Central African Federation have led a precarious life in recent years. When the Northern Rhodesian African Mineworkers' Union was engaged in a strike in September 1956 a state of emergency was declared though there had been no trouble in the copper mines. Within a few hours the majority of the union leaders were visited at their homes by the police and were arrested. Altogether thirty-two trade unionists were arrested and rusticated, including the general secretary of the union, a number of full-time officials and some part-time officials. The only official of

[15] *The Times*, 14 January 1959.
[16] Conversation with Mr Livchen, Director, Asia Field Office, 1 October 1958.
[17] ILO Correspondent in Pakistan, Report for February 1959.

the union who was not arrested was L. Katilungu, the union president who was in Southern Rhodesia when the emergency was declared. The continued presence of Katilungu ensured that the African Mineworkers' Union did not disintegrate entirely. But it was adversely affected by the arrests. Its industrial competence was reduced and, as the arrested officials were those who were politically active in the African National Congress, its political activities virtually ceased. Mr Katilungu was opposed to the union participating in politics. When the disturbances occurred in Nyasaland in the spring of 1959 several prominent union leaders in Northern Rhodesia, including Wilson Chakulya, general secretary of the Trades Union Congress, were arrested and detained for their alleged association with the Zambia Congress which was declared illegal. Union leaders in the rest of the Federation were arrested at the same time, particularly in Nyasaland. Moreover, in Nyasaland it was possible for union officials to be arrested on anonymously provided evidence. Employers, for instance, could provide such information.[18]

Devices to improve the supply

The restrictions on the supply of union leaders which have been mentioned above have been removed or eased in various ways. Men from outside the working class have been used; the existing supply of men from within the working class has been deployed widely; leaders have been given office in many unions; and long-term attempts have been made to provide Africans and Asians with courses in education for leadership.

The use of outsiders

The device of drawing on men from outside the working class is an obvious way of increasing the supply of leaders. It cannot be employed, however, unless there exists an educated, indigenous middle class containing men with both leadership qualities and strong social consciences, who have restricted avenues for exploiting their combined talents. Indeed this condition has only been fully satisfied in parts of Asia.

In most Western industrial countries intellectuals have played a relatively small part in trade union organization, largely because unions have evolved slowly as products of their environments. Unions did not reach the stage where detailed administrative knowledge was required until it was available within the working class.

[18] Conversation with C. Millard, ICFTU Director of Organization, 3 June 1959.

The working classes in these countries, moreover, have not been homogeneous. They have consisted of fairly distinct social groups which have received different standards of education. Thus the craftsmen were literate and educated long before the unskilled workers. The craftsmen organized first and then assisted the unskilled to organize; indeed in Britain they became the leaders of some of the unions catering for the unskilled.

The situation has been altogether different in the developing countries. The idea of formalized trade unionism was applied before the environments were ready for it; and it was applied not in a rudimentary form but in its Western industrialized mid-twentieth-century style. In most cases all the people within the community, except for a small élite, were illiterate when trade unionism was first practised. There was not even an educated middle class in most countries. India has been the main exception. The reason why there has been a substantial intellectual middle class in India and not in the other main developing countries is an historical one.

In principle all British colonial territories have been governed by indirect rule; that is, local indigenous institutions have been used as media for governing and administering by the colonial authorities. This principle, though consistently held, has appeared in different practical forms because the colonies have been acquired at different times, have been subjected to influences from a variety of economic and political forces, and have not developed at the same rate.

India was the first British colony to develop a system of local administration. The small amount of education which was undertaken there before 1835 was conducted in indigenous languages, in Sanskrit, Persian and Arabic. The English language was not taught there; it was the language of those who governed. A Committee of Public Instruction was in charge of education and there was a sharp division of opinion in the Committee over whether education in India should continue to be based on Oriental languages or be founded on the English language. There was a deadlock in the Committee for some time until the arrival in India of Thomas Babington Macaulay,[19] who, under the terms of the new India Bill, had become a member of the Supreme Council which governed India. The India Bill had stipulated that one of the members of the Supreme Council should not be a servant of the East India Company and Macaulay had been chosen to be that member. The deadlock was resolved by a minute written by Macaulay in which he put the case for educating the Indians in the English language:

[19] Later the first Lord Macaulay.

The claims of our own language it is hardly necessary to recapitulate. It stands pre-eminent even among the languages of the West. . . . What the Greek and Latin were to the contemporaries of More and Aschan our tongue is to the people of India. . . . The question now before us is simply whether . . . we shall teach languages in which, by universal confession, there are no books on any subject which deserve to be compared to our own.[20]

On 7 March 1835 it was decided that 'the great object of the British Government ought to be the foundation of European literature and science among the natives of India'. Macaulay, as president of the Committee of Public Instruction, set about making the decision effective and introduced an educational machine which, though small and limited, was to create an intellectual middle class too large for British needs.

The growth of an Indian middle class was a slow process. At first men were educated for the limited clerical tasks involved in local government administration. Later in the century commercial clerical posts became available to Indians. The opportunities, however, were limited and educated Indians could only be absorbed into economic activity if they were willing to undertake manual work. Most were not prepared to do this because they belonged to the castes which eschewed manual work. So they overcrowded the professions and sought other outlets which did not conflict with their caste traditions.

The British colonies in Africa, developed much later than India, have not reached India's position. There Government administration has remained exclusively in the hands of the European settler or the European civil servant. The Colonial Office district officer has acted as the representative of the British Government in all but the urbanized areas. And in those areas relatively few Africans have permeated the civil service. Education has been based on the English language as in India, but it has been largely confined to mere essentials. The educational provisions and the European needs have been related factors. The provisions have been dependent upon the needs and have expanded with them. An increasing demand for African administrators results in better educational facilities for Africans. Until the end of the Second World War the demand was contained by economic and political factors. Since 1945 these factors have been altered by the spread of nationalism, but not sufficiently to create an intellectual middle class which could not be effectively absorbed into

[20] G. O. Trevelyan, *The Life and Letters of Lord Macaulay*, Longmans, edn. of 1903, i, 409–10.

constructive economic activity. In the colonial territories which have achieved independence, the provisions for education have been extended and intensified; but so also have the occupational opportunities for educated people. The position in Africa then is that in British territories there is no intellectual middle class from which union leaders could be recruited; and in independent countries the growing intellectual middle class is fully occupied in the expanding and lucrative fields of industry and government.

French governments, through their policy of direct control over their African dependencies, have encouraged a flow of Africans to French educational institutions and have employed many of them on return as civil servants in the colonial departments of the French Government. In so far as there is an intellectual middle class in French Africa, it is mainly comprised of Government servants. There are few people from whom outsiders could be recruited. The situation has resulted in a union development described below.

Two factors brought the intellectual middle class in India into direct contact with the unorganized working class. The first was the Gandhian doctrine of political and social responsibility. Gandhi preached consistently that political and social service was an obligation on people—on those who were in a position to provide it. He was influential among the intellectuals and many of them regarded his doctrine as an article of faith. They regarded it as a duty that they should devote some part of their working lives to public service, and some saw the organization of labour as an effective means of rendering this service. Consequently many of them deliberately formed trade unions.

The second factor was the development in India of a cohesive, highly organized nationalist movement. The inspiration for the movement came from the British-educated Indians who were merely applying the concepts of freedom and democracy about which they had been taught in Britain, to their own conditions. These men became nationalist leaders. The movement extended beyond the confines of a class and became identified with a nation's struggle for political freedom; it brought together many people and organizations of different, conflicting, political views and, temporarily, it submerged class differences. Trade unions were regarded as legitimate organizations to use for the nationalist cause. There was no complaint, therefore, from the workers when middle-class intellectuals assumed their leadership.

The immediate postwar period (1918–20) [wrote S. D. Panekar] saw the emergence of Indian trade unionism. This period was preceded by the

Russian Revolution (1917) and succeeded by the Swaraj Movement (1920–24); the former provided to the infant trade union movement an inspiration and a goal, whereas the latter supplied young and enthusiastic leaders, who proposed to exploit the workers' organizations in their political struggle for freedom.[21]

Until India obtained its independence the two factors mentioned above were frequently combined in their operation. Indians satisfied their obligation to perform public service by becoming active in the nationalist movement as leaders of trade unions.

From the outset the role of outsiders in the Indian trade union movement aroused controversy. In most instances, however, the controversy originated from outside the movement. First it arose from the refusal of employers to negotiate with labour leaders drawn from outside the ranks of the trade union movement. In order to understand the employers' attitude it is necessary to appreciate the role which outsiders played. The outsiders formed unions, financed them, nurtured them and imposed on them their own social aspirations. Whether unions were highly organized, conciliatory or militant was determined by outside influence. The Ahmedabad Textile Labour Association was formed under the guidance of Gandhi. Its policy was consistently conciliatory. Many other unions were formed by Communists and they pursued militant policies. Interests, therefore, which were opposed to trade unionism focused their attention on the people who appeared to carry most responsibility for union activity.

Employers in India frequently stipulated that they would only negotiate with unions led by their own workers. Until 1920 the Government of India adopted the same attitude with regard to civil servants. The Indian Trade Union Act of 1926 gave legislative recognition of the right of registered unions to employ outsiders and to include them in their executives. This weakened the opposition of employers but did not remove it.

There was opposition too, from protagonists of the British type trade unionism who considered that the movement was unhealthy and unstable if it did not produce its own leaders. The activities of some outsiders gave these people evidence for their contention. There were some unions in the 1920s, the Royal Commission on Labour in India reported, which represented little or nothing more than the one or two men who filled the leading offices. These men were generally drawn from the professional classes. The Report stated:

[21] S. D. Panekar, 'Outside leadership of trade unions', *The Economic Weekly*, July 1958.

A few such unions can fairly be described as having had their main evidence of reality in notepaper headings. The object is to give a plat-form and a name to the leaders. The members, if not imaginary, are convened on the rare occasions when the endorsement of some resolution is required. This type of valueless growth, which is more characteristic of Bengal than of other provinces and is becoming rare even there, was stimulated by the belief that it would assist the leaders to secure nomina-tion in the labour interest to local councils or international labour conferences.[22]

But whatever the reasons for opposing outsiders, the Royal Commission stated that attempts to dictate to unions on the subject of their leaders or officials is 'equally short-sighted and unwise'.[23] The Commission elaborated:

We have referred to the great difficulties confronting the movement, which make the employment of a proportion of outsiders inevitable. In some cases victimization, and more frequently the fear of it, gives an additional value to the outsider. The claim to be allowed to deal only with 'one's own men' is frequently little more than an endeavour to secure that the case of the men shall be presented by persons who are not likely to prove assertive. In every country much of the active work of trade unions, particularly in their relations with employers, is carried on by persons whose livelihood does not depend on the employers' will. We recognize, as do outsiders themselves, the weaknesses of the position of persons who have no direct experience of industry. But this again is mainly a question for the unions themselves. . . . There is, however, still a disposition in some quarters to object to particular outsiders, and especially ex-employees and politicians. The dismissed employee, whose energy is whetted more by a sense of his own grievances than by a desire for the welfare of others, can be a severe trial to the most sympathetic employer. . . . But in actual experience the attempt to suppress such individuals by repressing their organizations or by insisting on their exclusion has seldom been successful. . . . The politician who hopes to divert a union to political ends can be equally trying, and it is frequently the case that his exclusion would be in the best interests of the men. But the employer, however pure his motives, is in a weak position when he attempts to protect his workmen by keeping their leader at arm's length. The leader who is not honestly working for the good of a union is not likely to have a long innings unless he is assisted by persecution.[24]

The sanguine expectations of the Royal Commission concerning outsiders were not fulfilled. Unions in India continued to depend for their leaders on social workers, lawyers and other professional and

[22] *Report*, 1931, p. 319.
[23] *Ibid.*, p. 324.　　[24] *Ibid.*, p. 325.

public men, for the education of the working class barely improved. The nationalist struggle, moreover, was intensified. The struggle, however, was characterized by different political approaches, projected on to the trade union movement through its outside leadership. After the independence of India was secured the trade union movement became, much more so than in 1931, a means of individual political advancement. Through trade unions outsiders could become prominent politicians and even members of the Government. The tendency for them to establish unions in their own interest increased. The controversy about them also increased.

Trade union law in post-independence India has stipulated that the majority of office bearers must be from the ranks of the unions,[25] but the dominant positions are filled by outsiders. The law relating to industrial disputes, until the late 1950s, defined a workman as one who earned less than a specified wage. This wage was so calculated as to exclude supervisory and technical personnel from the provisions of the Industrial Disputes Act and, therefore, from the membership of unions of manual workers. The effect of the definition was to exclude from membership those with the highest level of education. The Act was amended in 1958 to bring within its scope technical personnel and supervisory personnel earning a salary of up to R.500 per month. The amendment, it was claimed, would enable supervisors to become the natural leaders of the unions and so make it unnecessary for outside politicians to hold union offices.[26] The effect of the amendment is not yet known. Supervisors who play an active part in trade unions are faced with dual loyalties for they form part of the management hierarchy. Their loyalties are sometimes irreconcilable; one or the other has to be sacrificed. If it so happens, as is likely, that the loyalty to trade unionism has to be sacrificed then, no matter how well suited for leadership these supervisors are, they will not remain in official union positions for long. But it has been questioned whether the majority of the supervisors brought within the terms of the Act have the education and understanding necessary for effective union leadership. One writer was doubtful whether even 30 per cent of the supervisors were educated to a sufficient level to be considered for official union posts.[27]

The continued presence of outsiders in Indian trade unions depends on a number of factors. There is now a tradition of intervention by

[25] *Labour and Economic Development*, ed. Galenson, p. 41.
[26] Indian Institute of Personnel Management, *Industrial Relations' Journal*, May–June 1958.
[27] *Ibid.*, July–August 1958.

outsiders which has its own momentum. For this reason alone outsiders will remain in unions for a long time in the future. The
tradition, however, will be influenced by social forces. The reliance
of unions on outsiders for financial support may cease or lessen as the
unions become more effectively organized. At the moment this type
of support varies between unions and regions, but in many cases
outsiders contribute in one form or another. The most common form
of contribution consists of voluntary services. Many outsiders earn
incomes from non-union activities which support them in their union
work. Unions which are more effectively organized might be able to
finance staffs of full-time officials from their own resources. Another
relevant factor is the high level of intellectual ability which is frequently made available to unions by outsiders. An inquiry into union
leadership in Bombay in 1958 revealed that of the forty-five leaders
investigated only two had not matriculated and two-thirds were
university graduates.[28] The inquiry showed that some of the leaders
had had brilliant academic careers. Because of the reliance of unions
on the State-controlled legal machinery, lawyers have a prominent
place in unions. Eight of the forty-five leaders were lawyers. The
prominence of such outsiders in unions will depend on the prevalence
of specific needs such as that relating to the law and, more significantly, on the competition they meet for leadership positions. As the
level of education of the Indian workers is raised, so the competition
they meet for leadership positions will intensify. But there are
prejudices to be removed. It is said that Indian workers do not trust
their own kind in office because they suspect them of self-seeking,
and that they prefer to be represented by outsiders.[29] This prejudice
will undoubtedly be tested as Indian workers present themselves in
increasing numbers for leadership tasks.

A further factor concerns the supply of outside leaders. The
number of intellectuals who want to become union officials or who
desire to use unions as means to obtaining political positions will
decrease as the area of what is considered to be legitimate participation in economic affairs widens. Independence has brought a range of
new opportunities, but only the political ones have been exploited
fully by Indian intellectuals. Pre-independence attitudes, supported
by caste prejudices, have prevailed. When these change, then the
attitude of outsiders to trade unionism may also change.

Outsiders have not penetrated all spheres of trade union activity
for the law in India does not permit people who are not engaged in

[28] *The Economic Weekly*, July 1958.
[29] Conversation with Mr Ghatak, ILO, 6 November 1958.

the public service to become leaders of unions which organize public servants.[30] This restriction is not onerous because the public sector of the economy contains the highest proportion of workers with leadership qualities. But even public servants tend to be prejudiced against wholly inside leadership and they use outsiders to participate in negotiations with employers.[31]

The forces which resulted in outside leadership in India also operated to a large extent in Pakistan and Ceylon. The trade union movement in Ceylon has always been deeply political; it was formed by middle-class intellectuals and unions have been subsequently created by them for political purposes. The tradition of outside intervention has in some cases been influenced by an element of paternalism which has characterized relations between workers and employers. This has been particularly so on the plantations. In one instance a fusion of the two factors has led to the acceptance by workers of a large employer of labour as a union president.[32]

Away from the Indian subcontinent the presence of outsiders as union leaders has depended on a variety of factors. In a number of British territories trade union ordinances contain clauses intended to prevent outsiders holding office, though exceptions are made in the case of the position of secretary. The Ordinance in Sarawak, for instance, states that officers of trade unions are required to be persons actually engaged in the trade, occupation or industry concerned, although this requirement may be waived at the discretion of the public authority.[33] Similar provisions exist for Hong Kong, Kenya, Mauritius, Nigeria, North Borneo and Tanganyika.[34] In Malaya the Government changed the law relating to trade unions in 1959 so that all executive members of a union now have to be Malayan citizens who have been engaged in the industry for which the union caters for at least three years. This restriction does not apply to unions which have not established a political fund. The new law also stipulated that at least two-thirds of a union's officials would have to be actually engaged in the trade or industry for which it caters.[35] The Malayan union leaders had been consulted about the changes and approved of them. In this case the intention of the Government and the union

[30] Draft Report of Committee of Experts on the Application of Conventions and Recommendations, Part 1, 1959, p. 12.

[31] Mr Ghatak.

[32] The union is the Ceylon Workers' Congress, the largest union in Ceylon, whose president [1959] is S. Thondaman, a large employer of plantation labour.

[33] Influence of Article 35 of the Constitution of the ILO in the Application of Conventions in Non-Metropolitan Territories, March 1959, p. 174.

[34] *Report of Committee of Experts*, 1959, p. 40.

[35] ICFTU Information Bulletin, 18 April 1959.

leaders was not expressly to exclude outsiders but to prevent unions from being used as tools by politicians.

Where there were no legal restrictions the size of the intellectual middle class was the main delimiting factor. Asian countries had a greater supply of outsiders than those in Africa because of their earlier development. For this reason there have been varying degrees of outside intervention in Singapore and Indonesia. But outside intervention was possible in Africa so long as there were some intellectuals who for one reason or another were interested in unions. Thus in the British Cameroons the first full-time general secretary of the Cameroons Development Corporation Workers' Union was an Assistant Government Medical Officer. He left the union in 1950 to take up medical practice and then to enter politics. In 1958 he became the Premier of the Southern Cameroons.[36]

The greater the possibility of political advancement through trade unionism in an area, the more likely were intellectuals to be attracted into unions. Outsiders lead the trade unions in Liberia, but the reasons for this are wholly different from those prevailing elsewhere. The President of Liberia decided, for reasons which are difficult to discover but certainly not in the interests of the workers, that there should be trade unions. In consequence the Liberian Labour Union Incorporated was established by an Act of the Legislature in December 1949 and was provided with officials who were high-ranking Government officials.[37] The union became defunct in about 1952. After the visit of an ILO representative to Liberia in 1959 a second attempt was made to establish a trade union. This time it was called the National Congress of Labour and its chief official was the social secretary of the President of Liberia, who knew nothing about trade unionism. But Liberia is a freak case. There are other cases of government sponsored unions, but none where outsiders have been made the sole officials.

It is unlikely that outsiders will be used more extensively where they have not already established a practice of intervention, for in general current trade union opinion favours the development of internal leadership.

The deployment of working-class leaders

This is a method of utilizing the small supply of working-class leaders which involves the use of these men over a wide range of industries irrespective of their own experiences.

[36] Warmington, *A West African Trade Union*, p. 30.
[37] ICFTU, *Report on Trade Union and Labour Conditions in Liberia*, July 1954.

The circumstances which permit the use of outsiders in the trade union movement also enable officials who originate from the working class to be deployed. Unions in developing countries generally have neither rules, traditions nor prejudices against accepting as leaders men who do not come from their own ranks. Any literate man, regardless of his background and upbringing, is eligible for a union office. Where, then, there are members of the working class with an adequate standard of education they compete, to a large extent, with outsiders for union posts. In so far as there is competition it is restricted by a number of factors. First where there are caste prejudices they are likely to operate in favour of outsiders and against members of the working class whatever their qualifications, because outsiders will normally be members of the higher castes. This restriction will not operate in the case of tribal prejudices. Secondly, where there is a tradition concerning the use of outsiders and this tradition is established before a supply of educated working-class members becomes available, circumstances will favour the outsiders. Thirdly, where little or no significance is attached to membership of the working class as a qualification for union leadership then educational qualifications will figure prominently and outsiders, often with a university education, will be preferred. All in all, circumstances favour the selection of outsiders. The deployment of working-class leaders, therefore, is largely confined to those countries with small middle classes and no traditional use of outsiders by trade unions. That is, it primarily concerns African territories.

The literate members of the working class are concentrated in Government employment. This is because the Government has been both the largest employer of permanent wage labour and has provided the kind of employment which both needed literacy and attracted literate workers. In consequence the civil service has been the major source for union leaders. In French West Africa the leadership of the trade union movement has consisted mainly of civil servants and former civil servants.[38] In French territories this characteristic was encouraged by 'the French custom of allowing civil servants to serve as full-time union officials while continuing to receive their salaries from the government'.[39]

Because of the characteristics of Government employment mentioned above trade unionism has been practised in it for longer and more intensively than in other sections of the economy. Civil

[38] Elliot Berg, 'French West Africa', in *Labour and Economic Development*, ed. Galenson, pp. 213–14.
[39] *Ibid.*, p. 214.

servants, therefore, have had greater experience of trade unions than others. They are, moreover, often attracted by work in the wider trade union movement because that work offers opportunities for achieving personal ambitions and exercising power which Government employment denies them.

Holding office in more than one union

A characteristic which is found to some extent in most developing economies is for one person to be the chief official in a number of unions. This arises because of the acute shortage of officials, but given the shortage it can be accentuated by the desire of individuals to extend their influence and to obtain political power.

In a number of Asian countries—Indonesia, Malaya, the Philippines and Japan—a union official may be found to hold offices in two or three unions, or he may simply be an adviser to a union in addition to his own. This situation is uncommon in Western countries. In India the practice is extensive and occurs in an exaggerated form. The president of the Indian National Mineworkers' Federation in 1958 was the president of sixteen other unions catering for various types of workers. One of the unions organized power workers, another organized iron and steel workers, another clerical workers, and the rest mainly organized mineworkers in different areas. The general secretary of the same Mineworkers' Federation was the general secretary of one other union and a president or vice-president of four unions. One leader of the Indian National Trades Union Congress in Bombay was the president of seventeen unions in 1958 and the general secretary of two others; while an All-India Trades Union Congress leader who was a lawyer held offices in twenty unions. Many leaders in India hold offices in three to five unions and in addition undertake outside jobs to maintain themselves.

Where a person becomes the chief official in a number of unions simultaneously then his role in most of them becomes meaningless. If the offices which are held are sinecures the purpose of utilizing scarce leadership qualities is defeated. If administrative tasks are attached to the posts they must necessarily be neglected for the sheer physical task of coping would be too great. It may be that only enough administrative work is created in total as would enable one man to do it. If that is so the development of the unions is being retarded. The leaders, moreover, cannot possibly know the interests of the workers they purport to represent. They cannot be familiar with the various working conditions, the managements, even the workers themselves. Either they are union leaders in name only or the unions they are supposed to lead are organizations in name only.

Of all the methods for utilizing leadership resources this is the least effective. Indeed it is strongly defective. Fortunately when a real increase in the supply of leaders is obtained this method will give way for it has neither merit nor worthwhile tradition to maintain it.

Leadership training

All the methods for increasing and utilizing the supply of leadership resources so far described are expedients. They are devices which aim to make the best of a bad job. Leadership training is different for it is the only long-term solution to the problem of scarcity. It can overcome the defects of other methods. It can displace the use of outsiders and remove the need for deploying civil servants.

The process of learning by experience is too slow and inadequate in developing economies, for the demands which are made on union officials are immediate and intense. Moreover most Africans and Asians have little opportunity to gain experience; they are usually young when they take responsible union offices, sometimes without having held previous union posts; and their turnover is high. Training courses are necessary to equip effectively the existing officials as well as to increase the supply.

The nature of the task is set by the conditions in developing countries, but it must be understood that training courses cannot make leaders; they can only provide information and practice about and in trade unionism. In the process they can draw out and develop leadership qualities, but they cannot create them. For courses to be useful the students must be correctly selected. There is scope here for much error. The persons who are both willing to attend courses and able by their circumstances to do so, may not be the ones who will benefit most.

A number of attempts have been made to provide leadership courses. First, countries outside of Africa and Asia have endeavoured to do so. The British Government and the British Trades Union Congress have provided funds and scholarships to enable a small number of union officials from Africa and Asia to attend educational institutions in Britain. A government is necessarily limited in the kind of courses it can finance for trade unionists; it can only concern itself with the mechanics of trade unionism. Courses provided or financed by the British TUC were not similarly restricted. Trade unions from the USA have also provided funds to enable Africans to visit the USA either for the purpose of visiting a number of different institutions or of studying full-time at one of them.

The practice of taking union officials from their environments for training has been subject to much criticism. It has been said that the methods and ideas which have been learnt and assimilated have been alien to or unsuitable for application in developing countries and that the process of learning should take place within the countries concerned and should be conducted by members of the indigenous populations. Contentions of this kind have usually been made by nationalist Africans or Asians who have been conscious of the problems and conditions of their particular countries and they have had much supporting evidence. Apart from the general question of the relevance of Western ideas and institutions, there is the question of the effect on union leaders of being translated to Western environments. Union officials from Africa have often returned to take other than union posts, thus defeating the purpose of providing training. There is already a wide gap between the union officials and the ordinary members and courses of study under alien conditions tend to widen it. The question of the value of Western standards is irrelevant here. It is simply wise to avoid taking any action which tends to make it more difficult for union officials to understand, sympathize with, and interpret the actions and aspirations of ordinary illiterate or semiliterate workers.

The process of training union leaders will not resolve the main problem of supply unless it is based on a wide literacy and primary education campaign and proceeds from there in stages. Thus union training is part of a nation's social problem. Given an adequate level of national primary education, unions, either through their own efforts as in Ghana and India or through the help of international agencies, can implement their own educational programmes adapted to meet their particular needs. This entails a spread of resources over different regions and in the use of different methods. A single college in a continent or subcontinent can do little towards presenting a solution of one of the most acute problems facing developing trade union movements.

Problems of leadership

Many of the difficulties facing trade union leaders in developing countries are organizational and they have their origin in the nature of developing territories—in the values of non-industrial societies, the scarcity of economic resources, the low level of literacy, the habits of the labour force and other factors. And their removal to a large extent depends on structural changes in the societies in which unions operate. Some responsibility, however, rests with the union leaders themselves. The greater their imagination and organizational versatility the more readily will they overcome the difficulties. They need not only to assert their independence of Western notions about organization but also to be capable of formulating indigenously based ones. But they are caught up here in a vicious circle for this cannot be done unless there are men of ability at the head of trade union affairs and the rise of such men depends largely on the application of policies by able leaders. The circle can be broken by international help, but any international intervention which merely entrenches Western notions will be not merely superfluous: it could be damaging.

Here specific mention will only be made of leadership problems which have not been described elsewhere in this chapter.

(*a*) The scarcity of officials causes them to be concentrated at the head of organizations and thus places in their hands the power to exercise control. This power is increased by two factors. First, despite any constitutional provisions to equalize authority among the members, the absence of effective policy-making organs in practice in which ordinary members can participate leaves the chief officials in an isolated but strong position. Secondly, there is a large element of charisma in union leadership in Africa and Asia which gives them a power quite dissociated from their ability to organize and administer. Leaders with this 'gift of grace' do not have to account for their actions or justify the power they hold.

This situation can lead to an abuse of power. It can also result in the personalization of conflict within trade unions. Union officials may tend to regard their unions as their personal property and to look upon themselves as being more important than the cause they serve. They treat attempts to alter the policies they pursue as personal vendettas and the rise of leaders within their organizations as threats to their authority. Conflicts easily and frequently break out between personalities which have serious organizational repercussions.

(*b*) A problem which union leaders face in developing countries, particularly in Africa, arises from the attitude of inferiority with which they are often regarded by European employers and government administrators. Men who are not treated as being capable of running unions or of negotiating tend to search for some means of expressing their equality or asserting their superiority. In industrial relations the only alternative to negotiation is strike action. The European attitude, when it is determined by the idea of white superiority, encourages militancy where militancy is unnecessary and fosters the development of a rigid, uncompromising approach to labour problems.

(c) Because of the shortage of union officials there can be little division of labour within their organizations. Union officials, therefore, have to fulfil a variety of functions which are exacting and time consuming. Some of them have to spend time in other occupations, in order to finance themselves. Many are politicians. In addition to these commitments they are expected to undertake international duties which often take them away from their domestic tasks for many months in the year.

The fulfilment of international commitments is a necessary trade union function. It is important that the trade union movements in Africa and Asia should be represented on international bodies for their countries are newly developing centres of economic and political power and are attracting the attention of the Western trade union movements. A practical consequence of representation, however, is to weaken labour organizations. The unstable trade unions of Africa and Asia cannot afford to be bereft of their chief officials for months each year while they attend international trade union conferences, and conferences organized by agencies of the United Nations Organization. There have been instances where unions have collapsed because of the prolonged absence of even one important official. It has been likewise undesirable from the point of view of the organization for officials to be absent on educational courses. While officials are absent simple administrative tasks are often neglected, members are lost and action suspended. The authority which the union representatives claim is endangered because it is based on weakened organizations. Indeed some union leaders may be representatives in name only.

Clearly union officials must attend educational courses and conferences. But even Western trade union movements have to apportion their international commitments so as not to cause union leaders to neglect their domestic union affairs. The most frequent Western attenders at international gatherings are usually those whose domestic commitments are light. This kind of solution is not open to trade unions in developing countries. Obviously some solution must be sought.

(d) The last problem to be raised here concerns the kind of relationship which union leaders should attempt to establish with their respective Governments. This is an issue only in politically independent countries for where political power is in alien hands the circumstances force union leaders to adopt an attitude of at least a muted antagonism towards the Government.

The countries, by definition, need to organize their economic resources in order to increase production. The task is more easily tackled with collaboration from trade unions, for though the unions may not be pervasive in their influence they are usually influential in essential sections of the economy. Governments usually recognize the need for union collaboration. The Indian Government has done so. When, for example, Krishna Menon, as Indian Defence Minister, inaugurated a conference of the All-India Defence Employees' Federation in July 1958 and appealed for increased output, he said that 'as responsible trade union leaders, they were expected to assist the Government in stepping up production, especially in view of the difficult foreign exchange position. It was the ingenuity, skill and sense of appreciation of the workers that would go a long way to help increase production.'[40] Other governments have been more forthright in their attempts to gain the collaboration of unions.

There are also political influences which compel the governments of developing countries to seek the collaboration of union leaders. Newly independent countries are usually politically unstable and their governments endeavour to seek stability by removing, in one way or another, sources of opposition. Trade union leaders are a source of opposition.

The same factors do not influence the attitudes of union leaders. Their position is not clear cut because for them there is a case for and against collaboration with the Government. There are strong reasons making for collaboration. Trade unions have often formed part of nationalist movements and union leaders have been prominent nationalists with close connections with nationalist leaders. These connections have not always been broken when independence has been achieved. A close affinity has frequently been maintained between union leaders and the governing politicians. This was so in Ghana, in India and in Singapore. This affinity, however, does not indicate an identity of interests between trade unions and the Government.

Union leaders may recognize that any improvement in the economic state of the country could benefit trade unionists and they may realize that the closer their connection with the Government the greater the benefit might be. But a close economic and political con-

[40] *Indian Information*, 15 August 1958.

nection with the Government may also entail the loss of independent action. The union leaders may not be permitted to pursue the claims of their members freely, to call strikes, to criticize the Government's economic policies. They might, in the process, lose the confidence of their members and hinder the extension of their organizations by voluntary means.

In the West this independence has been highly valued for its own sake. In developing countries it may be an intangible factor subsidiary to the need to increase production. But there is one way in which it might have material consequences for union members and therefore be of consequence too for union leaders. Collaboration with the Government usually involves union restraint in seeking improvements in wages, hours and working conditions, and this could mean perpetuating workers in a depressed condition when through militant action they could gain some improvement in their state. Much depends in this respect on the policies the Government is pursuing and on its views about the distribution of the national income.

What Governments in developing countries want from union leaders is responsible action, and for this it is not necessary that union leaders should sacrifice their liberty of action. Liberty and responsibility are not incompatible qualities. The fear of Governments that nonetheless they may not be found together compels them to act as if they will not. And Governments, so much stronger than trade unions, can force their will on union leaders. On the other hand, union leaders in developing countries are often much more politicians than elsewhere and see little or nothing at fault in subordinating industrial action to political ends. This may be yet another instance of where a Western notion is inappropriate for the conditions of developing territories.

Index